A MATTER OF TRUST

ALSO BY LIS WIEHL

Snapshot

The Mia Quinn Mysteries (with April Henry)

A Matter of Trust
A Deadly Business (Available Summer 2014)

The Triple Threat Series (with April Henry)

Face of Betrayal
Hand of Fate
Heart of Ice
Eyes of Justice

The East Salem Trilogy (with Pete Nelson)

Waking Hours
Darkness Rising
Fatal Tide

"Book three in the wonderful Triple Threat series is a fast-paced thriller full of twists and turns that will keep you guessing until the end. What makes these books stand out for me is my ability to identify so easily with Allison, Nic, and Cassidy. I truly care about what happens to each of them, and the challenges they face this time are heart-wrenching and realistic. I highly recommend!"

—Deborah Sinclaire, editor-in-Chief, Book-of-the-Month Club and the Stephen King Library

"Beautiful, successful, and charismatic on the outside but underneath a twisted killer. She's brilliant and crazy and comes racing at the reader with knives and a smile. The most chilling villain you'll meet . . . because she could live next door to you."

—Dr. Dale Archer, clinical psychiatrist, regarding *Heart of Ice*

WAKING HOURS

". . . an exciting faith-based series that skillfully blends romantic tension, gripping supernatural suspense, and a brutal crime."

—*Library Journal*

". . . a truly chilling predator and some great snappy, funny dialogue will keep readers engaged."

—*Publishers Weekly*

"One word describes *Waking Hours* by Wiehl and Nelson—*WOW!* A gut-wrenching ride of supernatural suspense that left me breathless and wanting more. The book was a reminder that the battle between God and Satan is not over. Highly recommended!"

—Colleen Coble, best-selling author of *Lonestar Angel* and the Rock Harbor series

"A gripping plot, intriguing characters, supernatural underpinnings, and a splash of romance make *Waking Hours* a fast-paced and thoroughly enjoyable read. I want the next book in the series now!"

—James L. Rubart, award-winning author of *Rooms*

ACCLAIM FOR LIS WIEHL

A MATTER OF TRUST

"*A Matter of Trust* is a stunning crime series debut from one of my favorite authors, Lis Wiehl. Smart, suspenseful, and full of twists that only an insider like Wiehl could pull off. I want prosecutor Mia Quinn in my corner when murder's on the docket—she's a compelling new character and I look forward to seeing her again soon."

—LINDA FAIRSTEIN, *NEW YORK TIMES* BESTSELLING AUTHOR

"Dramatic, moving, intense. *A Matter of Trust* gives us an amazing insight into the life of a prosecutor—and mom. Mia Quinn reminds me of Lis."

—MAXINE PAETRO, *NEW YORK TIMES* BESTSELLING AUTHOR

THE TRIPLE THREAT SERIES

"Only a brilliant lawyer, prosecutor, and journalist like Lis Wiehl could put together a mystery this thrilling! The incredible characters and non-stop twists will leave you mesmerized. Open [*Face of Betrayal*] and find a comfortable seat because you won't want to put it down!"

—E. D. HILL, FOX NEWS ANCHOR

"Three smart women crack the big cases! Makes perfect sense to me. [*Face of Betrayal*] blew me away!"

—JEANINE PIRRO, FORMER DA; HOST OF THE CW'S DAYTIME COURT TELEVISION REALITY SHOW *JUDGE JEANINE PIRRO*

"Who killed loudmouth radio guy Jim Fate? The game is afoot! *Hand of Fate* is a fun thriller, taking you inside the media world and the justice system—scary places to be!"

—BILL O'REILLY, FOX TV AND RADIO ANCHOR

"As a television crime writer and producer, I expect novels to deliver pulse-pounding tales with major twists. *Hand of Fate* delivers big-time."

—PAM VEASEY, WRITER AND EXECUTIVE PRODUCER OF *CSI: NY*

A MATTER OF TRUST

A MIA QUINN MYSTERY

LIS WIEHL

WITH APRIL HENRY

THOMAS NELSON
Since 1798

NASHVILLE DALLAS MEXICO CITY RIO DE JANEIRO

Published in Nashville, Tennessee, by Thomas Nelson. Thomas Nelson is a registered trademark of Thomas Nelson, Inc.

Thomas Nelson, Inc., books may be purchased in bulk for educational, business, fund-raising, or sales promotional use. For information, please e-mail SpecialMarkets@ThomasNelson.com.

ISBN 978-1-4016-8806-6 (IE)

ISBN 978-1-59554-906-8 (trade paper)

Library of Congress Cataloging-in-Publication Data

Wiehl, Lis W.
A matter of trust : a Mia Quinn mystery / Lis Wiehl with April Henry.
pages cm.
ISBN 978-1-59554-903-7 (hardcover)
1. Women lawyers—Fiction. 2. Widows—Fiction. 3. Single parents—Fiction. 4. Female friendship—Fiction. 5. Serial murder investigation—Fiction. I. Henry, April. II. Title.
PS3623.I382M38 2013
813'.6—dc23 2013000713

Printed in the United States of America

13 14 15 16 17 RRD 6 5 4 3 2 1

For Jacob and Dani,
with my unconditional love always,
from Mom.

One may smile, and smile, and be a villain.

—Shakespeare, *Hamlet*, act I, scene 5

CHAPTER 1

If life was like a play, then the director had the ultimate power. The power to blight men's lives, or to give them what they most longed for. Even the power to utter the ultimate yes or no.

Tonight was a special engagement. One night only. Never to be repeated. The stage was a hundred-year-old two-story house, lit from top to bottom as if electricity cost nothing. The director watched from the quiet residential lane. At the director's side was the killer. It was a walk-on role with no dialogue.

Now for the lead actress to make her entrance.

Anticipation grew, thrumming like a bow string.

But where was she? Ah, there. In the basement by the window, phone clamped between ear and shoulder, pulling a box from a shelf.

The director nodded, and the killer raised the gun.

The lead bent over and set the box on the floor. Then she knelt beside it, dropping from view before the killer could take aim.

The director motioned for the killer to wait. Exhaling slowly, the killer lowered the gun.

"It was all right there on Facebook," Mia Quinn said into the phone as she tugged at the lid on the blue plastic eighteen-gallon storage tub. "Darin's dad made screen captures in case anyone tries to take anything down. He showed me a few of them."

"Facebook is God's gift to prosecutors," Colleen Miller said. "A couple of months ago I had this defendant on the stand. He swore on his mama's grave that he didn't sell drugs and that he'd never even held a gun. Then I asked him to explain why, if that were true, he had a Facebook status update showing himself holding a Glock, smoking a blunt, and flashing a sheaf of hundreds." Colleen laughed. "It was all over right there."

"It's hard to argue with proof that we can put right up on the screen in front of the jury." Mia finally managed to pry off the lid, revealing fishing supplies: a tan canvas vest, a tackle box, and a reel.

There, that wasn't so hard, she told herself. *This stuff can go in the garage sale, no problem.* The cold from the basement's cement floor seeped through her old jeans, worn soft as flannel. Outside, the dark pressed up against the windows, half set in the ground. Summer had passed in a blur, and now winter was coming.

Colleen said, "I love how defendants can't help but post incriminating pictures of themselves flashing gang signs and all the stuff they're not supposed to have. Now if only we could get our witnesses to stop using it. You know the other side is checking it as much as we are."

As prosecutors for Washington's King County District Attorney's Office, Mia and Colleen didn't get to choose their clientele. The hard truth was that sometimes the victims and the witnesses they built a case around were only a little bit better than the bad guys they were trying to put away. This was blue-collar law, not white-shoe. It was down and dirty, blood and guts, real people as opposed to companies squabbling genteelly over money.

But being a prosecutor also meant you made a real difference. Which was why Mia had been glad to go back to work at the same office she had left nearly five years earlier, even if the reason she needed to return was terrible.

"When I left, I don't think we were checking the Internet nearly as much." Still on her knees, the phone pressed up against her ear,

Mia dragged over another box from the nearest shelf. No matter how much she didn't want to face this, it had to be done. "Now everyone Tweets or has a blog or at least a Facebook page. Even my dad is on Facebook, although his picture is still that generic blue silhouette."

Mia pulled the lid from the second box. It held the vintage black pin-striped suit Scott wore when they got married. In the wedding photos he had looked all ears and teeth and Adam's apple—too young to be getting married. Over the years he had fleshed out to the point he complained about love handles.

Underneath the suit was a cardigan his mother had knit him in college, cream colored with two stags rearing on the back. He had never worn it. The sweater and the suit were like so much else down here, stuff Scott had never quite parted with.

"A lot changed while you were gone," Colleen said. "Frank's the district attorney, the murder rate is lower than it's been since 1955, even though the economy is in the toilet, and now a killer is likely to be some crazy guy with a grudge and a bunch of guns and a plan to take out a whole restaurant full of people. And of course everyone's on the Internet now, even bad guys. Right before you came back I prosecuted a guy who claimed he didn't even know the victim. Only I found photos of them together on his friend's Flickr account." Colleen's low laugh was tinged with sadness. "If there's one thing this job has taught me, it's to turn over rocks—but sometimes you don't like what you find underneath. Lately I've been thinking how flat-out ugly it can get when you start looking."

Mia nodded, forgetting for a moment that Colleen couldn't see her. A familiar smell teased her. And suddenly it was like Scott was right there in the room with her. She closed her eyes and imagined him pulling her to her feet, slipping behind her to lift her hair and kiss the back of her neck.

How long had it been since he had done that?

"Still there, Mia?" Colleen asked.

She shook herself. "Sorry. It's like every box I open is a surprise package. How about you? Have you found anything you want to add to my garage sale?"

"I'm rooting around in my basement, but all I've found so far are some old albums. I'm talking vinyl. Do you think anyone would want Fleetwood Mac's *Rumor and Sigh*?"

"You never know. I wish Gabe would start playing that instead of whatever it is he does listen to." Even from the basement Mia could hear her fourteen-year-old's music two floors above. Discordant, angry. It wasn't singing so much as yelling set to a thrumming bass line and pounding drums.

Colleen said, "You know, you could probably get more if you put your stuff on Craigslist."

Mia had thought about this when she sat up late at night with her computer and her calculator and her file full of bills. "Yeah, but then I'd have to set up meetings with every potential buyer. That takes too much time and just lets a lot of people know too much about me. A garage sale will get it all over with at once."

"Still, before you go pricing everything at a quarter, let me come over and look through it with you," Colleen insisted. "Some stuff might do great on eBay."

"Sure." Mia lifted her head and scanned the basement. It was overwhelming. Boxes and boxes and boxes, some filled with Scott's old files. A bench and a rack of weights. Gray Rubbermaid cabinets, some of them filled with pantry items, others with cans of paint, plastic bottles of automotive additives, baby food jars full of screws. And what about Scott's power tools? In the corner was an electric saw. That should definitely go before Gabe decided to make something one afternoon and sawed his fingers off.

Colleen cleared her throat. "And, Mia, I know things have been hard, so if you're tight for money, I could maybe—"

Mia cut her off. "We're fine," she lied. The hole was so big that no matter what she threw in, it would never be filled up. Just like the hole in her heart. She returned to her original question, the one that had prompted her to call Colleen on a Sunday night. "I want to file against those kids," she said. "I know you didn't get a chance to look at them, but their posts were like weapons. It hurt *me* to read them. I can't imagine what it was like for Darin Dane."

Mia was still trying to figure out exactly how the politics of her job had changed, and it was easier to ask Colleen off-line without worrying if she was stepping on toes. "Darin's dad has more than enough proof that these kids hounded his son to death. We can charge them with cyberstalking, harassment, violation of civil rights . . ."

"I don't know . . ." Colleen's voice trailed off. She had been the first to talk to Darin's father but had ended up asking Mia to step in because her caseload was too heavy. "I just keep imagining what Frank will say." Frank was Frank D'Amato, once just Colleen and Mia's co-worker, now the King County prosecutor. He prided himself on the office's winning record. But key to that record was taking on cases you couldn't lose. "This kid was fragile to begin with. He's been in counseling since, what—since he was eleven or twelve? Frank will say his demons were all in his head, not at the school."

"But those messages they posted about him were vicious. They said he was ugly, deformed, stupid, crazy. They urged him to kill himself." Mia regarded the shop vac. If she kept it, what would she use it for? If she tried to sell it at the garage sale, would anyone buy it? Or should she just give up and haul it to Goodwill? And then there were the leaf blower, lawn mower, and extension ladder. She had never used any of them. Even before Brooke was born, Scott had taken care of the outside part of their lives. Now she would have to get over her fear of heights if she wanted to make sure the gutters didn't overflow during Seattle's rainy season. Which was pretty much November through May.

"Some of the posts said the world would be better if he were dead," she continued. "It's a hate crime. Darin was gay, or at least everyone thought he was."

Her eyes suddenly filled with tears at the thought of Darin, the same age as Gabe, although the two boys could not be more different. And while she had no worries that Gabe was being bullied, Mia had made it clear to him that he had to show her his computer screen or share his passwords anytime she asked.

"Frank will say it's normal for teens to have spats, to have hierarchies, even to ostracize one kid," Colleen said. "And school's only been in session for, what—two weeks? Frank will say that short of a time period isn't enough to prove causality."

Mia took a deep breath. "Yes, but these kids had been targeting him for months. And it didn't let up just because school was out for summer. They were relentless, and the Internet made it easy to harass him around the clock. The only thing school being back in session gave them was easy access to his physical person. The autopsy found bruises consistent with his having been hit, kicked, and punched."

The silence spun out so long Mia thought their connection had been dropped. Then Colleen said carefully, "You might need to be realistic, Mia. Frank's up for reelection this fall. To win he needs a big war chest. And the kids you're talking about, the ones who went to school with Darin Dane, also happen to be the sons and daughters of some of Seattle's richest parents. People who are software engineers, doctors, lawyers. They're not going to let someone smear their kids, especially not right when they're trying to get them into good colleges. And they're not going to support a DA who lets one of his attorneys do that."

"Doesn't Frank want to do what's right more than he wants to win?"

"Nothing is black-and-white," Colleen said simply. "Nothing."

Mia lifted the top from the next box. It was filled with Scott's ski clothes. Just another hobby they hadn't had time for since Brooke was born.

Mia lifted a pair of black ski pants and blinked in surprise at what she found underneath. It couldn't be—could it? She pushed herself to her feet.

Mia must have made a little noise, because Colleen said, "Mia? Is something wrong?"

A head bobbed at the bottom of the window. There. Finally. She was getting to her feet.

At a motion from the director, the killer stepped out of the shadows, lifted the gun, and carefully lined the sights up on the white column of her throat. The director watched dispassionately. The lead wasn't a person anymore, but she hadn't really been one for a while, had she? She was a problem.

A problem that could be solved with a single twitch of the finger.

The director nodded, and the killer pulled the trigger.

CHAPTER 2

"Colleen?" Mia said after the sudden boom and clatter. "What the heck was that?"

No answer.

"Colleen?"

A gunshot, Mia thought. Her blood turned to slush. *That was a gunshot.*

No. That was impossible.

Wasn't it?

"Colleen?"

She must have imagined the boom. Or misunderstood it. The clatter, though, the clatter made sense. Colleen had simply dropped the phone. Any second now and she would pick it up, laughing and apologizing for her clumsiness.

Mia pushed back her memory's insistence that there had been a boom first. The memory that reminded her that the sound of the phone falling to the ground had come second.

Because the first sound could *not* have been a gunshot.

"Hello? Colleen? Hello?" Mia held her breath, straining to hear.

And after a second she did hear something. But it was another puzzle. A watery bubbling. Like the sound four-year-old Brooke made when she felt brave enough to put her face in the tub and blow bubbles. And then, terrifying and sharp and impossible to deny, a moan.

"Colleen?" she said again, but more softly. Part of her already knew there might not be an answer.

She had to call the police. But how? If she hung up on Colleen, she would sever her friend's only connection to the outside world.

Her cell phone. In her mind's eye Mia saw it on the kitchen counter. She raced up the basement stairs, rounded the corner, and snatched up the phone. The music thumped overhead. "Gabe!" she shouted as she dialed 911, still clamping the landline phone, the one connected to Colleen, between her right shoulder and ear. "Gabe, turn that off!"

"Police, fire, or medical?" a voice said in her left ear.

"Medical. And probably police." Overhead the music dropped a few decibels.

"What is the nature of your problem?"

"I was just on the phone with Colleen Miller, my co-worker, when there was a loud noise. I think it was a gunshot." Mia felt like she couldn't speak fast enough. "Our connection is still open, so I called you on a different phone, but Colleen's not talking. The only thing I can hear is her breathing, but it sounds all, all *wet*. And she's moaning."

Even the unflappable 911 dispatcher's tone changed at that. In answer to her rapid-fire questions, Mia provided her own name as well as Colleen's name, address, and phone number, and the fact that she lived alone. As Mia spoke she hurried up the stairs to the second floor. In her right ear she couldn't hear the moan anymore, let alone the sound that must be Colleen's sputtering breath. Had her friend stopped making sounds, or was it simply too noisy to hear her?

Mia flung open the door to Gabe's room. He was bent over his electric guitar, his too-long bangs a brown curtain in front of his eyes. At the sound of the door banging open, he scowled and then stabbed a button on his computer keyboard. The music abruptly ceased.

"I already turned it d—" He stopped himself when he saw Mia's expression and the two phones she held, one to each ear.

Mia answered another of the dispatcher's questions. "As far as I know, Colleen doesn't have any guns in the home." Suddenly she thought of an explanation. "She was looking for something in her basement right before it happened. Maybe her ex left a gun behind she didn't know about and she dropped it or something." Even though Colleen and Martin had been divorced for fifteen years, anything was possible, wasn't it?

Gabe's mouth fell open.

"Has she said anything to you?" the dispatcher asked. "Can you still hear her?"

Mia held herself perfectly still and was rewarded, if that was the right word, with a faint sound pulsing against her ear. "Just that bubbling sound of her breathing, that's all I can hear now. Nothing else. You've got to tell them to hurry." She couldn't bear to think of Colleen all alone and struggling to breathe.

"I've dispatched police and an ambulance to the scene," the dispatcher said. "Don't hang up, Mia. I need you to stay on the line and tell me anything you hear."

"Look, I'm going to give my son the phone and have him listen. I'll have him call you guys on his cell phone if she says anything. But I need to get over there, and I can't do that and listen."

In her ear, the dispatcher started to argue, but Mia was already hitting the button to end the call on her cell. Over the past few terrible months, she and Colleen had reconnected, becoming even closer than before. If Colleen needed her, Mia would be there, no ifs, ands, or buts.

With the sudden silence of no music and no 911 dispatcher, Mia listened again. Nothing except the faint gurgling sound that must be Colleen breathing.

"Mom—what's going on?" Gabe had pushed the hair out of his eyes, and Mia suddenly understood why he might wear it like that. Gabe wasn't old enough yet to have mastered how to hide his feelings, so he let his hair do it for him. His eyes were huge and dark, as vulnerable as a fawn's.

"Something's happened at Colleen's. Maybe an accident with a gun. I need you to do two things for me. One, be here in case Brooke wakes up. And two, stay on the line and listen. It doesn't sound like Colleen can talk, but if she says anything, I need you to listen carefully and write down exactly what she says. And if she can talk, ask her what's wrong, what happened, and then call 911 on your cell and tell them what she says."

Mia held out the phone, but Gabe didn't take it.

"Wait—where are you going?" His voice cracked.

"To Colleen's in case I can help. Look—all you have to do is listen." Mia pressed the phone in his hand and ran back into the hall and down the stairs.

A few months ago Mia wouldn't have asked Gabriel to watch his four-year-old sister, let alone insist he listen to those terrible sounds on the other end of the phone line. But a lot had changed in a few months.

She grabbed up her purse and car keys from the small table next to the front door and ran outside, twisting the lock behind her.

The drive to Colleen's house normally took a little less than twenty minutes. Tonight it took about twelve. A police car, siren wailing, passed as she pulled over to the shoulder, and then another. A block or two from Colleen's house, more lights slashed the night ahead of her.

Mia had to park a few houses back because of the number of police cars, marked and unmarked. She was at the top of Colleen's driveway when a young cop stepped in front of her, arms spread wide.

"Ma'am, stop. You can't go any farther."

"But I'm a friend of Colleen's. Is she okay?" Part of Mia already knew the answer. An ambulance was in front of the house, but it was just sitting there, no siren, not even any lights. Two paramedics leaned against the side panel, talking in low voices.

"Ma'am, I need you to get back."

"Look." Mia took a deep breath. "I'm an attorney with the King County Prosecutor's Office, same as Colleen. I was on the phone with her when something happened. I'm the one who called 911."

A man spoke behind her. "It's okay, Orkney."

Mia turned. Charlie Carlson, one of Seattle's homicide detectives, had just arrived.

A wave of nausea swept over Mia as her stomach crammed itself into the back of her throat. She put her hand to her mouth. From behind the shelter of her fingers, she said, "Oh no, Charlie. If you're here, it can't be good news for Colleen."

He didn't answer her directly. Instead he said, "I heard you were back. Heck of a way to see you again." He had a nose that bent at the tip and dark hair that Mia had always thought was really too long for a cop. But Charlie was known for coming close to the line—and sometimes crossing it. As Mia well knew.

"I was on the phone with her when she was shot. At least it sounded like a shot." Mia's thoughts suddenly flew to Gabriel. "In fact, my son—"

"You were on the line with her?" Charlie interrupted. "Did she say who shot her?"

"She wasn't doing anything beyond trying to breathe." She hoped Gabe hadn't heard the moment when Colleen's breathing must have ceased. "Look, my son could still be on the line with her. I asked him to listen in case she said anything. You've got to let me talk to him and tell him he can hang up."

She started down the driveway, but Charlie put a hand on her shoulder.

"Hold up, Mia. You can't go down there. This is a crime scene."

Who was Charlie Carlson to tell her what she was allowed to do at a crime scene? She opened her mouth to protest. If Gabe was still on the line, the next voice she wanted him to hear was hers.

Before she could argue, Charlie said, "I'll take care of it right now," and started to jog down the driveway while pulling a pair of blue vinyl gloves from his back pocket. He called back over his shoulder, "What's your son's name?"

"Gabriel."

Charlie ducked inside.

Mia waited in the darkness at the top of the driveway, hugging herself even though it wasn't that cold. Men talked in low voices and radios crackled. Down the street, three crime-scene techs were pulling on their identical boots and white Tyvek suits. Farther back, neighbors gathered in clumps, talking or standing with their hands over their mouths.

Here it was quiet and pitch-black. The nearest house to Colleen didn't have a single light on. It had been for sale for a couple of months, and now the For Sale sign listed to one side.

No stars out. Mia reminded herself that the stars were still there, just hidden by a blanket of clouds.

And suddenly Charlie was galloping up the drive to her, yelling as he went. "Mia, when I picked up the phone, no one was on it. But I could hear someone screaming in the background." He had nearly reached her. "It sounded like a little girl."

Mia's vision spun like water swirling down a drain. Brooke. He was talking about Brooke.

And Brooke was screaming.

Screaming.

Charlie grabbed her upper arm and tugged her forward. "Come on! I'll take you home with lights and siren."

CHAPTER 3

After his mom ran downstairs and rushed to Colleen's, Gabe sat very, very still. His suddenly sweaty hand pressed the phone against the side of his head.

In his ear was a sound like an aquarium. It was bearable if he thought of it like that. If he pictured bubbles rising through clear water filled with colorful fish and miniature plastic castles.

Not when he thought of it as a woman gagging on her own blood.

If there was one thing in the world Gabe didn't want to be doing, it was listening to what sounded like his mom's friend dying.

His shoulders hunched suddenly, and he shivered so hard the phone rattled against his cheek. Gabe felt like he had last winter when he had the flu. Shaky. Nauseated. Not quite real.

And this couldn't be real, could it?

Their home phone had a button you could push to put it on speaker. He pressed it and set the phone down on his desk. The wet, almost slurpy sounds were still there, but they no longer felt like they were part of him, rattling around inside his skull.

Gabe tried to turn the sounds into background noise. Like the hum of an air conditioner.

His eyes fell on his history textbook. He should be reading it, but of course he couldn't do anything right now. Just listen. Listen and hope that the ambulance people would get there in time to save Colleen Miller.

Three months ago Gabe would have said this was going to be a great year. High school instead of middle school. Getting a learner's permit in the spring. Making the football team, even though he wasn't that big. At least not yet.

But everything had changed, hadn't it? And Gabe was just expected to suck it up and deal with it. Overnight, it seemed, his mom had become the enemy.

She was crabby all the time now. Always nagging. Always yelling. Sometimes at herself, but mostly at him. Even when she was just asking questions, it sounded like yelling. Where had he been, who had he been with, what had he been doing?

But most of her sentences began with "Why didn't you . . ." *Why didn't you . . . finish your homework, make sure Brooke took a bath, tell me you had to bring in art supplies for class?*

Gabe started when the tone of Colleen's breathing changed. It roughened, paused—his stomach did a slow flip—then, after a watery gasp, resumed its rhythmic gurgle.

It was the most horrible sound he had ever heard. Gabe closed his eyes and tried to distract himself by thinking about how his mom wanted him to give up his whole entire life just because his dad wasn't around anymore. Just because she had to go back to work.

It wasn't like he didn't love his little sister. But everyone else on the team hung out together after practice, and meanwhile he was stuck being Brooke's unpaid babysitter. And there was dinner to start and the house to pick up, at least according to his mom.

She said they all had to pull together or they would fall apart.

But for Gabe, his new life was like being an adult without any of the good parts. He had all these responsibilities, but no money, no car, no freedom. If he were an adult, he could choose whether or not to have a kid. But he hadn't gotten to choose Brooke.

"Taxation without representation, dude," as his friend Tyler put it.

The only good thing that had come out of everything changing was his new phone. It could do everything, in addition to allowing his mom to call him a dozen times a day. She never texted him. She didn't get that no one called anymore. You didn't have to answer a text right away. Texting gave you time to think about what to say and a record of everything you had said.

From the landline phone on the desk, Colleen kept inhaling and exhaling in that strange, watery way.

He couldn't take this anymore. He couldn't just sit here and listen to these wet gasps.

Gabe picked up his cell and tapped out a text.

Gabe: You won't believe what I'm doing.

Tyler's reply came faster than he had hoped.

Tyler: What?

Gabe: Listening to some lady who's dying. It's horrible.

A faint groan rose from the phone lying on his desk. Bile flooded Gabe's mouth. The only thing tethering him to sanity was the cell phone in his hands.

Tyler: JK?

Gabe's thumbs flew over the tiny virtual keyboard.

Gabe: I wish. Mom was talking to friend on phone and then I guess she was shot. The friend, I mean. Now Mom's going over there and making me listen in case she says something. Only she can't talk. Just breathe. But it sounds all wrong.

Tyler: That's awful. Do you know her?

Gabe: Sort of.

Colleen was old, even older than his mom. She had a daughter in college but seemed to have forgotten how to act around kids. Her attempts at conversation had a slightly desperate quality. Every time she saw him, she asked him what his favorite subject was in school. And every time he said, "Lunch," she laughed in a fake-y, high-pitched way.

Only Gabe would give anything now to hear her fake laugh. Not this. He strained to hear sirens or footsteps or rescuers shouting in the background, but there was nothing but the harsh, irregular rasp of her breath. And then even that stopped.

Gabe: I just want to hang up and tell my mom we got disconnected.

But if he lied, his mom would probably know just by looking at his face.

Without warning, a scream shattered the night. Gabe's whole body jolted like he had just stuck his finger in an electric socket. He let his cell phone fall to his desk.

The scream hadn't come from Colleen's house.

It had come from right down the hall.

From the room where his sister slept.

Gabe's head whipped around. He saw no one in the hall. And he hadn't heard anyone come in, although he had been so focused on the two phones he had blocked out the rest of his surroundings. Could a burglar have snuck in after his mom ran out? Had she forgotten to lock the front door?

Another scream pierced the silence.

"I'm coming, Brooke! I'm coming." He jumped to his feet. At the last second he grabbed the landline phone, the one that was still connected to Colleen. As he picked it up, a new sound came from it. Something he didn't have time to think about now.

Instead he ran down the hall and opened the door to Brooke's bedroom.

Brooke was sitting bolt upright in her little pale blue wooden toddler bed. Her mouth was stretched wide in terror, and the whites showed top and bottom on her eyes. Her breathing was fast and shallow. She didn't even turn toward him. Instead her staring eyes were focused on one corner of the room. The corner where the window was. The corner he couldn't see because the door only opened three-fourths of the way and then was blocked by the dresser.

Gabe let the phone slip from his suddenly boneless hand. What was his sister looking at? Who was in the room?

Brooke screamed again, her hands coming up in front of her face, ready to ward off a blow.

Taking a deep breath, Gabe charged forward to put himself between whoever it was and his little sister.

CHAPTER 4

Dispatch informed Charlie Carlson that all available officers in the area had already been deployed—to Colleen Miller's house.

That meant that whatever was happening at Mia Quinn's house, Charlie would be the first officer on the scene.

Charlie and Mia, which might be a mistake. A kid screaming could mean a lot of things. Some of them very bad. Some of them things no parent should ever witness. He requested another unit to be scrambled from Colleen's, but knew he would still beat them there. Mia had already told him the fastest route to take. Made even faster by how Charlie was driving.

Going sixty in a residential area was a dumb idea, despite the fact that he had turned on the siren, the alternately flashing lights in the grill, and the red-and-blue light bar in the rear window. He was traveling too fast for any pedestrian—and most drivers—to react. Charlie goosed it up to sixty-five, his eyes scanning back and forth. One evening jogger dressed all in black except for white earbuds, and that would be all she wrote.

Meanwhile, Mia was speed-dialing a number on her cell phone. She pressed it to her head, the index finger of her free hand closing the other ear. Her lips were a tight line. After a long moment she shook her head and tapped a button to turn off the phone.

"Why didn't you take Colleen's phone with you?" she demanded.

"I need to know what's wrong." She groaned. "If something's happened to my kids . . ."

"I couldn't, Mia." He had to raise his voice to be heard over the siren. He and Mia had tangled when she first started working at King County, but that was a long time ago and it didn't matter now. Not when two kids were in danger. "It was a landline."

Colleen Miller had been sprawled on her side on top of a dozen record albums, her head turned to face the ceiling, a slick of blood painting her upper lip and chin. The bullet had caught her just below the hollow of her throat. More blood pooled like thick syrup under her head and upper torso, on top of the LPs. The phone rested on the floor near her bottom shoulder, just a few inches from her mouth. If Colleen had been breathing after Mia heard the shot, it didn't look like it could have gone on for very long.

Charlie had taken two quick photos of the phone—noting that there was no blood on the black-and-silver face—so he could put it back exactly where it had been after he told Mia's kid it was okay to hang up. That the boy could stop listening for the dead woman to name her killer.

With gloved hands, Charlie had gingerly picked up the phone. But when he put it to his ear, all he heard was a little kid screaming.

Now Mia asked, "Was Brooke saying anything?"

"Not that I could tell," Charlie said, hedging a little. It had just been wordless screams, seemingly without even a pause for breath. "I'm pretty sure I could hear your boy calling her name in the background." Again, he left out the panic in the older kid's voice.

"Did Brooke sound like she was hurt?" Mia's voice had gotten smaller, until it was barely audible over the thrum of the tires and the wail of the siren.

Parents seemed to know unerringly whether a child's cry was faked, whether it sprang from boredom or genuine pain. Charlie might not be a parent, but he knew what had been under the sounds he had heard.

Sheer terror.

"I don't know." Not knowing whether it was right or wrong to say even part of what he was thinking, Charlie just went ahead. "She was pretty loud. If your daughter's hurt, it didn't affect her lungs any." He thought of how the blood must have bubbled in Colleen's airway and then out through her mouth.

"Brooke walked in her sleep last week." Again Mia tapped on her phone and then held it to her ear, but Charlie could tell by her posture that she no longer expected anyone to answer. A few seconds later she put it back in her lap. "Maybe she fell out of bed and hurt herself. Our schedule has really changed since I went back to work. Her bedtime is all messed up."

Charlie just hoped that the reason for the screams would turn out to be trivial. Something that would seem like an overreaction tomorrow.

But then he thought of the horror and panic and fear he had heard in the little girl's voice. Crime was down all over the city, but just last month he had worked the case of a Yugoslavian immigrant who had gone crazy and stabbed to death three of his neighbors. Including a seven-year-old girl the guy had chased out into the front yard.

He pushed the accelerator up to nearly seventy. "You don't carry, do you?"

"No." Mia shook her head.

"Is there a gun at your house?" Maybe that had been what had happened. Mom was gone, so the kids decided to take out the gun and play cowboys or gangbangers? Or, even more likely, the older boy was jumpy because his mom had gone tearing off in the middle of the night, heard a noise, and accidentally shot his sister?

"No," Mia said again.

Nodding, Charlie blew air through pursed lips. Guns and kids didn't mix, not in his opinion. But when he thought of that little girl screaming, he found himself wishing that the other kid, the boy named Gabriel, had something to protect them both with. Something a little bit more powerful than a can of bug spray or a tennis racquet.

Mia's hands were braced on the dash. She leaned forward, her eyes fastened on the road, as if the extra few inches somehow helped her get to her kids faster.

"Put on your seat belt." Charlie was doing seventy in a twenty-five zone. His seat belt had gone on at the same time he turned the key in the ignition. He had once seen a rookie cop after a collision at 105 miles an hour. The kid had metal for hips and wasn't on the force anymore.

Mia didn't move. He grunted impatiently.

"Mia, come on, put on your seat belt. We need to get you there in one piece."

Slowly, like someone in a dream, she sat back and pulled the belt across her body, her eyes never leaving the road.

"Tell me about your kids." It might be useful information, but mostly it would keep Mia focused. Keep her mind off what horror might be going on at her house. Charlie saw gleaming knives, a tumble down an entire flight of stairs, a fast-moving fire, a meth-addled burglar. The trouble with their line of work was that your memory—not your imagination—could supply you with a million terrible vignettes.

Mia took a deep breath. "My son, Gabriel, he's fourteen. He's a freshman this year. And Brooke is four."

A long gap between kids. With anyone else, Charlie might have figured that the two kids were the product of different marriages, each husband wanting kids of his own. But Charlie had known Mia back in her first turn through the King County Prosecutor's Office, back before she decided to stay home and play house full-time. Her decision had always surprised him.

Then again, while Charlie had been married three times, he didn't have any kids, so he didn't know what it was like trying to be both a mom and a prosecutor.

"And what's Gabriel like?"

"He's a really good kid." Mia took a shaky breath. "I mean, he's been having a hard time with what happened, but what kid wouldn't? Normally I never would have asked him to listen to Colleen, but I didn't have much choice."

Single mothers. The world was full of them. Charlie had no idea how they did it all, how they wiped noses and packed lunches and reviewed homework and joined the PTA or whatever else it was they did.

Charlie didn't even have a cat.

"And your daughter? What's she like?" He hoped this wouldn't remind Mia about the screaming, but then again, it was clear that the screaming was all she could think about.

A smile touched her lips. "Brooke is four, but she thinks she's older. She's really proud of herself that she can put dishes in the dishwasher and help make her bed."

As she spoke, Mia's gaze never wavered from the dark road ahead of them. She was blond, blue-eyed, about five foot seven, slender. Not his type. He liked them short and dark and curvy. Plus she was far too rigid. She had never understood that sometimes you had to look at the big picture.

Charlie tore his eyes away. He had to be like Mia and keep his eyes on the road. So many bicyclists these days didn't have lights, let alone helmets. An ER nurse he dated said her hospital had a name for people like that.

Donors.

Mia continued, "All this change has been hard on Brooke too. Now she's in preschool full-time and then Gabe has to pick her up after school or football practice. Both of my kids are being forced to grow up too fast."

"What were they doing when you left?" Charlie asked.

"Brooke was sleeping. And Gabriel should have been doing homework. But when I went in to tell him about Colleen, he was playing his guitar to music on his computer." Mia fell quiet and hit Redial. After a few seconds she touched the button to end the call. Her next words burst out of her. "I never should have left them alone." Her eyes widened. "Charlie—what if it was all a ruse to get me to leave?"

"What do you mean?"

"How was Colleen killed?" Mia turned away from the road and stared at him wide-eyed.

"Shot in the chest."

"Where was she in her house?"

"In her basement." Charlie wondered where she was going with this.

"That's just like Stan." When she saw his blank look, she said, "You know. Stan Slavich. He used to work in my office. Until he was murdered."

Charlie hadn't thought about Stan in several years. He was pretty sure a homicide detective named Carmen Zapata had handled that case. Carmen was dead now. Breast cancer. Charlie said, "We never solved that one, did we?"

"No. And think about it, Charlie." Mia's back went rigid as she ticked off the coincidences. "Stan was a King County prosecutor. Just like Colleen. He was shot through the basement window of his home. Just like Colleen. And he was all alone when he was shot. Just like Colleen. What if someone is targeting prosecutors? What if they came for me next—and went after my kids when they figured out I wasn't home?"

"They would have to move awful fast." There were a lot of things Charlie thought were possible, but this wasn't one of them. "I don't think whatever's happening at your house is connected to Colleen, Mia. Maybe there is some kind of a connection between Stan and Colleen, but I doubt it goes any further than that."

The parallels between the two killings were too hard to ignore, though. Charlie didn't believe in coincidences. He didn't believe in much he couldn't see, hear, touch, taste, smell. "When did Stan die, anyway? Six years ago?"

"Four and a half. I know exactly because I was on bed rest with Brooke. They wouldn't even let me go to the funeral. Scott was really disturbed when Stan was killed. And then Brooke was born four weeks early. So Scott talked me into not going back." She gave a shaky laugh. "You probably heard how well that worked out." She turned back to look at the street. "It's right at the second light, and then it's just around the corner." Mia undid her seat belt.

Charlie cut the siren. If there was a bad guy in the house, he didn't want him to feel his back was against the wall. "Let me go in alone first and see what's wrong." And if it was really bad, maybe he could keep Mia away from it. There were certain sights no one should ever see.

Charlie had seen most of them.

"No way, Charlie." She was in full mama bear mode now, ready to rise up on her hind legs and swipe her claws at whatever got between her and her cubs. "Don't argue with me. Those are my babies in there."

She was out of the car before it had even come to a stop. Charlie barely threw it into park and ran after her, cursing himself. Whatever was happening in the house was bad enough.

He didn't need Mia to become a third victim.

CHAPTER 5

As she sprinted across her lawn, Mia heard muffled screams coming from the second floor of her house. The sounds gave wings to her feet.

What was wrong? She saw no strange cars, no flames, no smoke. The house was lit up from top to bottom, but the blinds were drawn.

Usually she liked how far apart the houses were here. But as she sprinted up the three stairs to the porch, Mia wished that she and her neighbors lived cheek by jowl.

She turned the knob and yanked the front door back. A shock ran up her arm and into her shoulder when it didn't budge.

The front door was still locked. No unlocked door, no strange cars, no flames, no smoke. No sign of anything amiss.

But somewhere above her, Brooke was still screaming, barely pausing for breath. At the end of each ululation, the sound was nearly a sob.

While Mia fumbled her key into the lock, Charlie peered through one of the door's small paned windows, one hand cupped around his eyes. His gun was out of its holster and by his side. The sight of it did not reassure Mia.

She twisted the key and threw open the door. "Brooke? Gabe?" she yelled as she ran into the empty entryway, Charlie at her heels. "What's wrong?"

For an answer, Brooke only screamed again.

"Mom!" Gabe called, his tone so desperate that tears sparked her eyes. "Something's really wrong with Brooke!"

Mia flew up the stairs. Her foot slipped on the fifth step and she half fell, banging one knee. Shaking off Charlie's hand, she bounced back up, not even registering the pain.

No blood, she thought when she reached the doorway to Brooke's room and tried to make sense of what she saw. *Thank God there's no blood*. But something was still terribly wrong.

Gabriel was kneeling on the bed, leaning over Brooke. His hands were on his sister's shoulders, trying to hold her still. Arms flailing, Brooke twisted back and forth, her body arching, her feet kicking under the covers. She let out another scream that made the hair rise on the back of Mia's neck.

"Oh, baby, no!" Rushing forward, she squeezed past Gabriel and tried to scoop up Brooke to comfort her. But at her touch, her daughter stiffened and bucked and scratched all the more, her back bending like a bow. She howled again, right next to Mia's ear. Her skin was clammy. Strands of hair stuck to her forehead. Brooke's gaze swung to Mia, but her eyes were oddly flat and unfocused.

"Watch out, Mom!" Gabe yelled.

Brooke's fist hit Mia in the temple so hard that for a moment one side of the room went black. "Brooke, it's okay," Mia shouted, trying to pierce through her daughter's cries. "Brooke, Brooke, Brooke—wake up!"

Instead Brooke kicked and thrashed as if Mia were attacking her. Wincing and tucking her head, Mia tried to grab her wrists, but Brooke fought back even harder, twisting her hands free. Finally Mia leaned her weight across her four-year-old's body, pinning her arms in place. She pressed her own face into the pillow, cheek to cheek with her daughter. Brooke's heart felt like it was beating so hard it might burst through her damp skin. Could a heart even beat that fast without causing damage?

Gabe pinned Brooke's legs in place under the covers, but she continued to fight them both.

Had she eaten some type of poison? Gotten into the sleeping pills the doctor had prescribed for Mia three months earlier? Was she having a seizure?

Her daughter's breathing was ragged and harsh, each exhale an explosion ending in another howl. It was so rapid that just hearing it made Mia's own breathing speed up.

"Brooke, baby, can you hear me?" she said, but her daughter's frenzy didn't abate.

"How long has this been going on?" Charlie asked from the doorway. Mia glanced back at him. He was holstering his gun.

Gabe jerked his head around, his eyes widening.

"Who are you?"

"That's Charlie Carlson," Mia said, still trying to hold her daughter's tiny body still. She had to raise her voice to be heard over Brooke's continued keening. "He's a cop. When he picked up Colleen's phone to talk to you, he heard Brooke screaming."

Gabe's gaze flashed to the phone that lay faceup on the floor a few feet from the bed. "Is Colleen okay? I didn't hear her say anything, and then Brooke started screaming and I dropped the phone. I'm sorry."

"We can talk about Colleen later." Mia tried to say it lightly, as if nothing were wrong. "Right now we need to figure out what's wrong with Brooke. What happened?"

"I was in my room when she started screaming. I thought someone had broken in or something, but she was all by herself." Gabe took a shaky breath. "It's like she's not really there. I mean, I think she's hearing something, seeing something, but whatever it is, we can't see it. It's like she's stuck someplace else."

Could a four-year-old be mentally ill? As if in answer, Brooke let out another terrified wail.

"Should I get dispatch to send an ambulance?" Charlie asked.

"No," Mia said. "I want to try something." Shouting and holding Brooke down weren't working. "Let go of her legs," she told Gabe. "Go stand in the doorway with Charlie."

She was working off instinct now, a guess that the exact opposite of what she wanted to do—shake Brooke awake, force her back into herself—was what was really called for.

She released Brooke, who continued to flail and screech, but no worse than she had been. Kneeling next to the bed, Mia put her face as close as she could to her daughter's without touching her and waited for a moment of silence. Brooke let out another half scream, and after it was finished Mia half crooned, half whispered into the pink shell of her daughter's ear. "Mommy's here, baby. It's okay now. You can go to sleep. You can relax."

There was a pause. Brooke let out another cry, but it was quieter and somehow held a note of sadness. She was on her side now, facing the doorway. Tentatively, Mia put out her hand and lightly touched her daughter's lower back. Sweat had soaked through her pajamas. Mia began to rub slow, small circles. Brooke continued to cry out, but there were pauses in between, and the volume was diminished.

"It's okay, baby. I'm here. It's okay."

Outside, sirens suddenly split the night. Mia's hand jerked. She had forgotten that Charlie had asked for backup. She realized with a little shock that it had probably been less than five minutes since they ran up the stairs.

"I'll tell them it's okay," Charlie said. "Right?"

"Right," Mia said, her attention still fully focused on her daughter. The sound of the sirens didn't seem to have penetrated. Brooke's screams had turned into something more like sobs.

Charlie went down the hall and murmured into his radio.

Slowly Brooke's cries faded away. In five more minutes she was breathing peacefully, seemingly deep asleep. Gabe tiptoed closer to the bed, and occasionally Mia met his eyes and they exchanged tremulous smiles. Charlie came back to the doorway and watched them without speaking. Even Charlie Carlson, it seemed, knew there were times when it was better to do nothing.

Finally the only remaining sign of whatever had happened to Brooke was a faint flush on her cheeks and a few strands of hair still stuck to her face. Her mouth was loose, her breathing easy.

Slowly Mia lifted her hand. Brooke's breathing didn't change.

Mia got to her feet. Looking down at her daughter, she found it hard to believe what had just happened, those moments of terror. She hugged Gabe.

Charlie cleared his throat softly, and they both turned to him. "I've got to get back out to the crime scene. We'll talk tomorrow."

"Talk?" Mia blinked. "Why?"

"Because you're a witness to Colleen's murder."

Gabe's head whipped around. Mia wanted to throttle Charlie. Her son did not need this terrible news. Not now.

Charlie winced and shot an apologetic look at Mia.

"But I never even saw Colleen tonight," she protested.

"Yes, but you were on the phone with her when she got shot. You might be the only witness."

CHAPTER 6

Mia walked Charlie downstairs. To compensate for her suddenly wobbly knees, she kept a firm grip on the handrail.

"So you're going back to Colleen's?" she asked.

"Yeah. I need to get a search warrant so the crime-scene techs can do their thing." He ran a hand through his hair, somehow managing to leave it even messier than it was before. "Sure you're gonna be okay?"

"I'm fine."

Charlie tilted his head and looked at her without speaking.

Mia laughed a little, surprised she was capable of it.

"Of course everything's terrible. I mean, Colleen's dead and Brooke just had the worst nightmare I've ever seen. But my family is safe. And if the past couple of months have taught me anything, it's how important that is."

Sadness pulsed through Mia at the thought of her little family, just the three of them. It was like she had lost a leg but had somehow gotten used to hopping and lurching, grabbing on to whatever she could for balance while still feeling the ache of the phantom limb.

Charlie held out his hand. "Give me your keys. I'll have someone run your car back here tonight and put the keys through the mail slot."

Her car. Mia blinked. She had completely forgotten that it was still parked on Colleen's block.

"Oh, thanks. That will be twice you've saved me tonight." Only where were her keys? She patted her flat pockets. The entry table was bare. "The thing is, I don't remember where I left them."

Charlie opened the door and there was a telltale jingle. The keys were still dangling from the lock. He pulled them out. "Be sure to lock up after I leave."

Mia felt a flash of irritation. She wasn't so far gone that she would see him out the door and then forget to throw the bolt. And to have Charlie, of all people, giving her advice about being cautious. She knew her annoyance was irrational, her subsiding adrenaline looking for an outlet, but it felt right.

"Don't worry, I will." It was all she could do not to roll her eyes, like Gabe at his worst, but Charlie didn't seem to notice.

"I'll be in touch tomorrow." He took his own keys from his pocket.

After turning both locks on the door, she climbed the stairs. Brooke was still asleep, curled on her side, breathing evenly. Gently, Mia closed the door.

She tapped on the door to Gabe's room. He grunted in answer. When she went in he was looking at Facebook.

She put her hand on his shoulder, then leaned down to hug him. When he stiffened, she straightened up.

"Look, Gabe, about tonight . . ."

Her son kept his eyes on the computer screen. "What?" How was it possible that a single syllable could contain so many layers of disdain and anger?

"I just want to say I'm sorry about what happened. What I asked you to do."

"Okay." He still hadn't turned in his chair. Hadn't looked her in the eye.

Mia took a deep breath. "Colleen didn't say anything, did she? Before she . . . she died?"

He bit his lip. "No. There was just that weird sound of her breathing. And then even that"—Gabe hesitated for a long time, and Mia's heart broke a little—"that stopped."

"Oh, Gabriel." She touched his shoulder, and he shrugged off her hand.

His voice twisted. "I was listening so hard, just, you know, hoping she'd start breathing again, but all I could hear was some classical music. And then Brooke started screaming."

"Maybe I should have stayed here. All I could think was that maybe there was a possibility I could help her." She sighed. "I'm sorry that I just ended up leaving you to deal with everything."

"Yeah, I know, Mom." A flick of the eyes, not quite an eye roll. The vulnerability had disappeared.

Thinking about her last conversation with Colleen, Mia gestured toward his Facebook page. "You know not to say anything about this, right, Gabe? It's an active murder investigation."

"Mom! What do you think I'm going to do, put it on my status update?"

"I was only making sure," she said, hearing a whine creep into her voice that was more appropriate to someone Gabe's age or even younger. How had everything turned around so fast? She had meant to comfort him, compliment him. Now all they were doing was irritating each other. "I'm going to bed soon, and you should too."

He nodded. Mia thought it likely they were both lying. There was no way she could go to sleep now, not after everything that had happened. She needed to get some distance from it, find a way to let some of the adrenaline dissipate. It was all too much—the house, the bills, Colleen dead, Brooke's nightmare, Gabe's standoffishness.

Maybe she'd get something to eat. She wasn't at all hungry, but that didn't matter. What mattered was that food would help quiet her thoughts. It seemed like most people couldn't resist chocolate, ice cream, cookies, candy. Mia liked sweets just fine, but she didn't crave them. Instead it was Ritz crackers that called to her, Pringles, Doritos coated with spicy powder that turned her fingers orange. Scott used to joke that Mia had been born with a salt tooth.

She went back down to the basement, planning to grab one of the bags of Kettle potato chips she had hidden in the Rubbermaid cabinet behind a twenty-five-pound bag of basmati rice from Costco.

A few weeks earlier PCC Natural Markets had had a special, so she had bought a half dozen bags of chips with flavors like Backyard Barbecue and Loaded Baked Potato and squirreled them away.

She told herself it was a bargain, but it was like an addict stocking up on crack cocaine because it was on sale.

At the bottom of the stairs Mia stopped. The plastic tub she had pried the lid from just before Colleen was shot, the one that had revealed Scott's little secret, was still open. She didn't have the energy to think about it tonight. After snapping the lid back on, she lifted the tub back into place. Just one more thing Scott hadn't quite been honest about.

Just one more hard truth she had learned since he died.

Back upstairs she sat at the dining room table with the bag of chips in front of her. Now that Scott was gone, no one really ate in here. Their house had a dining room nobody used, a living room she only dusted, and a family room that lived up to its name. She faced the sideboard that displayed a framed, enlarged photo of her family, the four of them on a beach in Kauai.

Two weeks after that photo was taken, Scott had died in a single-car accident after meeting with a client.

She ripped open the bag and stuffed a chip into her mouth. "I can't do this, Scott," she whispered around shards of chip. "It's too much."

He kept smiling, his eyes hidden by sunglasses. One arm was slung around her waist while the other rested on Brooke's shoulder. Gabe stood a bit to one side, as if already anxious to flee the family unit.

Mia and Scott had just . . . fit. Like two puzzle pieces, they had filled in the empty places of the other. Scott was methodical. Mia more impulsive. Scott came from a stable family. Mia only dreamed of one. At college freshman orientation they ended up seated by each other, and after that they hadn't looked at anyone else.

And now Scott was dead and everything was a mess. Mia put another chip into her mouth. How could she be both mother and father when it felt like half of her had died along with Scott?

Brooke would never remember her dad. Gabe was going to have to find his way to manhood without his father's advice, or even his presence.

She shoved three chips in at once. The crunch, the salt, the spices, the way they immediately turned to mush on her tongue—it answered some need. Or numbed it.

She reached for another handful.

And now Colleen was dead. And something terrible had happened to Brooke. And all Mia had were questions with no answers.

There was nothing to do with the energy and the emotions. Nothing to do but eat.

Mia knew she was eating her feelings. So what? It made her feel better. Emptied out her mind. As long as she was chewing and swallowing and licking spices from her fingers, there wasn't room in her head for thoughts.

She had talked about it with Colleen only a few days ago, complaining that her pants were getting hard to button. "Sometimes you just need a good food coma," Colleen had said with a smile that pushed up her plump, ruddy cheeks until they nearly obscured her blue eyes. Colleen loved to eat too.

Had loved to eat.

They had met when Mia joined the King County Prosecutor's Office right out of law school. She liked Colleen right away, first as a mentor and then as a friend. Colleen called herself a lifer. She had never worked anywhere else. Divorced, with one daughter, she was funny, smart, kind. Honest and real.

Mia had kept working after Gabriel was born, but after Brooke's birth a month too early, Scott had asked her not to go back, citing Stan's murder as just one reason. Mia had listened in something of a daze. Even though she had been on bed rest, the baby was so little. Not even five pounds. Brooke nursed and slept for a few minutes and then woke again, mewling.

Scott had left his accounting firm to start his own business two years earlier, and now, he pointed out, he was making good money. And hadn't they both agreed that these years were so important?

Mia said yes. Colleen had congratulated Mia with her mouth and asked questions with her eyes. Questions Mia couldn't answer.

For the last four and a half years Mia had put the nutritious food on the table, washed and ironed the clothes, taken Gabe to football practice and Brooke to Tumble Tots. And if there were times she missed putting on her suits, missed arguing in front of a jury, missed the challenge and the struggle of putting together a case, well, everything was a trade-off, wasn't it?

Then Scott died and Mia learned that Scott had been juggling trade-offs too. There had been far fewer clients to notify than she had thought. Now Mia wondered how often Scott had sat in his rented office space and only pretended to work. She had been lucky to get rehired at King County. She was sure Colleen had had a lot to do with that, even if she denied it.

A lot of staff had turned over in the time Mia was away. If you really wanted to make good money—or you had to, because of the law school debts you were carrying—your ultimate aim was to work in the private sector. Lawyers often started at the county, picked up a few years of experience, and left. Many a defense attorney bragged about the "insider knowledge" they had gained before crossing over to the other side.

But when Mia returned, Colleen was still at King County. In the two months since she started back at work, their friendship had blossomed again as if she had never been away.

And now Colleen was dead. Stan and Colleen. Was it possible that their deaths were related?

The two had been a study in contrasts. Every time Stan had a big trial, he lost thirty pounds in what was known around the office as the Slavich Trial Diet. He simply forgot to eat. He grew a beard for the same reason. For Stan, life had been black-and-white. The people he prosecuted were guilty and deserved to be punished. He didn't rest until they were behind bars for the maximum sentence he could get.

Colleen saw the shades of gray. For certain defendants, the ones who had grown up with no dads or a string of them, people who had never had a single decent role model, Colleen had exercised her discretion as a prosecutor, tried to find solutions that didn't leave them without a chance of turning their lives around.

Mia felt sorry for whoever got assigned to investigate and prosecute Colleen's case. It would be high-profile, nonstop. She remembered what Colleen had said only a few hours ago about Frank. He would want this solved before voters went to the polls.

As Mia reached for another handful of chips, a car pulled up in the driveway, followed by a second.

She froze, even as her heart began to beat wildly. Footsteps echoed on the porch. Who was it? What was wrong now?

She jumped as keys clattered through the mail slot. For the second time she had forgotten about her missing car. She tiptoed to the front door and peeped out. Charlie. Getting back into a patrol car. He hadn't delegated this errand but done it himself. Her earlier irritation was gone.

Charlie Carlson had always been prone to a generous interpretation of the rules. Early in her career, his actions had even resulted in one of Mia's cases being thrown out and Charlie being reprimanded. Charlie, for reasons of his own—or for no reason, you never really knew with him—had flushed Mia's case down the toilet. Even though he had been reprimanded, she had never quite forgiven him.

Tonight, though, she appreciated how he had bent the rules for her, not even hesitating to leave a fresh crime scene when he thought her children were in trouble.

She reached into the bag for more chips but found only crumbs. Folding the bag down as small as she could, she stuffed it into the garbage. Then Mia went upstairs to bed—but not to sleep.

CHAPTER 7

Get off the computer, Gabe," Mia yelled up the stairs as she dug a table knife into a jar of peanut butter. Her mouth tasted sour and sharp, a food hangover from the chips she had eaten last night.

"Just one more minute."

"Now!" He had been promising to come down to breakfast since six thirty. Her watch showed it was three minutes past seven.

Brooke sat unmoving in front of a bowl of cereal, her head propped in her hands. When Mia woke her this morning, Brooke claimed she felt fine. She seemed to remember nothing of the night before.

On any day, Brooke was not a morning person. Her bowl of Life cereal was still untouched. The squares of cereal were beginning to look like they were melting.

"Baby, you have to eat."

Brooke didn't look up. "I'm not hungry. And I'm not a baby."

"Just one bite, Brooke. One." Mia undid the twist tie and took a slice of bread from the loaf. Wait—what was that? The faintest green fuzz. Inside her head she swore, but mindful of Brooke, the only thing that came out of her mouth was a sigh. If she didn't have bread, what could she send her kids to school with? Sandwiches made with frozen waffles?

She slipped more of the loaf free. The mold seemed to be

confined to the first slice. Everything else looked fine. And hadn't she just bought this bread a few days ago?

Mia threw away the top few slices and made a mental note to buy more bread. Which, if she wanted her kids to have lunches tomorrow, would have to be on the way home from her part-time job as an adjunct professor at the University of Washington law school. Tonight was the first seminar of the semester, and Titus Brown, the program's director, had asked her to present a closing argument. When she had said yes, months ago, Scott had still been alive and her gig at UDub was just something she did to keep her hand in. Now it helped pay the bills. At least some of them.

Grabbing her heavy blue mug, Mia took another gulp of coffee. She hadn't had time to sit down and have a real breakfast since she went back to work.

The inside of her head felt swollen with the remnants of her dreams, a terrible amalgam of Colleen's bubbling breaths and Brooke's inconsolable cries.

Mia looked over. Brooke still hadn't lifted her spoon to her lips.

"Sweetie, you have to eat something. Studies show that kids who eat breakfast get better grades than kids who don't."

"You're not in court, Mom." Gabe walked into the kitchen wearing only a pair of jeans. He shook some cereal into the bowl she had set out for him. "Telling a four-year-old some boring statistic is not going to make her care." His gaze swept over the kitchen counter, bare except for her coffee mug and her lunch-making supplies. "Besides, where's *your* breakfast?"

"I'll eat a cereal bar in the car." Mia still needed to put on makeup, stockings, and shoes.

"That's not a healthy breakfast."

Was Gabe mouthing off or did he really have a point? Probably both. Mia decided to let it go. Maybe even label it a conversation, something they rarely had these days.

She used to pride herself on being good with her kids. But lately Gabe seemed to have zero interest in talking with her. Sometimes he would start walking out of the room while she was still speaking.

Head down, he began to shovel food into his mouth, barely pausing for breath. He hadn't really hit his growth spurt yet, but the way he had been eating lately, he must be on the edge of one. His bangs hid his eyes. If Mia tried to push them back, he would duck under her hand, but not before she saw the angry red pimples on his forehead.

"Brooke—you have to eat!" Mia said as she reached into the fridge for apples. A flyer on the fridge door reminded her that Gabe had another football game this Friday. This one was against Independence High School. She tried to remember if that was where Darin Dane had gone.

"What happened last night, Brooke?" Gabe asked his sister. "Did you have a bad dream?"

"No." Her tone implied that the question was ridiculous. She lifted a spoon with a single square toward her mouth.

"Because it seemed like you were having a nightmare."

"No, I didn't." She nibbled delicately on the edge of the sole piece of cereal.

Gabe leaned over. "Don't you remember screaming your head off? And you hit me. And Mom."

"I did not." Brooke set her spoon down.

"Gabe, leave Brooke alone. She needs to eat."

"I was just asking." He pushed back from the table, his bowl already empty. "Remember I've got football practice this afternoon."

"Well, don't forget to pick up Brooke at preschool before six."

He didn't answer her.

"Gabe?"

"All right, all right, I didn't say I wouldn't."

"And remember I'm teaching tonight. I should be home by seven thirty. Eight at the latest." She reached for her purse. "Let me give you some money so you can order a pizza from Pagliacci." That was another reason she had to go to the store. Frozen pizzas cost less than half of what delivery would, even though Pagliacci's were far better. Maybe there would be leftovers she could bring to lunch tomorrow. She handed him some bills along with his sack lunch.

He made a face. "I don't want to bring my lunch to school anymore. No one does that. It's for babies. I want to buy my lunch like everyone else."

Mia bit her lip. Couldn't he have said that while she was making his lunch? She still had her wallet in one hand. "How much do you need?"

He shrugged. "Five dollars."

Five dollars times five days equaled twenty-five dollars a week. But she had vowed to treat the kids the same as she would have if Scott were alive. Which meant handing out lunch money, if that's what Gabe wanted.

Since she had gone back to work, Mia had been brown-bagging her own lunch, begging off when co-workers suggested they go out to eat. Pinching pennies while the dollars slipped through her fingers.

Gabe started to leave the room.

"Aren't you forgetting to put away your bowl?"

He rolled his eyes. "I'm not done eating yet. I'm getting something I keep forgetting to give you."

He pounded upstairs and then came back down with a piece of paper. "It's due today." He thrust it into Mia's hand. "It's the bill for my school fees. Sorry. I forgot to give it to you last week."

Her eyes dropped to the total. $767.79. She blinked. "Why is this so much?" How much money did she have in checking? "That's ridiculous. You're supposedly in a public school."

He shrugged, not meeting her eyes. "It's extra money for lab fees and art supplies and field trips. Stuff like that."

Mia looked closer. Those expenses were on there, sure, but most of it was actually for football. The helmet was $248, the shoulder pads and the uniform were around $150. Each. A year ago she would have grumbled but paid the bill.

A year ago she might have fund-raised to help parents who couldn't afford to let their sons play football. Now she was almost one of them.

Not meeting her eyes, Gabe sat back down again and poured another bowl of cereal. His teeth, she saw, were sunk into his lower lip. He was afraid she would say no. It wasn't that he had forgotten about the fees. Instead he had dragged his feet, not wanting to ask her. She tried not to talk about money in front of the kids, but it was always in the back of her mind and sometimes on the tip of her tongue.

Brooke and Gabriel were getting Social Security survivor's benefits, and Mia made pretty good money at King County, but the amount that went out every month was mind-bending. Scott had always handled their finances. After all, he was the one with the undergraduate degree in accounting as well as an MBA. Mia had paid for groceries and other things she needed with a credit card that gave them airline miles, and Scott had then paid all the bills. She hadn't balanced a checkbook in years.

Going back to work meant that her costs had increased too. Brooke was in preschool full-time, plus before- and after-care. Mia had had to buy new work clothes. Gabe was starting to eat like he had two hollow legs. And it cost over sixty dollars just to fill the Suburban's tank, and sometimes she had to do it twice a week.

Even the funeral had been expensive. Just the catering for the gathering afterward had been over four thousand. But of course Mia had wanted trays of appetizers, and wine and beer, and servers old enough to serve the wine and beer, and a liability policy to cover anything that might go wrong because of the serving of the wine and beer.

Gabe had poured the milk on his new bowl of cereal, but he still hadn't taken a bite. "Just let me get my checkbook," she said, and he finally started eating.

She wrote what she was sure was a bad check. But their bank would pull money over from savings to cover it. Mia made a mental note to sit down and draw up a budget. Even though he had handled the money, it turned out Scott had not been organized at all. She was still getting a handle on where they stood.

As she handed over the check, Mia caught a glimpse of her watch. Time, like money, was slipping through her fingers. "We have to hurry." She took Brooke's full bowl away and set it in the sink.

"Come on upstairs with me and I'll help you put on your shoes." She lifted Brooke from the table and set her on her feet. "I need everyone dressed and in the car in ten minutes."

"That's okay," Gabe said. "You don't need to drive me."

Brooke was already going up the stairs, but Mia turned back. "What? You're going to walk?"

"Nah. I'll skateboard to school."

Mia mentally traced the route, gauging how busy the streets were. It was at times like this that she missed Scott most acutely. It took the voices of two adults to outweigh the voice of one teenager. "I don't know, Gabe." His mouth opened in protest. Something inside her said she had to give him some freedom sometime. And she was asking so much of him lately. "Okay, but wear your helmet. And I want you to walk across that last intersection."

"Walk?" he protested. "That's just lame."

"It may be lame, but it's safe. It's so busy there. People barely pay attention to other drivers. In rush hour they might not see you until it's too late."

"I'm not three feet tall, Mom." His neck reddened. She knew he hated being shorter than all of his friends. His tone was scathing. "You've got to stop babying me."

She touched his arm and he spun away, then pushed past her up the stairs. More slowly, Mia followed.

CHAPTER 8

When Mia hurried into the office, it was oddly empty. Only the secretary, Judy Rallison, was at her normal station. Her eyes were red-rimmed and she clutched a crumpled, mascara-stained tissue in one hand. She was scribbling on a yellow message pad while the console in front of her blinked with a dozen red lights.

"Of course I'll give Frank the message, Mayor," she was saying into her headset. "I'm sure he'll return your call as soon as he can." After pressing a button to disconnect, she looked up at Mia. "They're all in the conference room. Frank called a meeting about ten minutes ago." Judy pushed one of the dozen blinking lights on her phone. "King County Criminal Division," she said in a singsong voice. "How may I direct your call?"

Of all days to be late, this clearly wasn't one of them. But Brooke's teacher had wanted to talk to Mia about two "accidents" Brooke had had recently.

Without stopping to put down her raincoat or purse, Mia hurried down the hall to the conference room. Hoping to slip in unnoticed, she chose the door at the back of the room.

She could barely squeeze inside. All the seats around the long table were full, and around them people stood crowded shoulder to shoulder. Anne Rutter stepped to one side to let Mia crowd in between her and Katrina Nowell. All three of them had worked in

Violent Crimes with Colleen. When Frank caught sight of her, he stopped midsentence.

"Mia," he said, and the room fell silent. "We understand you were talking to Colleen on the phone when she was shot."

All eyes turned to her. She took a shaky breath. The room smelled of coffee and morning breath, but underneath she caught something sharper and more primal—the rank smell of fear.

"We were just having a normal conversation, and then someone . . . someone . . ." Mia stumbled, still shocked by it all. Anne put a comforting hand on her shoulder. Mia swallowed hard and managed to go on. "And then I guess someone shot her."

"Did you know what had happened?" Leslie Yee from Domestic Violence asked.

"Not at first. We were just talking about a case when there was this loud noise, and then Colleen dropped the phone. It took me a second to figure out what was going on, and even then I wasn't sure. I tried to talk to her, but she, she"—Mia decided not to say anything about Colleen's labored breathing—"really couldn't talk after that. And then I called 911 and drove over to her house, but by the time I got there it was too late."

DeShauna Mundy shook her head, setting her silver earrings swinging. She worked in the Sexually Violent Predator unit. "It's just like what happened to Stan," she said. "Somebody is gunning for King County prosecutors."

This assertion was met with murmurs and nods.

Jesse Sanchez raised his voice. "Until they catch whoever did this, none of us is safe." Jesse, a plump guy in his midfifties, worked in the Involuntary Treatment unit, which meant he spent his days focusing on the potential for poor outcomes.

"People," Frank said, "let's not get ahead of ourselves. Stan's and Colleen's deaths were separated by more than four years. We don't know that they are linked." A few people muttered in protest, and he held up his hands. "I'm not saying there aren't similarities. But right now it's too soon to say. If any of you has received threats, I want to know about them immediately. Or if you know anything about Colleen or Stan that you think might pertain to their deaths, come talk to me. And of course we should all remain alert and take reasonable precautions. If something makes you nervous, don't be afraid to ask for a patrol car to swing by your house or a security guard to walk you to the parking lot. Keep the doors locked in your car and at your home."

"A locked door didn't do Stan or Colleen any good." Tracy Lowe from the Juvenile Unit stabbed the air with a red fingernail.

"Folks, I promise you that we are going to get to the bottom of this. The Seattle police are going over the crime scene with a fine-toothed comb. We will be devoting every resource until we find the person or persons responsible for Colleen's death. We're already working with Crime Stoppers to put out the word of a ten-thousand-dollar reward for any tip leading to the arrest of a suspect."

Mia wondered if they should have waited. Rewards cut both ways. They encouraged the crazy, the lonely, and the vengeful as well as—perhaps—someone with real information.

Frank looked at his watch. "I know a lot of you have court dates this morning, so I'm going to end by saying that my door is open, and if you know something or have concerns, please come and talk to me."

Several people turned toward Mia. But before anyone could frame a question or ask for more details, Frank was by her side. "Mia, would you mind coming down to my office?"

"Of course," she said, feeling oddly guilty. Surely he wasn't going to get mad at her for being late? She followed his straight back, clad in one of his tailored suits, down the hall.

Frank was tall and fit, with black hair touched with silver at the temples. As Colleen had often joked, he looked like an actor who had been cast to play the part of district attorney—or president.

And who knew what heights he dreamed of scaling? Frank was a rising political star. He was campaigning hard, and it seemed likely he would be reelected. After that, there were rumors about what office he might run for next—attorney general, governor, even U.S. senator.

Once they were in his office, he closed the door behind her. Frank's furniture wasn't standard government issue, but instead made of cherrywood, a red so dark it was almost black.

Without saying anything, he waved at the visitor's chair as he walked around his desk. Photos of his two children were lined up along the credenza. The nearest showed his dark-haired son in a Little League uniform, his blond daughter in a gymnastics leotard. It was rumored that these photos were about as close as he ever came to actually seeing them. And now the son was a sophomore in college and the daughter a senior in high school.

Over the fifteen years Mia had known Frank, he had changed from being just one of her co-workers to being a brand that was as carefully managed as Colgate or Chevrolet. Only his brand was no-nonsense. Law and order. The man who kept you and your family safe.

Even speaking one-on-one, Frank still looked camera-ready. He took off his jacket, revealing sleeves already rolled up to show that he meant business. Despite the absence of a microphone, his words were still a crisp collection of sound bites.

He leaned across the desk to pat her hand. "Last night must have been terrible for you."

"It was. I didn't see her. After I got to her house, I mean. I didn't see Colleen after she was dead."

"Maybe that's better." Frank took his hand back. "You wouldn't want to remember her like that."

Mia wished she could forget about Colleen's labored breathing. "I have to talk to Charlie Carlson later today. He's the lead homicide detective, and I guess I'm a witness."

"A witness?" Frank sat back in his chair. "But you weren't there when it happened."

"I'm an aural witness."

"Oral?"

"Aural. You know, someone who hears something. But it's not like Colleen said anything. About all I can do is pin down a five-minute window when the shooting occurred."

Frank nodded, looking preoccupied. Finally he said, "I have a question for you, Mia, but I don't want you to answer it right away. Take the night and sleep on it."

"What is it?" Was he going to ask her to pick up Colleen's cases in addition to her own? Because Mia had only been back at the job for a couple of months, she probably had the lightest workload of anyone in Violent Crimes.

"You have the lightest caseload," Frank said, echoing her thoughts. "And that big case you had pled out on Friday."

Mia nodded. Nodded and waited.

"And you knew both Colleen and Stan. A lot of the district prosecuting attorneys who work here now came on after Stan died."

Mia wanted to protest she hadn't known Stan that well—she wasn't sure anyone had—but she kept quiet and just listened. She was beginning to have a feeling she might need to save her counterarguments.

"I'm going to need someone to head up the investigation into their deaths. If you say yes, I want you to team up with Charlie, figure out who did this, and get them convicted. If you take this on, I want you to hand off all your remaining cases. This will be your top priority."

Mia noted that Frank said *will*, not *would*. She had no doubt that in his mind, she had already said yes.

Talk about a blessing and a curse, all in one package. Visibility. Responsibility. And high probability for failure.

"Like I said, I want you to think about this," Frank continued. "I won't kid you, it's going to be challenging. You're going to need to give it everything you've got. But, Mia, I think you are absolutely the right person for the job. Remember when you came to me and asked to come back to the office?"

It had felt more like begging, but Mia nodded.

"You told me that losing Scott not only made you tougher, but it also gave you an even greater appreciation of what it's like for the people the victim leaves behind. I want you to bring that same determination and human touch to this assignment."

Mia's gut reaction was no. No, no, no. This case would eat her alive.

But it was an honor to be asked. And if she said no, she would look like a prima donna. Of course, if she said yes, half the office would resent her, wondering how she had managed to waltz back in and be handed such a big case.

But if she said no to Frank, how would he take it? Could he make things so bad for her that she would be forced out? Since the economy had tanked, even lawyers were having a hard time finding jobs.

"What about Darin Dane?"

"Who?" Frank's eyebrows drew together.

"Darin Dane. The kid who killed himself after being harassed. That's actually what I was talking to Colleen about when she was shot."

"That's very sad, but there's always going to be some kid who can't handle reality. Teasing comes with the territory when you're talking about teenagers. Kids will be kids."

"Frank, that's what they used to say about men who groped or harassed women. Boys will be boys. Now it's settled case law that it's assault."

He made a face. "I'm not sure we can make a case for going after those kids. This office has to set priorities. And you know what our number one priority is. It's finding whoever killed Colleen and, if we can, the same for Stan. That's what's most important. We can't let ourselves be distracted."

"But, Frank—"

He held up his hand. "I would feel the same way even if you decided not to help find justice for Colleen. And, Mia, I want to reassure you that if you do decide not to take on Colleen's case, I will understand completely." The words were right, but there was a dissonance with Frank's expression. "No matter what you decide, please keep this in confidence. I don't want anyone thinking they're my second choice"—he flashed her a conspiratorial smile—"even if they are. Katrina has already hinted that she's interested, but I think you're the best fit for the job. But it's still your choice, Mia. Sleep on it. And then give me an answer tomorrow."

CHAPTER 9

When Mia walked out of Frank's office, her head was spinning. He had just offered her what could be the coup of her career.

It could also possibly be the end of her career, at least at King County. If she took this on and failed, Frank might hang her out to dry.

Even if she was successful, how could she handle the immense amount of work it was sure to mean? She was away from Brooke and Gabe too much now as it was.

Her thoughts skipped back and forth. If she said no, what would her next performance review look like? And once word got out that she had turned it down, people would lose respect for her. They would whisper behind her back that she thought she was too good to get her hands dirty. Some of the men and the childless women would complain that the moms always took the easy way out.

When she turned the corner, she stopped short. It wasn't the knot of people huddled at the end of the hall that made her hesitate. It was the sight of Colleen's office, the closed door crisscrossed with yellow crime-scene tape. A fist closed around her heart and squeezed.

This was real. It was more than office politics. More than her career. Her friend Colleen was dead.

Scott was dead and Colleen was dead and there might be something wrong with Brooke.

Mia forced her feet to start moving again. As her co-workers caught sight of her, they fell silent, looking at her and then at each other. Mia realized she had never taken off her coat.

Holding a file folder, Katrina came out of Mia's office. "Oh, I was looking for you." She drew her into a one-armed embrace. Mia hadn't really gotten to know Katrina that well—she had started at the office while Mia was home with her kids—but now she found herself clinging to the other woman as if she had just saved her from drowning.

Anne, Leslie, Jesse, Tracy, and DeShauna crowded around, murmuring their own condolences. Mia closed her eyes as she felt light pats on her hands and shoulders.

Finally she opened her eyes and pulled back. She looked at Colleen's office and then away. "It's just going to take a long time for it to sink in."

"I know," Katrina said. "Colleen was just such a life force." She leaned in closer. "What did Frank want to talk to you about?" Katrina's parents were German immigrants, and she seemed to have inherited a practical bluntness from them, along with her frizzy blond curls and bright blue eyes.

Mia cast around for a truth that would avoid a lie. "We were discussing Darin Dane."

Katrina's eyes lost their sparkle. "That boy who killed himself? You should let that one go, Mia. It's too hard to prove it crossed the line, and the other parents will fight it every step of the way. It's terrible, sure, but those kids' parents will make sure little Johnny and Janey don't even get a slap on the wrist."

It was Colleen's argument, slightly rephrased.

"We're all wondering which one of us Frank will assign Colleen's case to," DeShauna said.

Tracy snorted. "Someone with no home life." Tracy, with her talon-like nails and her ever-changing cast of boyfriends, had more of an away-from-home life than a home life, but everyone knew what she meant.

Anne nodded in agreement. "At least they won't have one after this. It's going to be a lot to take on." She and her husband had four kids, two of them younger than Brooke. Whenever Mia thought she couldn't do it, she thought of Anne, who always looked put together, with her long dark hair pulled back into a low bun. Anne would never come to work in one brown pump and one blue, the way Mia had last month.

Jesse said, "It's an election year. Frank will want this wrapped up as soon as possible. He doesn't want anyone saying that not only can't he keep Seattle safe, he can't even manage it with his own staff."

"Still, the assignment could be worth it," Katrina said thoughtfully. "It could be a career-maker."

"Or a career-ender," Leslie countered, putting her hands on her hips. "Four years ago they couldn't figure out who killed Stan, and the trail's only gotten colder since then."

"But now there's a new trail," DeShauna pointed out.

Leslie shrugged. "And who knows if it even leads back to Stan? By trying to make the evidence fit two cases, you could end up muddying the waters on both. And say the shooter was the same person—then who do you think they're going to want to kill next? No, I wouldn't want to put myself in this guy's targets."

Frank came around the corner to talk to Judy, and the conversation broke up as people went back to their offices. Only Katrina stayed. Her office lay just past Colleen's.

She put a hand under Mia's elbow and steered her into Mia's office, then took her purse, set it down on her desk, and helped Mia off with her coat. Mia let it all happen. Katrina might be nearly ten years younger, but right now Mia felt like she needed a mother.

Or what she really needed, she thought, sitting down heavily in her chair and closing her eyes, was Colleen. If Colleen were here right now, she would listen to her without asking too many questions. And only when she was all talked out would Colleen give her excellent advice.

Mia started when Katrina spoke. "So you were on the phone with Colleen when it happened?"

Mia thought back. "We were talking about that garage sale I'm going to have." It seemed so ordinary. So *banal*. "And about Darin Dane. And then I heard the shot."

Katrina shook her head. "That must have been awful."

Mia tilted her head back to meet the other woman's concerned gaze. "It *was* awful." She swallowed. "I could hear her trying to breathe."

Katrina's eyes widened. "The connection wasn't broken when she dropped the phone?"

"No. I tried to talk to her, but she couldn't answer. I guess the phone didn't fall too far away, though, because, like I said, I could hear her breathing." Mia thought of how she had handed the phone to Gabe, forced him to listen to Colleen's last, labored breaths. The fewer people who knew that, the better. It had been traumatizing enough for him to hear it. If he had to testify about it, it would be even worse.

"First Stan and now Colleen." Katrina walked over to Mia's door. "It just doesn't feel safe. Who knows who will be next?" With a shake of her head, she turned and walked down the hall, leaving the thought hanging in the air.

Finally Mia was alone. Normally her day would have been filled with phone calls, texts, e-mails, preparing witnesses for trial, and meeting with investigators. But she had just plea-bargained a big case the week before, and now she couldn't summon the energy to focus on any of the many less-urgent items that remained on her to-do list. If she took Frank up on his offer, she would be buried again tomorrow.

Mia went to KIRO-TV's website to see what was already out in the media. They hadn't released Colleen's name yet—Mia's heart contracted when she thought of Sue, Colleen's mother, and Violet, her daughter—but they did have the bare facts of a local prosecutor dying at home after being shot through a window.

It was the anonymous and often angry comments on the story that sickened her. Half of them weren't even rational.

Sweetbob wrote: *What was she thinking, not having her curtains closed? She was just asking for some weirdo to come along and target her.*

Rainyday said: *If she had been armed, this wouldn't have happened.*

And Lilywhite opined: *All liberal cities are garbage dumps for insane thinking and actions. The devil has taken over the minds of these godless heathens. The Bible teaches that Satan goes about seeking who he may destroy.*

But it was True Patriot's comment that made the hair on Mia's arms stand up: *Now if only the same would happen to a few thousand more anti-American, anti-constitutional traitors mooching off the public's dime.* She made a mental note to see if there was any way to track down True Patriot's IP address—and real identity.

Mia was still shaking her head when her phone rang. When she answered, Judy said, "Charlie Carlson's here to see you."

Didn't he know to call first to give her a heads-up? Typical Charlie, playing by his own rules. Mia ground her teeth in annoyance as she walked back down the hall.

CHAPTER 10

At Starbucks, Charlie leaned back in his chair and rested one foot on a low table off to one side. Across from him, Mia Quinn shot him a look.

His shoe was only on the edge, for crying out loud, and it wasn't as if anyone was using the table anyway, except as a place to pile old sections of the *Seattle Times*. Still, his foot went back down on the floor.

He slurped his mocha, enjoying the sweet, dark taste. The sugar and fat would help keep him going. In the old days, three hours of sleep would have been plenty, but those days were gone.

Mia took another dainty sip of her nonfat latte. Didn't she know that fat was the good part? The only surprise had been her request for an extra shot of espresso.

She was wearing a navy suit and a white blouse with an extra-wide collar. Last night, dressed in faded Levi's and a scoop-necked blue T-shirt streaked with dust, Mia had seemed a different person. Today she had reverted to the conservatively dressed, by-the-book prosecutor he had long known, if not exactly loved.

"I still don't understand why we couldn't do this in my office," Mia said, tapping her fingers on the round white faux-marble table.

Charlie took another sip. Say what you wanted about 'Bucks, they made pretty good coffee. And Charlie enjoyed this location, with its floor-to-ceiling windows showcasing Pioneer Square's usual mix of tourists, office workers, and homeless people. "We're less than three blocks from your office, and anyone who needs you can call your cell. Besides, I don't know about you, but after last night I desperately need some good coffee. Right now there's far too much blood in my caffeine stream."

One side of Mia's mouth quirked, there and gone so fast he almost missed it.

"How late did you have to stay?"

"I was at the house for about six hours, and back there again after the autopsy." Charlie took another gulp from his cup—he had ordered the venti size, with enough caffeine for a whole pack of Mias—and followed it up with a bite of his double-iced cinnamon roll. It was the first thing he had eaten since—since when? He wasn't sure. He had been eating last night when dispatch called. Leftover pad thai while watching a *Seinfeld* rerun. The pad thai was probably still sitting on the coffee table next to his remote.

Once he got back from Mia's, it had taken an hour to get a search warrant. It was legal to make a warrantless entry to aid a victim or search for a killer. After that, you needed a warrant. During that time he had posted two officers outside the house and then drafted another into helping him return Mia's big SUV. He'd been surprised—and oddly pleased—to see how much of a mess it was, with broken crayons and plastic toys and a couple of those sippy cups scattered around the booster seat strapped in the back.

"So tell me more about when you were on the phone with Colleen." Charlie sucked an errant wad of icing from his thumb. A little noisily, because he could tell it bugged her.

Pausing only to take measured sips of her coffee, Mia talked. There wasn't much to tell. She and Colleen had spoken about Facebook, about a case Mia wanted to pursue, and about a garage sale Mia was planning. The garage sale explained the old albums he had found under Colleen's body.

"But after she was shot, she never said anything. I don't think she could."

Charlie nodded. The autopsy had confirmed this. Speech would have been nearly impossible. The bullet had caught Colleen just below the hollow of her throat. It was a .22, which meant that each time it hit bone it had bounced around inside her like a pinball. He tried to divorce this knowledge from any thought of the real Colleen he had known and liked, with her loud laugh, red hair (dyed, he was pretty sure), and perpetually flushed cheeks. They had worked six or seven cases together over the years, the last one a double homicide that proved an open-and-shut case—an ex-husband who had taken offense to a current boyfriend.

"Was Colleen still audibly breathing, moaning, anything like that, when you handed your son the phone?"

A long pause. Mia gave him the stink eye and finally, reluctantly, nodded.

"So your son heard her stop breathing?" He thought of the panicked kid he had seen last night, hair hanging in his eyes.

An even longer pause. "Yes. But you and I both know that just because he couldn't hear her breathing, that doesn't mean he heard her die."

Charlie thought she was talking to herself as much as him.

Mia squared her shoulders. "It was bad enough I handed him the phone. I should have just stayed put and called 911. I don't want Gabe dragged even further into this." She leaned forward and lowered her voice, even though the espresso machine and the dozen conversations around them gave her plenty of cover. "Look, Charlie, Colleen didn't say anything to Gabe. Can't we just keep him out of the report?" The word triggered a thought, and her brows pulled together. "In fact, shouldn't you be taking notes?"

"I don't need to."

She sat back. "Come on, everybody needs to."

He set down his now-empty cup and raised his hands. "If I take notes, they just get subpoenaed."

"But if you don't take notes, how do you know what was said?" She looked like a disgruntled schoolmarm.

"Oh, that's not a problem." He pitched his voice high, higher than hers, and quoted her own words back to her. *"But you and I both know that just because he couldn't hear her breathing, that doesn't mean he heard her die."*

Mia looked taken aback. "You have a photographic memory?"

"Not quite. But it's pretty good. And if I don't put something in my report, it's not discoverable." The defense couldn't subpoena Charlie's memory. Not yet, anyway. And her kid had to be traumatized, after everything that had happened last night as well as this past summer. No point in making it worse.

He watched Mia wrestle with this. If it had been anyone but her son, would she have had such difficulty? Finally she said, "Thanks. It would be too harrowing for him if he had to take the stand. You've probably heard about Scott. My husband."

"Yeah. Look, I should have said something earlier, but I'm sorry about what happened to him." What Charlie had heard was that it wasn't too clear what had happened. A little bit of alcohol in the guy's system, but not enough to be drunk. A cloudy night, but visibility hadn't been bad. So why had he left the road, hit a tree, and died on impact?

"It's been a tough year."

He could believe it—losing her husband and now her friend, a few months apart. "I turned up a neighbor who heard the shot. She was watching TV, and she remembers what was happening in the program. So we've got the time pinned down pretty well." Charlie popped the last bit of cinnamon roll into his mouth. "Do you know if anyone was in the house with her?"

"No. Colleen lived alone."

"That doesn't mean someone wasn't with her last night," Charlie pointed out. "Did you hear any noises in the background—voices, a doorbell or a knock?"

"No."

"Has Colleen received any threats?"

"Not that I know of." A lawyer's answer.

"Any problems at work?"

She shook her head.

"Had her demeanor changed in the past few months?"

At this Mia hesitated. "Maybe. A little. I knew something was bothering her, but she hadn't said what it was—oh!" She started as a memory hit her. "She said something about turning over rocks and not liking what you find underneath. I just thought she was talking about the people we prosecute. Sometimes the victims and even the witnesses aren't as lily-white as you wished they were."

"But it could have been about something else?"

"It could have been. But if it was, I don't know what. Colleen could play her cards awfully close to her vest."

"How long have you known her? How close were you?"

"Were," Mia echoed with a sad smile. "You can't imagine how strange it feels to use that word about Colleen." She took a deep breath. "I met Colleen when I got hired by King County about fifteen years ago. It was my first job out of law school. Initially Colleen was more like my mentor. She was married and had a five-year-old, and I'd just gotten married. She loved it when I got pregnant. She wanted to have another baby and her husband didn't, so I think she was living vicariously through me. Then her husband wanted a divorce, and it really blindsided her. And after that, we were more friends than anything."

Charlie was familiar with work friendships, how you could be so tight with a partner but then find you had nothing to say to each other when you no longer worked together. "Did you and Colleen stay friends when you left the office?"

"We kept in touch, but it wasn't really the same while I was at home. But when I came back to work a few months ago, we picked right up again."

"Did she have any problems in her personal life? Drugs? Alcohol use?"

Mia snorted. "Colleen?"

"Her cheeks were always so red."

"She had rosacea, Charlie." Whatever rapport they had been building a moment ago seemed to have broken. "It's a skin condition." Her tone was condescending.

"Oh. Okay. Any other problems? Gambling? Debts? Any known enemies?"

"No."

"Was she dating anyone?"

"Colleen hasn't dated in a while. She tried some of those online sites, but she said it was impossible, that women in their fifties were competing with women in their twenties and thirties. And of course for a long time her daughter came first. Violet's in college now, at Evergreen."

"Yeah," Charlie said, "we had campus police and a chaplain notify her last night. She's coming home tomorrow, after we release the crime scene. I'll interview her then. What about Colleen's ex-husband?"

"Martin? He's married to the woman he left Colleen for. There was a lot of drama at the time, but that was almost fifteen years ago." She drank the last of her coffee and wiped her lips with a napkin. "Were there any clues at the scene?"

It was weird to be questioned by a witness, but given the circumstances and her job title, he supposed Mia had the right. "As far as we can tell, there was no entry. The responding officer had to break down the door to get inside."

Pristine crime scenes didn't exist. TV CSIs were the only ones who investigated crimes where every thread or hair was an important clue. In this real-life scenario, you had officers responding to the report of shots fired, forcing entry, searching for suspects and victims, and trying to render aid to the woman they found. Only then had they looked for evidence of a crime.

The problem with a killing without a clear motive was that they didn't know what was or wasn't evidence. Still, last night Charlie had gone through Colleen's bedside drawers, desk, and filing cabinets. Her computer had gone to the forensics lab. After he was done talking to Mia, he would conduct a similar sweep of Colleen's office.

"We've got plenty of fingerprints, but once we rule out friends and family, I don't think any of them are gonna be meaningful. The one big clue we have is that the killer didn't pick up their brass," he said, referring to the shell casing. "We found it in her yard, but they weren't stupid enough to load the gun with bare hands. They used a .22. But the bullet's probably too mangled to compare the rifling."

"Any footprints?"

"No." That had struck Charlie as odd—the ground was relatively soft—but the killer must have watched where he or she stepped.

"So how will you approach this?"

"I'm gonna get the murder book for Stan and look for similars." From what Charlie had heard about Stan Slavich's murder, it had all come to a dead end. "How many of the staff who are working at King County now do you think were there when Stan was killed?"

"Well, Frank for one. Back before he was the DA. But there are at least a dozen of us who worked with both Stan and Colleen." She looked at her watch. "Are we almost done? I've got to stop by the office before I leave for the day."

He checked the time on his phone. It was three fifteen. "This early?" And then it dawned on him. "Oh. Because of your kids."

"No, Charlie. It's not because of my kids." Whatever distance he had closed between them yawned wide again. Mia looked like she wanted to spit. "I'm an adjunct law professor at UDub."

CHAPTER 11

Have you even heard of a napkin?" Mia asked.

Charlie didn't answer. Probably because Mia was alone in her car, inching forward. The University of Washington was only five miles from the King County Courthouse, but today was one of those days when it might be faster to walk. While Mia was technically on the freeway, traffic was crawling.

Now every driver who cut her off, every minute that ticked by, every inexplicable holdup just made her angrier. Not only with the traffic, but with Charlie. He was her age, but clearly he was a Neanderthal who didn't believe women with young children should be working. And if they were working, he thought they kept hours even a banker would envy.

With his loose grasp of the rules, Charlie Carlson had been just what she needed last night when Brooke and Gabe seemed to be in danger. Even if that meant he left a fresh crime scene. Even if it meant he drove with no regard for the speed limit or the limited visibility offered by the curving residential roads. Charlie had dropped everything to help her. And she appreciated it, she really did.

But if Mia said yes to Frank, she would be yoked to Charlie for weeks or even months. His laxity would no longer be an asset, but a liability. She would have to babysit him, make sure he didn't screw anything up by blazing his own path. As he had more than ten years ago.

"I already have two kids at home, Charlie," she said, thumping the steering wheel. "I don't need another." The older woman in the car next to her turned and stared. Mia pressed her right hand against her ear as if adjusting a Bluetooth.

The cop-prosecutor relationship was often likened to a marriage. If Mia were ever married to Charlie, the first thing she would want would be a divorce.

Less than a mile to UDub now. Mia looked at her watch again. The seminar was just starting. Titus was not going to be happy. And the other presenter was a new professor. Talk about making a bad first impression.

When Mia was in law school, Titus Brown had been the professor she most admired. She still remembered his words about being punctual. "Why should lawyers strive to be on time with clients, prospects, fellow counsel, and staff?" he had asked in his trademark cadence. "Because being punctual builds credibility and trust."

Mia had last taught spring term. Back before her life had been turned upside down. Then she had been teaching to keep her hand in. To give her a little spending money she didn't feel she had to justify to Scott. When she returned to King County, Frank had had to sign off on her continuing to teach, but it had been a formality. Having a prosecutor who doubled as a professor added to the office's prestige.

Mia finally slipped in ten minutes late. If you could call it "slipping in" when you sat up front facing a hundred and fifty students. She took the seat next to what must be the new professor. He was tall and slender, with high cheekbones and eyes even bluer than her own. His blond straight hair was nearly military short. He nodded and gave her a smile.

Titus shot Mia a look, but his voice, which had the rhythm of a preacher's, never faltered. He had shed his suit jacket to reveal a crisp white shirt and gray-striped tie.

"You might wonder why I'm up here talking about closing arguments," he said, prowling back and forth, microphone in hand. "Why not start at the beginning, for example, building your case or choosing a jury? Because without your closing, you have no theory of the case. You've got no game plan. All the evidence you present and everything you argue must lead you, step by step, to your closing. You have to know what you're going to ask for before you even start."

Mia looked out over the students. Some were slouched, some attentive. Some took notes, while others appeared to be texting. In the second row, a guy leaned over and showed a girl something on his cell phone. She giggled. Mia gave them the same look she would have given Gabe, narrowed eyes, lips pressed together. They both straightened up, eyes front.

"Your close is the only time during the entire trial," Titus continued, "that you have the opportunity to sum up the evidence and argue it to the jury." He turned toward Mia and the new professor.

"Now two of our section instructors are going to model closing arguments. You won't be seeing full closing arguments, which can take several hours or even days. I've given each of them about ten minutes. So they'll be dispensing with the usual space fillers of 'May it please the court,' or 'Ladies and gentlemen of the jury.' Instead, I've asked them to distill a closing argument so it goes to the heart of the case. First up will be Mia Quinn, who works for the King County District Attorney's Office. She'll be followed by Eli Hall, who has just joined King County's Public Defender's Office."

So this was Tami Gordon's replacement. Interesting. Eli gave her an encouraging nod as she got to her feet and took the microphone from Titus.

"This is a case about a woman who was found murdered, killed by someone she thought was a 'friend,' the defendant."

Mia slipped into the rhythm of the words. "The defense has said that there is no one to tell you what happened that evening down by the river. But that's not true. There is one person who is telling us the truth of what happened that night. And that person is Amber Smith."

Mia switched to the first name of the fictitious girl to help the imaginary jury begin to think of her as a friend. "Amber is telling us what really happened that night. The medical examiner and the police officer told you about her body. Amber had no defensive wounds on her. None. There was no sign of struggle. And look at this picture of Amber." She held up an imaginary photo. "Are her clothes torn? Has she been dragged or forced here?" She shook her head. "There is absolutely no evidence of that.

"As I said, the medical examiner told you that there wasn't a single defensive wound on her body. No skin under her fingernails. But everybody has called this girl a fighter. Somebody who pushes for what she wants. A girl who is quick to act. Even the defendant agreed with that characterization. Amber was not forced to go down by the river. She went willingly with someone she knew.

"What else does this picture tell us? What is Amber saying? The defense has tried to tell you she was killed by a mysterious stranger, some random act of violence.

"But that's not what Amber tells us. Amber's body tells us she was killed by somebody she knew, somebody she was not afraid of. Somebody who suddenly shot her in the face without any warning. And remember? The shot was front to back." Mia tapped her own forehead, trying not to think of Colleen. Which was worse—being shot in the head or the throat? The head, she supposed, would have been quicker. "Amber was looking straight at whoever shot her. The angle of the wound is slightly upward. What would you do if somebody you knew came up to you with a gun? What would your reaction be? You would lean back." Mia demonstrated, raising her hands as if in shock. "And that's what Amber did. That's all she had time for. That explains the angle of the wound. Amber is trying to tell you that the defendant was this man, the man whom we already know bought a gun two weeks before Amber died. The man who even his parents describe as impulsive. The man who decided that the best way to get Amber out of his life was to kill her."

Mia continued for another few minutes, adding fact to fact, inference to inference. She closed by telling the jury what she wanted them to do: return a guilty verdict.

After she was finished, there was a round of applause. Then it was Eli's turn.

"This is a case about a man facing a murder charge, with only circumstantial evidence linking him to the crime," Eli said. He didn't pace like Titus, but his quiet intensity commanded attention.

"It is a sad fact that in America violence has unfortunately become a way of life. Every year hundreds of people are murdered. And when this sort of tragedy happens, we count on the police to take charge. We expect our police department to be competent. To be efficient. To not be corrupt. We expect them to carefully investigate without rushing to judgment.

"We expect all of this. And the victim's family demands it. But in this case, unfortunately, the police had another agenda. From the very first orders issued by the top brass, it's clear they were more concerned with their image. With public relations. Not with professional police work. Not even with justice.

"But your verdict will send them a message. Your verdict will tell them that justice is important above all things. Your verdict will tell them that no one is above the law—not even the police.

"You have heard how, from the very beginning, professional police work took a backseat to expediency and sloppiness. Untrained officers literally walked through the evidence. They ignored obvious clues. They left a piece of paper at the scene, and that evidence—and the fingerprints it might contain—is now gone forever.

"Once they realized their mistake, they had to find someone to blame it on. They chose Mr. Doe. They implicated an innocent man, and they never, ever looked for anyone else. We believe that if they had done their job, Mr. Doe would have been eliminated as a suspect months ago. We believe that the real killer would have been apprehended. But their bungling denied justice not just to Mr. Doe, but to the victim and the victim's family."

As she listened to Eli, Mia had to admit it was a good argument. A generation earlier, the average jury wouldn't have entertained the idea that the cops could have screwed up. But there had been enough overturned convictions, enough coerced confessions and bungled evidence, that that was no longer true. By now the public knew that even the good guys were sometimes bad guys.

Mia had been in the zone while she spoke, but by the time Eli finished and the students started asking questions, she was thinking about Colleen's murder, Frank's question, Charlie's intransigence, and the conundrum she faced. Twice she had to ask students to repeat their queries.

Finally class was over. Students clustered around Titus. Back when she was in law school, she would have been one of them. She still trusted him as she did few others.

She turned to Eli and offered her hand. "As you've probably figured out, I'm Mia. Mia Quinn."

"Eli Hall." He gave her a firm handshake.

"I apologize for being so late. So you just joined the public defender's office?"

"Yup. My daughter and I moved up from Portland three weeks ago."

No wedding ring, she noted. Mia still wore hers. She supposed there would come a time when she took it off, but right now it would feel like too much of a betrayal. Even after everything that had happened.

"You must be replacing Tami Gordon?"

"She's, um, left the office."

Mia wondered what the real story was. Tami was a true believer, with no life outside of her job. She didn't shy away from the toughest cases. Pedophiles with years of victims in their wakes would find that at least one person—Tami—believed their stories of playful wrestling.

The last of the students left and Titus came over. "I see you two have already met." He was in his early sixties, with a shaved head, dark eyebrows, and a salt-and-pepper mustache and beard. His warm brown eyes nearly matched his skin tone.

Mia winced. "I have to apologize to you for being late."

"I know you have a lot on your plate."

"Speaking of that, I was wondering if I could talk to you for a minute."

"Sure." He turned to Eli. "Do you have any questions about tonight?"

"No. If I think of anything, though, I'll come in early on Thursday to talk to you."

"Thursday?" Mia echoed. "We must be teaching the same day."

"You are," Titus said. "And, Eli, Mia's been with the program for four years. She can help you if you have any questions."

After Eli left, they went down the hall to Titus's office. How many times had Mia sat opposite him and asked his advice? She felt closer to him than she did to her own father.

She took a seat in his worn leather visitor's chair. "You heard about Colleen's murder?"

"Yes. I'm sorry." He shook his head. "What a year of loss."

"This morning Frank asked me to head up the investigation into her death and whether it's linked to Stan Slavich's."

Titus kept silent, regarding her. His face was creased and folded in a pleasant way.

"I know it's a good catch," Mia finally said. "But I don't think I want it."

"Why not?"

"Titus—there're so many reasons not to take this. For one thing, the detective is Charlie Carlson, and he can be a loose cannon. Plus it's going to mean long hours just when my family needs me. And four years ago they were never able to find out who killed Stan. Who says I'll do any better?"

He closed his eyes for a moment, then reopened them and focused on her.

"You were close to Colleen, right?"

"Before I left the office, yes. And since I've come back, we've become tight again. She's been such a big help to me since Scott died. But if I say yes, then how can I do it all?"

"I don't know that you can. I don't know that anyone can. But I believe that you can be a good mother *and* be a good prosecutor."

Mia nodded. But she wasn't so sure that Titus was right.

CHAPTER 12

Mia's first thought as she turned down her street was that there was a burglar on her roof. Her heart sped up, even as her rational mind reminded her that there was no access to the house from the roof.

It wasn't a burglar. It was her dad. Her sixty-seven-year-old dad. Who had about as much business being on her roof in the gathering darkness as a burglar.

She parked next to his black pickup and got out. He didn't seem to have heard her arrival. He was on his knees, chiseling off lumps of emerald moss and tossing them over his shoulder. One almost hit her.

Mia cupped her hands around her mouth. "Dad! What are you doing on the roof?"

"What?" He turned toward her, and his right foot slid down several inches. Silhouetted against the expanse of gray shingles, he looked smaller than she remembered.

"Dad! Be careful! You should come down!"

"I'm almost done. Go inside and check on Brooke." He turned back and levered up another green lump.

Check on Brooke? Where was Gabe? Biting back her questions, Mia walked past the ladder and into the house.

Downstairs was deserted and quiet. In a sudden panic, she ran upstairs. No sign of Gabe, but Brooke was in her room, surrounded by approximately three thousand pieces of molded plastic, most of them pink. A pink Barbie car. A pink-and-white xylophone. A Hello Kitty radio. A pink-and-purple shopping cart tipped on its side.

Brooke had a doll in each hand. Mia knew that her daughter called them the mother and daddy dolls, although one was really some sort of Transformer and the other a Barbie. The Transformer loomed over Barbie. In a gruff voice Brooke said, "I've had a hard day. All I'm asking for is a little peace and quiet."

Anything Mia had been thinking of saying evaporated at Scott's words, channeled by a four-year-old.

Brooke turned toward her, her blue eyes unreadable.

Mia found her voice. "What're you doing, honey?"

"Just playing."

"With the mommy and daddy dolls?"

Brooke shot her a look that wouldn't have been out of place on Scott's face. She turned and regarded the Transformer for a moment, then looked back up at Mia with a wary expression.

"Will he ever come back alive again?"

Mia's heart seemed to stop beating. "Do you mean Daddy, honey?"

Brooke didn't answer, just kept watching her face.

"No, honey, I'm sorry," Mia said slowly. "He won't."

Brooke blew air through pursed lips. "I knew that." Her tone was almost sarcastic.

Mia dropped to her knees and tried to gather up her daughter, but Brooke wriggled away.

"I want to keep playing."

Downstairs, the front door closed and her dad called up to her. Mia got to her feet and went down.

"I got your mail." He handed her a stack, which she put on the entryway table. Gabe's skateboard was underneath it, instead of in the hall closet. How many times had she asked him to put it away? Lately she might as well be talking to herself.

"Dad, I don't think it's a good idea for you to be up on the roof like that."

"Are you saying your old man's an old man?"

Yes.

"Of course not, Dad, but the roof has a pretty steep pitch. I can hire someone who specializes in that kind of thing and has special tools and safety gear." To avoid an argument, Mia switched topics. "Where's Gabe?"

"Oh, I told him he could go out with his friends after practice. You've got him watching Brooke every day—a boy needs time to be on his own."

And what if something had happened to Brooke while her dad was on the roof? "It's not like I have a lot of choices, Dad."

His mouth turned down at the corners. "Oh, Mia, you're right. I'm sorry."

Mia blinked. When had her dad ever apologized?

"Don't worry about it." She looked past him to the kitchen, where saucepans covered most of the counter. Her kitchen used to smell like chocolate chip cookies and long-simmering stews. Now there were whole weeks when it smelled like delivery pizza and takeout Chinese. "Did you cook dinner?"

"I tried. I'll have to admit it was more heating things up. Brooke seemed to like it, though. I can fix you a plate." He headed for the kitchen.

"Now you're waiting on me?" Mia tried to make a joke of it. "Who are you and what have you done with my dad?"

His face lit up. "I'm glad you noticed. I am different. God is working in me."

She wanted to roll her eyes. God was working in her father? All his recent talk about God and church was just her dad trying to find something to do now that he was retired. Without a job at the center of his life, he was lost.

Her dad had dedicated most of his waking hours to his job as a manager at a packaging company. His retirement funds had been invested solely in company stock. When the company went bankrupt a year after he retired, the company CEO got jail time and her dad had been left with nothing but Social Security.

Six months ago he had started going to church. Church! Mia couldn't have been more surprised if he had taken up belly dancing. Now he plopped some broccoli in bright yellow cheese sauce onto a plate. "If you wanted, you could come with me to church sometime."

"I don't know." Was Peter getting the same sales pitch? Somehow she doubted it. Her brother had even less patience than she did. Mia had joined Scott's church when they married, but over time their attendance had dwindled to Easter and Christmas.

"I think the kids would enjoy it. They've got special classes for different ages." He mounded some mac and cheese on her plate. It was slightly more orange than the broccoli's cheese sauce.

When Mia and Peter were little, their mom would get them up and dressed in stiff clothes and take them to church—while their dad, more often than not, slept in. He had said it was the one morning he could get a little peace.

Mia tried to be polite. "I'll think about it." She pushed aside dirty plates and sat down.

"I used to think that if there was a God, He was way off in heaven someplace." Her dad opened the dishwasher and slid in a dirty dish. "But now I know that God really cares about each of us. Not just in some global way, but down to what we eat and wear. Jesus said that He counted each sparrow."

Then where had God been when someone shot Colleen? When Scott lost control of his car?

Mia took a deep breath. "I appreciate that you feel that way, Dad, but can we not talk about it right now? I have had the most awful twenty-four hours."

"Really?" His forehead creased in concern. "What happened?"

In between bites Mia told him about her phone call with Colleen, how she had gone to her, and how she and Charlie had raced back to the house, sure that something terrible was happening to the kids. "Brooke was having what must have been the worst nightmare I've ever seen. She was screaming and fighting, but I couldn't get her to wake up. It was awful."

Her dad nodded. "You used to sleepwalk." He fit a smeared glass onto the top rack of the dishwasher. "And a couple of times you did that whole screaming with your eyes open thing too."

"Are you sure? I don't remember that."

Smiling, he reached past her to grab the dirty plates from the table. "You never did then either. We'd try to talk to you about it, and it was like it had never happened."

Mia's anxiety about Brooke receded a little. "Now Frank wants me to head up the investigation into Colleen's death. I'm really torn." She forked up another clump of broccoli and waited for her dad to tell her what to do. He had never been shy about sharing his opinions.

"I know you'll make the right decision." He cleared the last few dishes and then looked at his watch. "I probably should be getting back. The dog will be wondering where I am. Tell Gabe I'll see him at his game on Friday."

Just as he got to the door, Brooke scampered down the stairs and crashed into his legs. She wrapped her arms around his knees. "You know what, Grandpa? We should have a sleepover party!"

Mia's dad smiled down at her, his face lighting up. "Not tonight, honey bun. But maybe sometime."

Had her dad ever smiled at her like that when she was little? Mia let him out the front door and then picked up the stack of mail to sort through while she ate the rest of her meal.

Two minutes after he left, tires squealed up outside, followed by a fusillade of honks and shouts. Since when did Gabe have friends who were old enough to drive?

He slouched into the kitchen carrying a white plastic bag. Mia looked closer at his clothes. His black T-shirt had something silk-screened on the front.

No. Hadn't she talked to him about not wearing that shirt to school?

It was a drawing of a kitten. Printed in block letters above it were the words *I hate everyone*. Mia knew it was supposed to be ironic, but it did not offer the best impression to the students and teachers who were just getting to know her son.

"Gabe! Don't tell me you wore that to school today." This must be why he had come down bare chested to breakfast and then insisted on riding his skateboard.

He just shrugged and grinned.

She didn't have the energy to be angry. "From now on, I don't want you wearing that to school." She held out her hand. "Since your grandpa made dinner, you can give me back the money I gave you for pizza."

He shrugged. "I spent it. Sorry."

"On what?"

"Protein powder. I had to use part of my allowance too." From the bag he pulled out a blue canister and set it on the counter. "But if I drink this twice a day, it will help me get bigger."

"Bigger? You're nearly eye to eye with me now."

"Most guys on the team are way bigger than me. Not just taller, but heavier. I need more muscle. You can't play football if you're skinny."

She was too tired to argue. Later she would have to Google the stuff to make sure it wasn't dangerous.

Gabe went into the family room, where she heard him greet Brooke and then turn on the TV. It was the first time Mia had been alone all day, if she didn't count being in her car. She dished up the last of the macaroni and cheese and sorted the rest of the mail. *Redbook* for her, *Outdoors* for Scott (she had to figure out how to cancel it), political mailings, pleas from charities, and then something that looked like a bill, addressed to Scott. The return address was their local post office. She slid her finger under the flap.

It was a bill for a post office box. But why had Scott had a PO box?

Scott's keys were upstairs on their dresser, nestled in the silver dish where he had put his change and keys every night. Hadn't she seen a small, unfamiliar key on it?

Still chewing, Mia went upstairs and grabbed his keys. Yes. A small brass key engraved with the number 306. That matched the box number mentioned in the letter. What could be in it? Their post office lobby was open around the clock, even when the counter service was closed.

She stuck her head into the family room. "Gabe, I need you to keep an eye on Brooke for a second. I have to run an errand." He started to mutter, but she kept going.

Mia told herself she wouldn't think about what she might find, but still her imagination immediately conjured up images of scented letters from a woman. Maybe even several women.

Five minutes later she was standing in a hallway-sized space lit by fluorescent lights and lined on both sides by little metal boxes. They reminded her of the mausoleum niches the funeral director had shown her after Scott died.

She fit the key in the lock and turned it. Her eyes widened. The box was stuffed full. She pinched a dozen envelopes and tugged until they finally came loose, spilling everything on the floor. Leaning over, she gathered them up. Some envelopes were stamped "Third notice" and "Urgent!" in red letters.

A sudden surge of vertigo made it hard to straighten up without staggering. Bills. All bills. No wonder Scott had been keeping the existence of this post office box a secret.

Mia was going to lose everything.

CHAPTER 13

At 8:35 the next morning Mia stood outside Frank's office waiting for him to finish a phone call. DeShauna walked in the main door and gave Mia a look that was frankly curious. Mia nodded and then turned her back on the reception area.

Staring at the dingy beige carpeting, she made a conscious effort to clear her mind. She would not think about how her co-workers might view Frank's offer or her decision. Or about Brooke's nightmare on Sunday. Or about Gabe's obsession with fitting in.

Mia most especially would not think about what she had learned from Scott's post office box. She would not think about how the Suburban was actually leased—leased!—for $599 a month. Or how it was already two months in arrears.

Ever since Scott died, Mia had been paying bills as they came in—gas, water, electric, newspaper, cell phone, Internet. She should have wondered where the credit card bills were, both for the single card she carried as well as the cards she had found in his wallet when it was returned to her. Although she had been vaguely aware that Scott carried more credit cards—she remembered signing a few forms he had handed her over the years—it had been a surprise to see how many there were. Even so, the number of bills stuffed in the PO box was a shock. After she had gotten home, Mia had locked her bedroom door, spread the envelopes out on the bedspread, and methodically made her way through an entire box of Better Cheddars while adding everything up.

Even though many of the paper bills were duplicates, the ultimate total on the calculator was staggering: $53,727.

And each time Mia hit the plus sign, it became clearer.

She had to say yes to Frank.

It wasn't just that she owed Colleen justice. She also couldn't afford to risk her job. Not now. Not when she had to do everything she could to somehow pay off the bills and hold on to the house.

The house was the key to everything. If she lost it, her family would continue to unravel. If she were reduced to a rental, chances were that the schools in whatever area they could afford would not be nearly as good. Gabe probably wouldn't be on the new school's football team. Mia would have to find a new preschool for Brooke. Both kids would have to leave their friends, neighbors, the park just two blocks away . . .

How could Mia have missed the red flags? Three months before Scott died, her credit card had been declined at the grocery store. Brooke was whining for some of the Wheat Thins that had already been bagged when the clerk loudly announced that her card had been rejected. The woman had looked at Mia with narrowed eyes, as if she were a thief. With a great show of reluctance, she had finally accepted a check.

When Mia called Scott from the parking lot, he said, "Oh, didn't I tell you? I lost my card last week when I was out of town and had to cancel the account. Sorry. I thought I mentioned it."

"You didn't." Mia had stared at a small bird with drab black feathers pecking at something in the parking lot. Behind her, Brooke was stuffing Wheat Thins into her mouth. "I feel like I never see you anymore, Scott. Maybe we can start sitting down at night with a glass of wine and catching up on our days like we used to. Sometimes I feel like I don't know what's going on with you."

"What do you mean, what's going on?" Scott's voice had an edge to it.

"Like how your business is going. You never talk to me about that anymore."

"The last thing I want to do when I'm home is talk about the business. We made a deal, right? You take care of the kids and the house and all of that, and I take care of the financial parts of our lives. Well, I've kept my part of the deal. And it's my long hours that make our lifestyle possible. Isn't that what you wanted?"

Now Mia knew the truth behind Scott's words, that he had been scrambling, robbing Peter to pay Paul, and then borrowing from Perry to pay the interest on the loan from Patrick.

Since Scott died, there had been one surprise after another.

None of them good.

Startling her out of her reverie, Frank called out, "Okay, Mia, come in." Once again she sat facing the framed photos of his kids. After today, would her kids be as close to her as Frank's were to him?

Frank steepled his fingers. "Have you made a decision?"

"Yes." Mia took a deep breath. "I'll take on Colleen's case." He started to say something, and she held up one hand. "On one condition."

"Condition?" He raised an eyebrow, his expression hovering between amusement and annoyance.

"We talked about Darin Dane yesterday. I still want to take his case to the grand jury. See if there's enough evidence for an indictment."

"Mia, you've got to be practical." Definitely annoyance. A muscle in his jaw flickered. "If you're going to investigate Colleen's death, it will demand your full attention."

"I'm not saying we file charges against the people who harassed Darin. I'm saying we let the grand jury decide whether there's a case. That's all. Gabe's the same age as Darin." She pointed at his daughter's photo. "We're talking about a boy only a couple of years younger than Caitlin. And now he's dead."

"Mia, realistically speaking, that's a waste of resources. We can't bring that kid back."

Was Frank thinking about the department's record? The best

won-lost records did not come from amazing legal work. They were built by cherry-picking only the strongest cases for trial and pleading out the rest. Or, in some cases, never filing charges at all. But the public didn't understand those nuances.

"And if it's a dead end, then I promise you I'll let it go," Mia said. "But I am not going to look Darin's father in the face and say, sorry, those kids may have tormented your son until he killed himself, but there's nothing we can do. Don't worry, Frank, I plan on devoting all of my time to figuring out who killed Colleen. I'll just fit this in the cracks."

Frank sighed and nodded, as part of her had known he would. The new Frank was a much more political animal than the man she had met when she first started working at King County. But underneath his worries about resources and perceptions she sometimes caught flashes of the idealistic thirty-year-old she had worked alongside all those years earlier.

"I still think it's a waste of time, but as long as you give Colleen's death your full attention . . ."

"Of course I will, Frank. But there's one more thing we still need to discuss. What if I'm called to testify about what I heard on the phone? Do we need a second on this case?" Mia meant a second prosecutor.

Frank winced. "We're stretched thin as it is. Also, when it comes to trial we don't want to look like we're bigfooting the defendant by having you, Charlie, *and* your second at the table, not when the defense only has the defendant and his attorney." He sat back, laced his fingers over his belly, and thought about it. "Actually, I don't think we need to worry about it. We're not going to put you on the stand, and why would the defense? The prejudice outweighs the probative value. The death is self-evident, and your testimony might be considered gratuitous."

Frank was right. Taking the jurors through those last horrible moments would be bound to influence them—which meant no judge would allow it. And even if the judge would, the defense was certainly not going to want to dwell on the gritty details.

"I guess I'm in all the way then, Frank."

"I always knew you would be."

There was no point in being annoyed, not when he was right. "How long did you work with Colleen?" she asked.

"Over twenty years. That's why it's just so hard to believe that she's gone. I mean, you actually heard it happen, so I guess you must believe it. I just keep thinking about how it used to be. Remember? You and Colleen and I, we're part of the old guard. We remember the go-go years, when Seattle had all that Microsoft and Boeing cash. When even the government could spend money and nobody complained too much." He made a sound that was a cross between a grunt and a laugh. "Sometimes I miss those days. Things were simpler then. Now there are so many decisions, and whatever I do, somebody's going to be unhappy."

"You mean because you gave me Colleen's case?" Mia thought of the way people had looked at her yesterday after she emerged from Frank's office. Looked at her and looked away.

"There's that. There's also being in the public eye. I mean, look at this." He tapped on his keyboard and then half turned his computer screen so that she could see it. It was a Facebook page, and the profile photo looked like a screen capture of Frank from a video. She guessed he might have been talking. His mouth was open and his eyes half-closed. He looked more than a little crazy.

He stabbed at the page's title with his finger. Mia started to read it out loud. "Frank D'Amato is a—" She stopped. "Huh, I thought that word was an obscenity."

"Things have changed," Frank said bitterly. "I've heard people use that word on TV. Not even cable. Network."

She looked at the comments. Posters called Frank a fat cat and an imbecile and a blowhard. So much naked hate, but much of it hid behind names that were obviously fake, like Scarlett O'Hara.

"Who even knows who these people are, Frank? It could even be the same person posting under different user names."

He nodded, but his expression was still miserable. Suddenly she was reminded of Gabe, of how he would obsess over a pimple—that same sense that the whole world was watching and judging. Only in Frank's case there was far more truth to it.

"You can't change their minds. You just need to stay away from looking at this kind of thing. All it will do is stress you out." She sounded more like his mother than his employee, but Frank nodded.

"Speaking of computers, I'm going to need Jonas to help me go through the database," Mia said. "I want to see if Colleen and Stan had any cases in common."

Frank waved his hand. "Of course. Tell him it's top priority."

When Mia left Frank's office, Tracy, Jesse, and Katrina were talking next to Colleen's closed door with its yellow crime-scene tape. They fell silent as soon as they saw her. Tracy threw Jesse a meaningful look, and Jesse raised his eyebrow. They left, but Mia guessed what they had been saying. That it wasn't that long ago that she had walked away from this place. And now that she was back, far from having to repay her dues, a high-profile case was being handed to her on a silver platter.

Katrina grabbed her arm and pulled Mia into her own office. "Frank gave it to you, didn't he? Colleen's case."

Mia hesitated, trying to think of an answer that wasn't a lie.

"He did!" Katrina cuffed Mia's arm. "I asked about it, but I figured you were the one who would get it. Everyone knows how close you and Colleen are. Were. If anyone can figure out why they were killed, it's you."

Feeling grateful that Katrina didn't seem jealous, Mia said, "There are a lot of downsides. It's going to mean a ton of extra hours. And Charlie Carlson's the homicide detective on the case."

"Charlie?" Katrina raised an eyebrow. "I've always thought he was kind of cute."

"Cute?" Mia snorted. "I can think of a lot of words for Charlie, but cute isn't one of them. Let's just say we have some history."

Katrina leaned closer. "Tell me about it."

"Not that kind of history. About ten years ago, before he was in homicide, a robbery case we were working together got tossed because he took something from the scene."

Katrina looked scandalized. "He stole something?"

"But nobody knows what. He admitted to taking it, but that was all he would say. Just that it wasn't material to the case. So of course the case got tossed out. And the guy was back out on the street and robbing again as soon as he got released."

Both their heads turned at the sound of a rap on Mia's half-open door. She started when she saw that it was Charlie, while Katrina managed to look composed.

How much had he heard? How guilty did she look?

"Hey, Mia, can I talk to you when you have a minute?" Charlie's expression betrayed nothing.

CHAPTER 14

Hey, Charlie," Katrina said easily.

Her face was as innocent as an angel's. Mia was sure that she herself was blushing furiously.

"Katrina, Mia." He stepped just inside Mia's door and nodded at them.

"I was just leaving," Katrina said.

Charlie closed the door, leaned against it, and crossed his arms. Mia was uncomfortably aware of his body, of how his suit jacket tightened over his biceps.

"So Frank tells me you're gonna be heading up the investigation." Charlie did not sound as if this was a plus.

Better to grab this bull by the horns. "Actually we're going to be working on *two* cases together."

His brow furrowed. "Two? What are you talking about?"

Leave it to Frank to leave it to her. He never liked saying things other people didn't want to hear. "We're going to be investigating two deaths. Colleen's and a high school freshman named Darin Dane. Darin killed himself last week."

Charlie's brow furrowed. "So there's doubt about whether it was really a suicide?"

"No. But Darin's been tormented by the same group of kids since middle school. The day after he died, his father came to me with evidence that these students cyberbullied him. I want to bring it to the grand jury to see if there's enough evidence for them to be indicted. And to do that, I need you to help me interview witnesses and gather evidence."

Charlie shook his head. "Mia." It was amazing how much weight he could load onto a single word.

"Hey, we're already working one case. We're going to be fastened at the hip anyway."

"You said he killed himself—how is that someone else's fault?"

"The medical examiner found bruises consistent with beatings," Mia said. "And his father has evidence that his Facebook page was hacked in a really vile way."

Charlie sighed. "Just tell me what you need done and I'll do it. But my priority is gonna be finding whoever killed Colleen."

The cop-prosecutor marriage could be a rocky one, but ultimately the prosecutor took the lead. Mia figured she had better set some ground rules. "Actually, I think your priority is going to be doing what needs doing, whether it's helping me learn if anyone is to blame for Darin's death or figuring out who killed Colleen and if it's related to Stan's murder."

He uncrossed his arms and opened his mouth, but she didn't let him say anything. She knew he thought she was harping, but if she didn't stand firm with Charlie Carlson, he would push her a little one day and a little more the next until ultimately they would be following Charlie Carlson's path.

"And I'm going to want briefings at least once a day on what you've turned up. Why don't you start by telling me what you've learned so far about Colleen?"

He gave her a little mock salute. Mia gritted her teeth and smiled pleasantly. Then he sat down at her visitor's table. She pulled her desk chair closer and sat opposite him.

"There's not a lot to say that I didn't tell you about yesterday." He ticked off the paltry evidence. "No signs of forced entry to the house. No strange fingerprints or footprints. About the only evidence we have is that .22 slug, and it's too mangled to be of much use. However, it is the same caliber as the bullet that killed Stan. And Colleen was shot in her home, alone, at night, just like Stan. Unlike with Stan, we did recover the brass, but there're no prints on it. Colleen's work and home computers, as well as her cell phone, are at the computer lab, and the forensics people are gonna give me printouts of whatever they find." Charlie's eyes, which were a stormy gray-blue, met hers. "Since we're coming up empty-handed forensically, we need to start with the victim and work out from there. So who would want Colleen dead?"

"That's a good question. The problem is that I can't think of anyone."

Charlie tilted his head and narrowed his eyes. "Hey, nobody's perfect. Not even Colleen. I'm sure she ticked off someone at some point."

"I'm just thinking of Colleen as a person. Everybody who knew her liked her. Even that crazy Tami Gordon from the public defender's office liked Colleen, and Tami thought all prosecutors were Satan's minions. Colleen was funny, she was kind, she was generous." Tears pricked Mia's eyes. Charlie was right. She was losing objectivity. But Colleen had been killed because of her job, Mia was sure of it. Not because of *who* she was, but because of *what* she was.

Leaning forward, Charlie countered, "I knew Colleen too. And she *was* generous, and funny, and kind. She could also be loud. And nosy. She also had a lot of opinions. Those things are also true, Mia. And just because they're true, they don't make any of the good things you just said about Colleen any less true. You've got to put on your prosecutor hat. You know people can be killed for the smallest of reasons. People have been murdered for their pocket change."

Mia matched him stare for stare. "But that's a spontaneous crime. And to me it looks like whoever did this planned it out in advance. I don't think this was someone who happened to be out walking with a gun and decided it might be fun to shoot a stranger through a basement window. So when I put on my prosecutor's hat, I still have a hard time thinking of why anyone would want to kill Colleen the person. It's a lot more likely that she was killed because she was

Colleen the prosecutor. You know as well as I do that attorneys in this office have been physically attacked in court by defendants or stalked by their families after we sentenced them."

"Okay, if that's your working theory, that she was killed by someone connected to her job, how does that fit with what happened to Stan?"

"It sure fits a lot better than your theory, because that one doesn't explain what happened to Stan at all."

"It's not *my* theory, Mia," Charlie said. "I'm just saying it's too soon to rule anything out."

"Okay, okay, you're right. We don't know what really happened." Mia held up her hands in surrender. She had to work with this guy, and if she kept jumping down his throat, he might find ways to keep her out of the loop. "As soon as we're done, I'm going to ask our database guy to cross-reference Colleen's and Stan's cases to see whether they prosecuted any of the same defendants."

Charlie nodded. "There've been times we worked something as a single case, closed it, and then later realized we'd really been looking at a serial rapist or a serial killer at the beginning of their career. But that doesn't explain a nearly five-year gap in between."

"Maybe some guy killed Stan, got picked up for something else and sent to prison, recently got released, and decided to come back and settle a score with Colleen."

Charlie looked thoughtful. "Time in prison would explain why the two crimes are so far apart. I'm also gonna reopen Stan's case, see what's changed. People who may have kept quiet four or five years ago might be more willing to talk now." He blew air through pursed lips. "Did Colleen's and Stan's personal lives overlap at all?"

"Oh, they both believed in the same progressive causes, although Stan tended to get a little more intense about them. And Colleen mothered him, the way she did all of us." It sickened Mia how easily the past tense came to her now, as if it were normal and accepted that Colleen was dead. Not forty-eight hours earlier she had been fully, vibrantly alive. "When Stan was in the middle of a case, there were times she would literally force him to eat. She found this restaurant that made pierogies like he used to have when he was a kid, and she would swing by at lunch and get a takeout order and then stand over him until he finished every bite."

"Wish I had that problem," Charlie said, getting to his feet. "I'm gonna go through Colleen's office one more time. I'll ask you if I come across something that needs clarification. And I'm interviewing Violet at noon at their home if you want to be on hand for that."

"Of course I do." It might be easier for Violet if she was there.

Mia found Jonas Carvel in his cubicle. Jonas was always in his cubicle. He was a doughy young man with round glasses, a round head, and hair shaved down to a blond stubble. He spent his lunch hours playing some kind of multiplayer game on a tablet computer he brought from home. Mia had learned it was better not to ask about it unless she wanted to hear a lot of confusing talk about elves, spells, gold coins, and battle axes.

"Jonas, I need you to do a central case file database search for me. Frank said you should make it your top priority."

"What kind of search?" He began ticking off possibilities on his fingers. "I can search by case type, party names, attorney names, criminal charges or the type of civil case, the judge who was assigned, and whether the case is open or closed."

"I need you to cross-reference Colleen's and Stan's cases and look for any that had the same defendant."

Jonas's eyes lit up. "Because they were killed in the same manner! And you believe that the same person may have taken his or her revenge against both of them."

"That's right. And wherever you find an overlap, I want you to request the actual paper files." Even though everything had technically gone digital, in practice a lot of prosecutors took handwritten notes when they interviewed witnesses. And those notes ended up in the paper file, but not the digital.

"I can write the code and run it for matches today," Jonas said, "but I probably won't be able to get the paper files pulled until tomorrow."

"Okay. Just let me know when you do."

When Mia walked back down the hall, it was a shock to see Charlie sitting in Colleen's office, slowly thumbing his way through a file drawer. As she watched, he slipped something yellow into his mouth. With an exasperated sigh, she knocked on the door and stepped inside.

"What is that you're eating?" As long as Mia had known her, Colleen had kept a cache of wrapped butterscotch candies in a silver dish on her desk.

"What?" Charlie said absently. Then his eyes followed her gaze to the bright yellow cellophane wrapper he still held in his hand. The light dawned. He swallowed with audible effort. "Oh, sorry."

"You're eating a dead woman's candy?"

"It's not like she needs it, Mia."

She knew it was irrational, but seeing Charlie eat Colleen's candy was like seeing a vulture settle on fresh roadkill. Afraid to open her mouth in case she couldn't control what came out, Mia just gritted her teeth and shook her head again.

"Hey, I liked Colleen. A lot. And I will do everything to make sure her killer is caught. But it's not like this is a crime scene. I'm not contaminating evidence. I'm just eating a butterscotch candy. As I have in Colleen's office before, because she offered them to me. And which, I would like to point out, there are dozens more of. But if you are really that upset, I can drive over to Safeway right now, hit the bulk bins, and get a replacement candy."

"No. You're right," Mia made herself choke out. He was right. She was being irrational. "It's fine."

He got to his feet. "Look, we have to work together, right? And we both want to catch whoever did this, right?"

Feeling ashamed, Mia nodded but didn't meet his eyes.

"So if I do a few things that bug you, you have to let it go. And the same goes for me. If something you do gets on my nerves, I'm not gonna pay any attention. The only thing that matters is catching the person who did this. Right?"

Mia raised her eyes to his. "Right." For a second she held his gaze, then she turned away. "I'll see you at Colleen's house at noon."

CHAPTER 15

Charlie had gone to Colleen Miller's house so many times in the past three days that his car could probably drive itself there. Now the drive passed in a blur as he ground his teeth over Mia Quinn. She was a real piece of work. Some goody-two-shoes who had probably never had a single piece of Colleen's candy, not after considering the nine calories or whatever it might cost her. He was sure she ironed her jeans and never, ever did a rolling stop at an otherwise empty four-way intersection, the way Charlie was doing right now.

He pulled up behind Mia just as she was getting out of her big SUV that badly needed a wash. And for a moment, before she realized he was there, Charlie saw Mia's face when it wasn't animated by anger. Instead, it was naked, vulnerable, contorted by loss upon loss.

Maybe Charlie should give her the benefit of the doubt. First of all, she had been close to Colleen, and Colleen had good taste in people. And second, and more important, what he had told her back at the office was true. They had to work together if they wanted to solve Colleen's murder.

When Mia turned to face him, she had her professional mask firmly back in place. He gave her a nod.

The crime-scene tape was gone, but the signs of the murder and its aftermath were everywhere. The ground still bore the boot impressions of the techs. The window through which Colleen had been shot was boarded up with plywood. All the windowsills were covered with black fingerprint powder. The frame for the front door was smudged gray.

Mia rapped on the door. A second later it was answered by a tall girl with short hair that was most definitely violet.

Charlie had never met Violet before, but in some ways her face was now as familiar to him as any minor movie star's. Searching Colleen's home and office, he'd seen hundreds of snapshots documenting Violet's first twenty years on earth, from sleeping infant to graduating high school senior. But none of them had shown her with purple hair.

"Oh, Violet!" Mia reached out for the girl, but Violet stepped back and crossed her arms.

"Mia." Her tone was cool. "What are you doing here?"

"I'm actually working on your mom's case." She turned to him. "Along with Charlie. Violet, this is Charlie Carlson, the homicide detective. Charlie, this is Violet."

He put out his hand, but she stared at him without moving.

"So does that mean you're a cop?" A single small gold hoop pierced Violet's left nostril. Tasteful, if you could consider those things tasteful. Charlie wasn't sure he ever would, which made him feel old.

He let his hand fall by his side. "I'm with the Seattle Police Department."

She sucked in her breath and then put her hands on his chest and shoved him. Charlie was too startled to resist. Besides, he had enough weight on her that he didn't budge.

"Violet!" Mia said in a scandalized voice.

"I thought the jerk who killed her was the one who left everything a mess, but they told me it was actually you guys! The cops! So first my mom was murdered, and then the cops went and trashed everything." Her hands were fisted, her breathing ragged.

Charlie had made sure his team put things back, at least more or less. So clothes had gone back into drawers, but probably not folded.

Papers had gone back into the filing cabinets, or at least been left in a neat pile. Charlie wasn't like some detectives, who would just toss drawers and leave stuff lying out, not just for suspects but even for victims. But the truth was that even conscientious investigators weren't expected to clean up after themselves. That was the victim's—or their survivors'—responsibility.

Still, Charlie felt oddly ashamed. "I'm sorry. We do the best we can." And it wasn't as if they had found anything that shed light on the murder. No scraps of paper with mysterious notations, no answering machine messages from cryptic callers. He had even gone through Colleen's key ring, looking for a strange key that might open a powerful secret: a safety deposit box, a PO box, a secret lover's apartment. But every key had fit into a known lock.

"Violet, I don't think I've seen you since this summer," Mia said brightly, trying to press the restart button on the conversation. "I can't get over your hair." She reached out to ruffle the bottom edge of it.

With a grimace Violet stepped back. "I figured I had to live up to the stupid hippie name Mom gave me. As soon as I got back to school I dyed it."

Mia and Charlie exchanged glances, then followed her into the living room with its worn but beautiful oriental carpet in shades of red, royal blue, and gold. Charlie and Mia took a seat on the red velvet couch, while Violet sat on a brown leather Morris chair and hugged her knees to her chest. It was a strange feeling to be back in a room you had only recently searched. Charlie knew what was on the bookcase, on the shelves, in the drawers.

"So who did it?" Violet demanded. "Who killed my mom?"

"We're working on a number of angles that involve her work as a prosecutor," Charlie said. "But we could use your help figuring out more about your mom's personal life."

She snorted. "So you're saying you have no idea?"

"Violet!" Mia said.

Charlie took a deep breath. "I'm not saying that at all. I'm saying we are pursuing a number of leads. And we need your help. To start with, when was the last time you saw your mother, talked to her, e-mailed her, texted her . . ."

Mia shot him a look. It was a question you would ask a suspect, and she had already informed him that there was no way Violet could be one. But she had also said Violet was a sweet, quiet girl, so her judgment was suspect. And it was possible, if Violet had driven very fast, that she could have driven up to Seattle, shot her mom, and arrived back in Olympia in time to be notified by the campus police about her mother's murder.

Still, this crime felt oddly impersonal. People who killed family members usually acted out of an outsized anger that had built up for years. An anger that didn't dissipate until the victim had been nearly obliterated—stabbed dozens of times or beaten past all recognition. But here death had come through a single shot. There had been no overkill. And no shame afterward, no need to cover the victim's face with a rug or sheet. A pane of glass had separated the killer from the victim, both in reality and symbolically. This felt like an execution, carried out by someone who came away with clean hands and experienced no guilt at the sight of Colleen sprawled on her old vinyl LPs, gargling her own blood.

"My mom called on Saturday night but I was kind of busy, so we didn't talk long. It was all her just wanting to know stuff about my life and all." Violet pressed her lips together. "I've told her that nobody else I know talks to their mom that much."

There. Charlie hadn't imagined it. Her lower lip was trembling. This girl was all hot emotion. Although he had seen killers weep before.

Mia leaned forward. "Has your mom seemed upset about anything lately?"

A shrug. "I don't think so." Her face was very pale, making the smattering of freckles across her nose stand out.

"Has she talked about any case that bothered her?" Mia asked.

Violet shook her head. "Mom doesn't ever talk about work. Maybe she didn't think I was old enough."

"Maybe she just didn't want to worry you," Mia said gently.

"Maybe she was afraid it would make you think the world was a dark and scary place."

"Isn't it?" Violet said. "Someone just assassinated my mom."

"Assassinated?" Charlie echoed.

"Maybe that's not the right term." Her mouth twisted. "But somebody must have killed her just for doing her job."

"Aside from people she prosecuted, do you know if your mom had any enemies?" Charlie asked.

"Mom? No. My mom?" Violet smirked. "Mom just wanted people to be happy. She always had some stray she was taking care of. I'm not talking animals, I'm talking people. If someone at church looked lonely, she'd ask them home for dinner. I remember one Thanksgiving she invited this old man with no teeth. I had to sit across from him and watch him slurp oatmeal." Violet shuddered, secure in her belief that such a fate could never befall her. "And when the lady across the street lost her job, Mom used to get Costco packs of mac and cheese and leave them on the porch for her and her two kids before they got evicted." She straightened up and put her feet on the floor. "This neighborhood isn't as safe as it was when I was a kid. There's lots of empty houses now, because of the recession. People have had their cars prowled, and someone up the street said she saw a strange guy in her backyard. Do you think that might have something to do with what happened to Mom?"

Charlie and Mia exchanged a look. Car prowls were usually kids with too much freedom, trying door handles until they got lucky and could make off with meter change and a few CDs, maybe an MP3 player. But the idea of a stranger standing in a backyard in Colleen's neighborhood gave Charlie pause.

What if Colleen's death *was* the result of some unstable homeless guy's whim—a brightly lit window, a figure walking past it, a voice telling him to pull the trigger? That kind of crime—motiveless, with no connection between the killer and the victim—was almost impossible to solve, unless the killer struck again and again.

It was also extremely rare.

"Break-ins, car prowls—those are crimes of opportunity," Charlie said. "But I don't see how a stranger would benefit from shooting your mom. And in my experience, people are murdered for reasons. Maybe not good reasons, but still reasons. Is there anyone your mom hasn't gotten along with lately?"

"Yeah. My dad. But Dad would never, like, what, kill Mom?" Violet snorted to show how ridiculous the idea was.

"What have they been fighting about?" Mia asked. "I thought Colleen got along pretty well with Martin."

"He and his wife adopted a baby this summer. Did Mom tell you that?"

Mia nodded.

"I guess they finally gave up on that in vitro. Which I don't know why they didn't before, because they are, like, old. And this baby of theirs—*I'm* old enough to be its mother. The whole thing must have cost a lot, because Dad started complaining when it came time to write the tuition check." She turned to Charlie. "See, when they got divorced, my dad told my mom he would pay for my college. It's not like I expect him to do everything. I work part-time, and my mom helps pay for my room and board. But even though it's a public college, it still costs twenty thousand a year, and what I make isn't enough to cover tuition and books and all those other things."

Could that be a motive? But if Violet's dad had wanted to stop paying his kid's tuition, wouldn't it have been a better solution, if far more cold-blooded, to kill the daughter rather than the mother?

"This term," Violet continued, "Dad's only paid part of the tuition. The last time I talked to him I could actually hear his wife in the background telling him what to say."

"Your stepmother," Charlie supplied.

Violet made a face. "I guess so, but I've never called her that. Gina's only fourteen years older than me, but she likes to pretend it's even less than that."

"How about your mom's other personal relationships?" Charlie asked. "Do you know if she was dating?"

When Violet nodded, Mia blinked. "Really?"

"Right before I went back to college, I went into her office. Her computer was open to that dating website, eHeartMatch, and some guy had sent her a flirty note. At first I couldn't believe it. I mean, my mom? She's over fifty."

Charlie had the feeling that in Violet's eyes he and Mia were both practically in the grave.

"Maybe she was worried about being lonely. I'd already made it clear to her that I wasn't going to be coming home very much this year." Violet set her jaw. "I told her that I have my own life now." Her eyes told him that she heard the irony in her own words.

"We're checking to see what forensics can get off her computer," Charlie said. "You don't remember this guy's name, do you?"

"No. It was like a jokey name, you know, a screen name." She took a deep breath. "Do you have to look at everything from my mom's computer?"

"Why?" Charlie asked. Was there something Violet had written her mom that she was afraid they would find?

"Because it's private. I mean, when my mom wrote all her e-mails, she didn't imagine someone else reading them."

The dead didn't have any privacy. Maybe it was a good thing they were dead. "Think of us like doctors," Charlie said. "We've seen it all before."

Violet frowned. "That actually doesn't make me feel any better."

Thirty minutes later, having gained no real insights, Charlie and Mia left. As he opened his car door, Charlie had the sensation he was being watched. He froze and looked all around him. The street was deserted. Still, he couldn't shake the feeling.

CHAPTER 16

From this window on the second floor you could see into nearly every room in Colleen Miller's house.

And if you didn't have a TV set, it was nearly as good as one. Although you didn't know what you would get and you couldn't change the channel even if you wanted to.

You could watch the policemen swarm over the house with their cameras and their brushes and their fingerprint powders. They spent most of their time in the basement, although they appeared in other windows too. And then they went away.

Violet roamed from room to room, crying.

The neighbors came bearing casserole dishes.

Today the woman with the blond hair who had been here so many times before came back, even if there was now no Colleen to visit. She was with the dark-haired detective who had conferred with the policeman.

But none of them knew they were being watched. This house was empty. Had been for months.

That was what they thought.

But they were wrong.

CHAPTER 17

As she sat at her desk trying to triage her e-mails, Mia couldn't get over the idea that Colleen had been dating. Or maybe what she couldn't get over was that Colleen hadn't said *anything* to her about it. Had she been embarrassed about using an online dating service? Or had they not been as close as Mia thought?

Charlie knocked on her door, interrupting her thoughts. Police headquarters was just three blocks from the county courthouse. "I asked our computer forensics guy to separate out anything related to Colleen's love life and make two copies," he said. "He said to give him an hour."

Mia nodded, distracted. Charlie smelled like french fries. He must have hit the drive-through on his way back. Her stomach rumbled. There hadn't been any leftovers to pack this morning, and breakfast had been a cereal bar eaten in the car. This was going to be one of those days when lunch came from vending machines.

"Okay," she said. "And I made an appointment for us to meet the Danes at their house at four. The mom's a nurse and she gets off at three thirty."

Charlie remained on his feet. "Let's talk about what we know so far. Do you have a flip chart? It helps me think."

"There might be one in the supply room." Mia went into the hall, and Charlie followed. The supply room was jammed, mostly with discards—broken printers, chipped laminate bookcases, discarded binders. These were piled haphazardly among items that were still actually useful. Sometimes it was easier to put something in the supply room than to fill out the paperwork required to get rid of it.

In the far corner Mia spied a silver flip chart. She picked her way toward it, Charlie at her heels. Reaching for it, she stepped on something small and round that rolled away from her, suddenly pitching her backward. She crashed into Charlie. He caught her with one hand on her shoulder and the other on her waist. Mia jerked upright, her cheeks flaming. She grabbed the flip chart and thrust it into Charlie's hands. On her way out, she snatched up the brown marker that had nearly caused her to fall.

Back in her office, Charlie set up the flip chart. She handed him the errant marker, and he made two lines down the paper, dividing it into three. With blocky handwriting he labeled the first column *Colleen,* the middle *Stan,* and the last *Both.* Then he drew in horizontal lines to create a grid.

"Okay, you've got your guy checking the database to see if they have an angry defendant in common." He wrote *Angry Defendant* in the *Both* column. "And we know from Violet that Martin was arguing with Colleen about money. And Violet wasn't getting along that well with her either." *Martin* and *Violet* went under Colleen's name. Mia didn't agree with putting Violet down, but she didn't argue. "We also know Colleen was dating." *New Boyfriend* went in the Colleen column.

"What about Violet saying there'd been a prowler in the neighborhood?" Mia said.

"This doesn't feel random," Charlie said, but he still added *Prowler* under Colleen's name. "But better to start with too many suspects than too few."

"Maybe Colleen was the target of some fringe group," Mia suggested. "She's prosecuted guys from the Mongol biker gang and the Aryan Nation and probably a few more. I'm sure Stan did too." She wrote a note to herself on a yellow sticky. "That reminds me to ask our database guy if he has a way of teasing that out."

Charlie added *Fringe Group* to the *Both* column. After a pause, he added *Angry Defendant* to both Colleen's and Stan's columns. "I guess we shouldn't overlook the idea that they were killed independently by different defendants."

"Both of them were shot with a .22 at night, at home, through a window," Mia said. "Both of them Seattle prosecutors. Don't you think that's too many coincidences?"

With an edge of impatience Charlie said, "Like I said earlier, we can't rule anything out, Mia. Not at this stage."

She knew he was right, but something about Charlie made her want to argue. "But we can't draw the circle so wide that *everyone* is inside it. Otherwise pretty soon you'll be putting my name up there."

His mouth twisted, but he didn't argue any further. He also didn't change anything on the flip chart. "So when will your guy have those files for us?"

"It'll be tomorrow before Jonas has the paper files. We need them because there are prosecutors' notes that don't make it online."

"So much for the paperless society." Charlie stepped back and regarded the chart. "We also need to figure out if there was anything outside of work that Colleen and Stan had in common. Were they friends? Lovers? You told me she bought him pierogies."

"That was just Colleen being motherly. I don't think they really had that much in common." Something had been nagging at her, though, and Mia's eyes widened as she remembered what it was. "Wait a minute. They were both pretty active in Safe Seattle."

"The gun control group?"

"Right. They both worked on that measure that made it illegal for people who've been in a mental hospital to buy guns."

"So you think somebody on the other side decided to take them out?" Charlie pushed out his lips, looking dubious. "That's taking it pretty far. That's when you try to get the law repealed. Not go around shooting people. And that law passed when? Ten years ago? Why wait all this time to kill Colleen?"

"Maybe because she was working with Safe Seattle on a new

ballot measure." Mia tried to remember the specifics. "Something about mandatory trigger locks or background checks at gun shows." Mia turned to her keyboard, her hands suddenly trembling. She was onto something, she knew it. "Look at this comment some guy calling himself True Patriot left on KIRO's website."

Charlie leaned over Mia's shoulder, close enough that she could feel his breath on the side of her face. He read out loud, "'Now, if only the same would happen to a few thousand more anti-American, anti-constitutional traitors mooching off the public's dime.'" He let out a whistle. "We need to track down that jerk. Can you get a subpoena for the TV station's website?"

"Yeah, I'll do that today." Mia should have done it yesterday, but she hadn't been thinking clearly. "Although you'd have to be pretty stupid to post something like that if you're the one who killed her."

"Someone who decides to solve their problems with a gun is not necessarily accessing their higher mental functions." Charlie wrote *Gun Rights* in the *Both* column, then looked at the empty spaces under Stan's name. "Stan never married, right? Did he have a girlfriend? Guyfriend?"

"Stan? As far as I know, Stan was married to his job. If he had a love life, he kept it really quiet."

"Carmen Zapata worked Stan's case, but you probably heard she died of breast cancer last year. I need to find out where Stan's murder book ended up." A murder book was a fat binder with crime-scene photos, the autopsy report, investigators' notes, and transcripts of witness interviews. "Then we need to reopen the case. Have you ever worked a cold case before?"

Mia shook her head.

"Basically what you do is throw out any ideas from five years ago and start from scratch. Things change, and sometimes you can leverage that. You might interview somebody who lied then, but by now they've forgotten exactly what they said. Or they're no longer in love or in business with someone, so they don't feel the same pressure to keep quiet."

Mia thought back. "The problem is, I don't think there were

that many people to interview. I was out of office when they were investigating his death, but Colleen told me they were coming up empty-handed. They had no witnesses, no death threats, and no obvious enemies."

Charlie tapped the butt end of the marker against his teeth. "We also need to follow the money. Violet and Martin both benefit financially from her death. Violet is the named beneficiary of Colleen's life insurance and inherits everything from her mother. Martin had only an informal arrangement with Colleen to pay for Violet's college. He could have figured that getting Colleen out of the way got him off the hook."

Mia nodded. Even if the idea of Violet killing Colleen made her queasy, she had to consider it. "We need to talk to Martin."

"I'll set something up," Charlie said. "Do you want to be with me for the interview?"

"I didn't know him that well, but it might be useful not to let him know I'm involved just yet. Why don't you see if you can get him down to the station? Then I can watch from an observation room."

Charlie turned back to the flip chart. "How about Stan? Who benefited the most from his death?"

Mia tried to remember. "I don't think there was much of an estate. Stan had an older brother, but that was about it."

"I'll track him down, see if there's any other family I can talk to." Charlie started to say something else, but Mia's stomach let out a rumble and he broke off, laughing. "Sounds like someone's hungry."

"Maybe a little." Her cheeks were hot. "Do you mind if I grab something from the vending machine?"

"No problem. I'll make some calls to figure out where Stan's murder book is. And if they have any Fritos, could you get me some?"

In the break room Anne was heating a bag of microwave popcorn. She turned toward Mia. "I hear you're going to be working on Colleen's case. I sure hope you can get the guy who did it."

"Me too." The sign for her garage sale was still posted on the bulletin board next to the vending machine. Surrounded by notices for piano lessons, coast house rentals, and cars for sale, it read: *Cleaning out your attic, basement, or garage? Mia's having a garage sale.* Tears stung her eyes as she remembered how Colleen had offered to loan her money.

She blinked and turned to scan the vending machine's choices, looking for something vaguely healthy that would last for a few hours. After feeding bills into the machine, she pressed the button for Fig Newtons, figuring that they at least counted as a fruit. "I'm kind of worried about how I'm going to do it all and still take good care of my kids. How do you do it with four, Anne?"

"Do it?" Anne laughed. "Some days I don't. Some days it seems that no matter where I am, I should be someplace else. Like if I'm at work, I think of everything I need to do at home. And when I'm home, it's easy to think of everything I should be doing here. But then I realized that the result was that no matter where I was, I was only half there. So what I tell myself now is, 'Wherever your feet are, that's where your heart is.'" Anne looked down at her flats. "So when my feet are at work, my heart stays at work. And when I'm at home, my heart stays at home. I don't split my attention anymore."

The microwave dinged.

"But what about when you're at work and your kid texts you and says the coach doesn't like him?" Mia needed protein. The closest thing the vending machine offered was Peanut M&M's. Mia would kill Gabe if he ate this way, but she was an adult. She'd already been through her growth spurt. She stabbed the button. "Or when the only way you're going to have time to read up on a case is to do it at home?"

Anne's smile was rueful. "I didn't say it was perfect."

Mia pressed the button for Charlie's Fritos. "Don't worry, these aren't all for me," she said, pushing open the metal swinging door a third time. Anne smiled, but Mia didn't know if she believed her. They left the break room together.

Back in her office, Mia spread out her bounty. Charlie ignored the Fritos and opened the Peanut M&M's instead. He nodded at the photo on her desk. "That your husband? I never met him."

"Yeah. That's Scott. But that picture's probably ten years old." Sometimes Mia felt like she had stepped through the looking glass. Scott was dead, they were broke, her dad wanted to talk about his feelings, and her son no longer wanted to have anything to do with her.

"Your kid looks a lot like him." Charlie's eyes flashed up to hers. "That must be hard. Good and hard, both."

Tears prickled in Mia's eyes. She nodded, unable to speak. Charlie patted the back of her hand, still munching on her M&M's, and for a minute she forgot that she didn't like him.

CHAPTER 18

Charlie was a fast walker. Fast enough that Mia, who thought of herself as quick, was having a hard time keeping up. Although her pumps had sturdy two-inch heels, Mia found herself wishing she were wearing flats. Thinking of her shoes made her think of her feet, and Anne's rule. Mia's feet were on James Street. But where was her heart? Or maybe Anne's rule didn't apply, since the sidewalk was neither home nor work, but a place in between.

Most of the people around them also did not seem to be heeding Anne's advice. Aside from Mia and Charlie, no one seemed to be really present on this sidewalk in Seattle, underneath these maples turning scarlet, walking past these people with all shades of skin, including colors made by tattoo ink.

The other people on this crowded city sidewalk seemed to be embracing distraction, as if they wanted to forget exactly where they were. A number were listening to music through white headphone wires. Some blundered forward blindly as they checked smartphones. Most of the rest were talking animatedly on cell phones. Mia heard snatches of conversation ranging from "She said what?" to "It was ginormous" to "Tell me if he hits you again," which made both her and Charlie do a double take. Not noticing their stares, the young man who had said it kept walking. Charlie and Mia looked at each other, then Charlie shrugged and they continued on.

At the police station they passed through the metal detector and then went upstairs to Charlie's office. It wasn't really an office, just a cubicle in a large room filled with two dozen cubicles separated by tan chest-high walls. The air was filled with the buzz of conversations, the clack of computer keys, the ringing of cell phones and landlines—so much sound it was like white noise.

"Looks like they turned up Stan's murder book," Charlie said.

The fat binder sat in the middle of his desk. There were also two tall stacks of printouts bound by rubber bands, which Mia figured were from Colleen's computer. Otherwise, the space was surprisingly neat. Mia had half expected to see a jumbled desk covered with discarded takeout wrappers and teetering stacks of paper.

Charlie flipped open the murder book. As was standard, the first page was a color photograph in a plastic sleeve, a reminder that the victim had been a living, breathing person. It showed Stan in a maroon tie and a short-sleeved white tattersall shirt. Mia thought it might be an enlargement from his employee badge photo. He had gold wire-framed glasses, a bristly mustache, and brown close-cropped hair that stood straight up like fur.

The next page showed Stan dead, sprawled next to a small desk. The contrast was almost painful. Charlie flipped it closed. "I'll take this home tonight and read it." Pushing one of the stacks of paper on his desk toward her, he said, "Now let's see what was up with Colleen's love life."

Mia sat in Charlie's visitor's chair, which was crammed in between the side of his desk and cubicle wall, and undid the rubber band. The first page was Colleen's eHeartMatch profile. In her profile photo Colleen's hair was a different shade of red than Mia was currently familiar with. Her face was thinner and her complexion creamy, without the flush that had marked her skin in the last few years. Only the bright blue eyes were the same.

Mia looked up and met Charlie's eyes. "How old do you think that photo is?" he asked.

"I can remember when Colleen looked like this. You probably can too. But it was awhile ago." A long while.

Next to the photo was a list of stats. Colleen had taken years off her age and pounds off her frame, while at the same time adding two inches to her height. Remembering Violet's words, Mia felt her face heat up. If Colleen were still alive, she would have been mortified to know that friends, co-workers, and even strangers were poring over the hidden sides of her life. In pursuing Colleen's killer, Mia and Charlie could end up exposing everything she had wanted to keep secret. All in the name of justice.

Colleen's profile read:

I'm a redhead, with the temperament to match. I'm passionate about my job, Italian food, and movies and books that make you think—or leave you gasping in surprise. I believe sarcasm is a spice of life, so if you have a sarcastic sense of humor, bring it on. I'm looking for someone who says what he means and means what he says. Someone who already has a life he likes, but who would also like someone to share it with.

Mia glanced up and met Charlie's gaze. If he felt pity or disgust, she couldn't see it. Just sadness.

"A long time ago Colleen told me she had tried online dating," she said, "but she gave up when she realized she was competing with women who were twenty years younger. I guess she decided to become one herself."

Charlie was paging ahead. "Well, it looks like the time-capsule photo worked. She got tons of responses. The way eHeartMatch works is that there's a dedicated website where members read and respond to e-mails. That probably gives the company a little bit of cover in case one of their clients turns out to be a complete nutcase."

Mia looked at her own copies. Some were e-mails from men who offered to take Colleen to coffee, to dinner, to the movies. Others were from men who had sent back cruder offers along with self-portraits snapped in their bathroom mirrors with cell phones. The parade of headless torsos in various degrees of muscularity and hirsuteness made her queasy.

"Ugh. I don't remember Colleen saying this was what she was looking for," she said, tapping on one photo of a shirtless guy with a hairy chest and beer gut. "She wanted a relationship, not some guy who was advertising himself like a hunk of meat."

Charlie exhaled through his nose. "I guess I'm old-fashioned. I like to know someone in person before I ask them out on a date. Plus, I've been in this line of work long enough to know that most people on these sites are probably lying about something—their weight, their height, their age . . ."

Mia completed the thought. "Or all three."

"Or all three. You meet somebody online and you'd better leave room for surprises."

"Maybe Colleen figured that made it okay for her to fudge things a little." Mia turned back to the photo of her old friend before time had knocked some of the shine off her. "Maybe she figured she would just be trading lies with someone." Did lies cancel each other out?

"You ever see that *New Yorker* cartoon?" Charlie asked. "It shows a dog sitting on a chair in front of a computer with its paw on the keyboard. And it's telling another dog that's sitting on the floor, 'On the Internet, nobody knows you're a dog.'"

Heat rose in Mia face. "Colleen was hardly a dog."

Charlie sighed in exasperation. "I'm not insulting her, Mia. I'm just saying that you can't trust people."

"You mean strangers."

Charlie thought about it. "No, I'm pretty sure I mean people. Now dogs, dogs you probably *could* trust. They're not very good liars."

Together Mia and Charlie continued to read through the pages. Even though dozens of men had responded to Colleen's ad, it seemed like she had only gone out with a handful of them. And then after one or two dates, one of them would come up with an excuse for the other as to why it wasn't working. Mia wondered how many were really covers for Colleen or the guy—or both—being disappointed by reality.

But one man kept turning up over and over again: Vincent. Mia paged back to his photo and profile, which was labeled *Tall, Dark, and Handsome.* He was in his midthirties, with dark straight hair, strong black brows, high cheekbones, and a wide smile. If Colleen had still been the same woman she had been in her photo, they would have made a beautiful couple.

Colleen and Vincent had shared hundreds of messages, some as short as a sentence, some that went on for several pages. The e-mails were flirty, funny, serious, and romantic. Mia's eyes picked out random phrases.

> Do you realize we've been e-mailing for an hour?
> What are you wearing?
> You are one fine-looking woman.
> You have got a wicked sense of humor.
> I can't wait to get my hands on you.

"Look at this." Charlie stabbed at the printouts with his index finger. "They were e-mailing each other just an hour before Colleen was killed."

Mia found the same page.

The surprise was that it seemed to have been Colleen who wanted to meet and Vincent who had demurred.

> Colleen: You're married, aren't you?
>
> Vincent: I'm not, I swear. It's just that I think I would be a disappointment to you.
>
> Colleen: Don't I already know you, Vincent? If there's something you're not telling me, let's just try being honest with each other.
>
> Vincent: I like you, Colleen, I really do. But I don't know if I can give you the kind of relationship you want. Give me awhile. Let me think about it.
>
> Colleen: I don't know if I can. I want you so much. And I'm tired of waiting. I want to make this real.

The pages ended there. That was the last thing either of them had written.

"Maybe Vincent is married," Mia said. "Maybe he was worried his wife would find out and figured he had to nip it in the bud."

"Or maybe he found out that the woman he was having an online relationship with was nearly old enough to be his mother," Charlie said. "I'll subpoena eHeartMatch for his full name and address. They should give it up pretty easily. They don't want to get a reputation for being a great place for serial killers to meet their next victims."

Mia paged back and took another long look at Vincent's open, handsome face. Had he snapped when he realized that Colleen was not what she had pretended to be? Or had he acted to protect his own secrets?

CHAPTER 19

"Is your kid on Facebook?" Charlie asked as he parked in front of Darin Dane's house. The neighborhood was a mix of houses—some a century old and stately, others reflecting the styles of more recent decades. Darin's was a yellow ranch.

"Gabe has an account, but he knows I can look at it anytime." Although when was the last time Mia *had* looked at it? "Some parents don't let their kids go on Facebook, but there's a downside to that too. After my parents got divorced when I was in seventh grade, my mom wouldn't let me go to the mall, which is where all my friends hung out. After a while I didn't get invited to anything." Mia remembered what it had been like to come to school on Mondays and hear about birthday parties and trips to the ice skating rink that no one had invited her to. "I guess my mom was worried about me hanging out with no supervision. But since she was at work, it wasn't like I was being supervised when I stayed home. And the times I've worried about Gabe and Facebook, I imagined some pervy guy trying to friend him. I wasn't thinking about what the other *kids* on Facebook might do to him."

Was Gabe being picked on? Was that why he was suddenly obsessed with bulking up?

"How old does a kid have to be before he can get an account?"

"Thirteen. But that's a joke. Most kids can do enough math to figure out how many years to subtract from their real birth date to make themselves eligible. According to Gabe, half his friends were on Facebook before they were thirteen. And I read somewhere that there are five million Facebook users under the age of *ten*."

On Darin Dane's doorstep, both of them went to push the doorbell, but Charlie got to it first. *Typical Charlie,* Mia thought. He hadn't wanted to be part of this investigation, but now he wanted to be in charge. He had even insisted on driving, but since the county paid for his gas and not hers, she had been glad to say yes.

She had thought she could simply give the Suburban back to the dealership, maybe pay a small fee after she showed them Scott's death certificate. It turned out not to matter if he was dead. Even if she turned the car in, she would still owe everything he would have paid if he had driven it to the end of its lease, plus a penalty. His estate was on the hook for it—which meant she was. Just thinking about it made her stomach clench.

A man in his midforties and dressed in a flannel shirt and jeans opened the door, releasing a fug of stale cigarette smoke. His face was unshaven, his eyes sunken. He looked even worse than when Mia had spoken to him last week.

"Nate, this is Charlie Carlson. He's a homicide detective. Charlie, this is Nate Dane, Darin's father."

The two men shook hands, and then Nate stepped back and waved them inside with the hand holding an unfiltered cigarette. "Laurie should be home soon."

Nate had told Mia that his wife was a nurse, which seemed kind of strange given how much smoking he appeared to be doing. All Mia knew about Nate was that he didn't currently have a job.

The reek of cigarettes was overpowering. Not one but two overflowing ashtrays sat on the coffee table, next to a photo album and an inch-high pile of papers, facedown. The curtains were drawn, the blinds pulled down. It felt like dusk even though it was only four o'clock. It took a minute for her eyes to adjust to the darkness. Nate took a seat on a plaid recliner, and Charlie and Mia sat on the navy blue couch. A gray tabby skittered around the edges of the room.

Nate handed the photo album to Charlie. "These are photos of my son."

Setting it on his lap, Charlie started to flip through the pages while Mia leaned over to look. Darin as a big-eyed baby, wearing a yellow-and-blue-striped knit hat. A three- or four-year-old Darin, grinning while he piled sand on his dad lying stretched out on the beach. Darin, a slender blue-eyed boy with small gold hoops in his ears, showing off a plateful of decorated cupcakes.

Then Charlie turned to the last photo and recoiled. Mia gasped, feeling like she had just been punched in the stomach. Darin lay on his back on the floor, a rainbow-striped scarf next to him, a wide red mark around his neck, his blue eyes half-open.

"What in the—! Did you take that photo?" Charlie demanded.

"Yes." Nate's face was stony.

"Why on earth did you take it?"

"Why did I take it? Why did I take it?" His words grew more agitated. "Because I wanted them to see what they did to him. They killed a beautiful boy just because he was different. They couldn't stand that. So they killed him."

A voice behind Mia made her jump.

"Don't tell me you are showing those people our son like that. No one should remember him that way." Laurie Dane was a plump woman with brown hair scraped back into a ponytail. She wore blue scrubs printed with cartoon butterflies.

"They need to see it so they'll be motivated to take down the bullies that did it to him."

Laurie didn't answer, just made a show of waving her hand as if she was trying to rid the room of some of the cigarette smoke. But the air was so saturated it had no place to go. Tonight Mia would hang all her clothes in the garage in hopes of airing them out rather than having to pay for dry cleaning.

"You said Darin was different," Charlie said. "Was he gay?"

Nate's hand clenched so hard that it bent his cigarette. "What difference does it make? Are you saying if he was, what they did was okay?"

"No." Charlie didn't seem flustered. "I'm saying if he was, there are hate-crime laws that might also apply."

"Who knows what they are at that age?" Nate said. "If he thought of himself as gay, he didn't tell us."

Laurie picked up the cat and then sat down on a brown ottoman. "He's always been a little different."

"He's still our son," Nate said. "A long time ago I realized I could spend all my time wishing for the son I never had or I could love the son who was standing right in front of me. But those kids—they pushed him and pushed him and pushed him, and finally he fell over."

"I understand he's been in counseling since he was twelve," Mia said softly, trying not to phrase it like an accusation.

"As he got older, the kids got meaner," Laurie said, stroking the cat so hard that it bent under her touch. "In elementary school, everyone knows everyone. He went to a small school and there were always parents around volunteering or picking up their kids. But things changed in middle school. The kids are on their own more. They have more secrets, and they get sneakier. He seemed depressed, so I took him to a counselor. He put Darin on medication."

Mia made a note. Some antidepressants had actually been shown to put a small percentage of teens at greater risk for committing suicide. The defense would be sure to bring it up. "Would you give me permission to talk to his therapist?" Patient-client confidentiality would probably preclude a lot of discovery, but Mia still might be able to tease out something if she phrased her questions as hypothetical.

"Of course. It's Dr. Thorensen," Nate said. "Harold Thorensen."

"Do you know if Darin had ever talked about killing himself?" Mia asked gently.

"No," Laurie said. "At least not to us. He did keep saying he didn't know how he could do four more years. He wanted us to homeschool him, but how could we do that? I work full-time and Nate never even graduated from high school." A look passed between husband and wife.

"I know this is painful," Mia said gently, "but can you go over some of the bullying that went on at school?"

Nate took a deep breath, coughed, and then began. "Last year, when Darin was in eighth grade, things started getting really bad. They pushed notes into his locker. They called him names. They tripped him in the hall. Once I went into his room when he was changing into his pajamas. I saw bruises on his chest. He said he fell. I knew that was a lie."

Charlie, who normally seemed unflappable, looked ill.

"He used to beg me to call in and say he was sick." Laurie was petting the cat faster and faster. "He said he could help Nate with the yard work."

"But it was Facebook that was the last straw." Nate lit another cigarette. "We thought letting him have a Facebook account would be a good way for him to stay in touch with his cousins or friends who had moved away. He was on it a lot at first, but then he stopped using it as much."

"The novelty wore off," Laurie said.

"'The novelty wore off,'" Nate parroted. "Get your head out of the sand, Laurie. It wasn't that Darin got bored. It's what they started doing to him. He'd put something on his wall, and kids would chime in with sarcastic comments, and then other kids would 'like'"—he made air quotes—"those comments but not his original post." He took a long drag on his cigarette before continuing. "But the worst is that someone hacked into his account two days before he died."

"What do you mean?" Charlie leaned forward.

"Someone pretending to be him posted disgusting messages on his wall." Nate's lip curled. "They invited kids—boys—from his new school to come over to our house and have sex with him. Only it looked like it was Darin doing it. Kids he didn't even know. He had been hoping that things would be different because he was in high school."

Laurie added, "They even put up his address and phone number. We're just lucky some pedophile didn't come over here and try to take advantage of him."

"What do you mean lucky, Laurie?" Nate snapped. "Darin is dead. You can't get any more unlucky than that."

Laurie didn't answer, but she stroked the cat so hard it let out a yowl and shot off her lap.

Mia tried to get them back on track. "And no one told Darin that his Facebook had been hacked?"

"No." Nate spit out the word. "It took him two days to realize what was going on. Whoever it was, they were smart. They unfriended his real friends, unfriended anyone who was a relative. So no one who might clue him in knew. Meanwhile, it seems like everyone else in school not only knew about it but kept it going. These kids weren't innocent bystanders. And you can't tell me that just because they're in high school they didn't understand what they were doing. When he finally figured it out, he tried to tell everyone it wasn't him, but no one believed him. So he came home and killed himself."

"Was he home alone when it happened?" Mia asked. It felt too cruel to spell out what *it* was.

Nate flinched as if he had been slapped. "No. I was right here. I was twenty feet away. He came home, yelled hello, and went into his room. I was on the Internet, if you want to know the truth. I was just killing time, looking at stupid stuff, and meanwhile my son's looping his scarf over the closet rod. It was probably almost an hour before I went in to talk to him and I found him. His skin was already cool to the touch. I can't help thinking if I had been paying attention . . ." His voice trailed off. "And when I touched his laptop, the screen came to life and I saw his Facebook page. I saw what they had done. I printed it all off in case someone went back and tried to delete things once they heard what happened. Facebook deactivated his account the next day, but not before a few people posted on there saying they were glad he was dead. Glad."

Nate picked up the stack of papers and started paging through them. "I mean, look at this." His voice cracked. "'You queer! I'm going to tie you to a pole with a rope, then tie another rope around your stomach and tie the end to my bumper and drive off. I'll rip you in half.'"

What Darin's father had been describing already met the state's definition of cyberstalking. But Mia hadn't seen the death threat before, which took it from a misdemeanor to a Class C felony.

"By making examples of these kids, we can help make it so that it's no longer acceptable to do what they did," Mia said.

"Make examples?" Nate echoed sarcastically. "That's not much punishment, is it? Considering that my son is dead? You sound as wishy-washy as that first woman I talked to."

Mia froze. "Do you mean Colleen Miller? Colleen is dead. She was murdered in her home on Sunday."

Nate had the grace to look away. "I'm—I'm sorry."

Mia didn't want to lose her focus, so she turned the conversation back to Darin. "We're going to do our best to hold these kids accountable. Do you have any idea who they were?"

"Darin would never tell us the names of the kids who picked on him. He said it would just make it worse."

"Well, can you give us the names of some of his friends so we could ask them?" Charlie asked.

Laurie said, "There's these two girls, Shiloh and Rainy. They've known Darin since grade school." She turned to Nate. "And maybe they should talk to Jeremy."

After a moment Nate nodded. "Jeremy and Darin were best friends in grade school. In middle school they started growing apart. Or at least Jeremy started pulling away from Darin. Darin was only over at Jeremy's house once this summer and that's it. They used to be really close. But Darin talked to Rainy and Shiloh nearly every day."

Mia said, "I have a son who's about the same age. A lot of the time they'll tell their friends things they might not tell their parents."

"You have a son." Nate's eyes skewered her.

"Yes." She was suddenly sorry she had mentioned Gabe.

"You still have a son." He took a long drag on his cigarette. "These punks left me with nothing."

CHAPTER 20

At the beginning of second period, Gabe broke out his two peanut butter sandwiches. Mrs. Schmalz was cool and let them eat in class. He had made them after his mom left for work, so she wouldn't ask why he was bringing sandwiches to school but still needed lunch money. She wouldn't understand.

This morning she had seemed upset about something, yelling at herself for forgetting to buy fresh bread. But Gabe hadn't seen anything wrong with the bread they already had. And he needed the 680 calories and 18 grams of protein that he could get from two sandwiches.

Today Mrs. Schmalz showed a boring video about geometry while Gabe doggedly chewed and swallowed, chewed and swallowed. After he finished, it was all he could do not to fall asleep. Even after the lights were turned back on, the talk about postulates and theorems made him prop his head in his hands while trying to keep his eyes open.

In American history they had to pretend they were reporters at a muckraking newspaper and write articles about tenements. In ceramics they made fish out of clay. For lunch Gabe had two vanilla milk shakes and two slices of sausage pizza, for a total of 1550 calories and 42 grams of protein. Then it was on to Spanish I, which was a bunch of verbs he couldn't remember two minutes after he parroted them back to the teacher.

At least biology was all easy stuff like cell parts, and Tyler was in this class. Tyler wasn't on the football team—he only cared about basketball—but Gabe and Ty had been tight since elementary school. He had been texting Tyler when his mom made him listen to Colleen's last minutes. Of course that night, after everything was over and his mom was in bed, he had texted back and forth with Ty, told him what really happened. His mom had said not to tell, but it was too late for that. By then Ty already knew most of it. Gabe had just filled in the blanks.

Before class started, Ty leaned over. "I heard Mr. Washington played basketball at Wake Forest." His eyes were wide with excitement.

Yeah, but now Mr. Washington was a teacher, not a pro. Maybe that was why he had pinned a quote from Horace Greeley, whoever that was, above his whiteboard: *Fame is a vapor, popularity an accident, riches take wings. Only one endures, and that is character.*

While that might be true, Gabe thought as he munched on a protein bar on the way to football practice, he wouldn't mind fame, popularity, or riches. Even if they didn't last, still, you would have had them for a little while.

Right now he didn't have any of those things. The high school was four times as big as his old middle school, and he still felt a little lost. But Coach Harper had picked Gabe for the team, so he must have seen something in him. Gabe wished he knew what. It seemed to have disappeared between being picked for the team and actually playing in a game. Once Coach saw how scrawny Gabe was compared to everyone else, he had probably realized his mistake. If he got bigger, maybe Coach would put him in.

Practice started with warm-up drills: lunges, sprinting, jumping jacks. Then Coach had them running up and back around a backstop. As Gabe huffed and sweated, he hoped the running part would be over soon. It was basically cardio, and everyone said cardio burned calories. Next they did monkey rolls and practiced running into dummies. Gabe was feeling pretty good about things—he might be little, but he was fast and limber—but then Coach had them do punts and punt returns. Eldon hit Gabe so hard he ended up on his back with all the air knocked out of him. Then Coach told them to run pass routes, and Rufus just turned around and threw Gabe down like he was nothing. When practice ended, Gabe's ego was as sore as his body.

After showering, Gabe stepped on the scale. He was pleasantly surprised. He had already gained three pounds! He had set up a diet plan, and it was working. He was on a roll!

A cuff to the shoulder sent him staggering sideways off the platform.

"Hey," Gabe yelled, fists balling. Then he turned and saw that it was Zach, one of the guys he had hung out with the night before. Zach was a year older, four inches taller, and seventy-five pounds heavier. The cool thing about high school was that you got to hang out with older kids. The classes weren't filled with babies, little sixth and seventh graders who didn't even come up to your armpit, the way it had been last year. Some of the guys on the team were the size of adults—and not regular adults either, but football player adults.

"Beefing up?" Zach asked, grinning. "Drinking that protein shake like I told you to?"

Eldon and Rufus were listening as they got dressed. They were both sophomores and friends of Zach's. Eldon didn't say much, and his eyes were continually at half-mast, but he was always smiling. Rufus was big, over two hundred pounds, not all of it muscle. But that didn't matter very much when he had just run into you and he weighed nearly a hundred pounds more than you did.

"I made one of those shakes last night." It had tasted terrible.

"You should have another one as soon as you can after practice. Try mixing it with grape juice. It's a fast-absorbing carbohydrate, and that means it'll replace the glycogen in your muscle cells that you lost when we were pushing you up and down the field today." Zach probably knew more about biology than Mr. Washington.

"Okay." Gabe pulled on his boxers and jeans.

"So what are you going to do now?" Zach asked.

Gabe looked around to make sure he was still talking to him. He thought last night had been a fluke, just him happening to be next to Zach and his friends when Grandpa called with the word that he was free.

"Just going home."

Zach's eyes flashed over to Eldon and Rufus, then looked back at Gabe. "There anybody at your house?"

"Only my little sister. I have to pick her up from preschool on the way home. My mom doesn't get home from work until kinda late." He hoped no one would ask about his dad—or worse yet, knew what had happened and would say they were sorry—but nobody did. "And then I'm going to lift. There's a whole weight setup in my basement."

Zach took the bait, as Gabe had hoped he might. "Cool. Maybe we can come hang out at your place?"

"Sure." He tried to hide his grin. "Like I said, all I need to do is go get my sister."

"We can pick her up in my car."

Gabe was still impressed that Zach had a car. They had all gone to the mall together in it the night before. Gabe was studying for his learner's permit, which he wouldn't be able to get until he turned fifteen in February. Wasn't there some kind of Washington law about drivers under eighteen not being able to carry more than three passengers under the age of twenty who weren't members of their immediate family? Once they added Brooke, it would be four. Plus there wouldn't be any car seat. But it was only four blocks, and she would be sitting between him and Eldon and they would be like cushions. And he could throw his arm across her if they had to come to a sudden stop. As they walked out to the parking lot, Gabe gave Zach directions to the preschool.

His new friends stayed in the car while he went inside to get his sister. It was five forty-five, so there were a lot of parents running in and out. He hoped no one noticed that he wasn't walking her home.

Brooke gave him a big smile with her tiny white teeth. But when they went outside and he opened the passenger door for her, she hung back. Eldon smiled at her encouragingly and patted the empty seat, but Gabe could feel her back stiffen against his knees. "Come on, Brooke, get in," he said, nudging her. She wouldn't budge. The only way he got her inside was to have her sit closest to the door while he squished in next to Eldon. Meanwhile Zach drummed his fingers on the steering wheel and sighed.

"Dude, this is nice," Eldon said appreciatively after Gabe unlocked the front door and they all trooped inside. He looked around, seeing the wood floors and old oak furniture with new eyes. Maybe it was nice. He didn't know.

"Hey, Brooke, go on and watch TV for a little while, okay?" She went into the family room without protest.

"Time for you to drink that shake," Zach said. Gabe ended up following him into his own kitchen. While he was making the shake—with milk, since they didn't have any grape juice—Zach started rooting around in the fridge. "The only way you are going to get big, dude, is to eat lots and lots of protein. Eggs, cheese, milk, peanut butter. And meat. Get your mom to start buying steaks." He emerged from the refrigerator with an unopened two-pound orange loaf of Tillamook cheddar cheese. "Now that's what I'm talking about." He grabbed a knife from the block on the counter and started cutting off hunks and handing them to Eldon and Rufus, in between stuffing bites into his own mouth.

By the time Gabe thought to say anything, the cheese was already half-eaten. His mom had been complaining lately about how much he ate. Zach was opening cupboards now, looking for crackers to go along with the cheese. It seemed like a good time to remind them about what was in the basement.

"So you want to check out the weight set?"

"Let's go," Zach said, grabbing his pack and another hunk of cheese.

"Yeah, bro," Rufus said.

The basement smelled musty, a smell that must have always

been there but that Gabe had never noticed before. Some people had basements with carpets and TVs and gaming systems, but in this part of Seattle during the rainy season most basements were, at a minimum, damp. The weight bench was in a dry corner, along with a rack of dumbbells that ranged from ten pounds all the way up to fifty.

Zach sat on the bench, hooked his legs behind the pads, and started doing leg extensions. Eldon picked up the twenty-pound weights and began doing bicep curls. Rufus did the same thing, only with thirty-pound dumbbells that he handled with ease. That left the ten, fifteen, forty, and fifty-pound dumbbells for Gabe to choose from. He grabbed the fifteens, glad he hadn't been the first to pick up weights. Nobody could blame him for not taking the forties. Even still, if the other guys ended up doing more than twenty-five reps, it was going to be hard to keep up.

Zach already seemed bored. He stopped lifting, got off the bench, and started walking around the basement, touching things while Gabe bit back the urge to ask him not to.

"I saw you hanging out with that Tyler McCabe at lunch today." Zach picked up a bottle of paint thinner, undid the cap, and took an experimental sniff. "Are you friends with him? Because he's queer. You can tell."

Gabe smiled uneasily. "Tyler's not gay." He had known Tyler since kindergarten. "He's just a little different, that's all."

"Different as in gay," Zach pronounced. He put the cap back on the paint thinner and set it down.

"Different as in he's just a little intense. He's got some specialized interests." One of them was Legos. Ty still played with Legos, only now he incorporated little motors inside so the things he made actually moved. Over the summer he had made a spider that skittered across the floor. Gabe hadn't known it would move, or even that it *could* move, so when Ty had shown it to him, he had screamed like a girl.

"Specialized interests like other boys, you mean."

Gabe realized it was futile to argue.

"We did something fun over the summer." Zach grinned.

"What?" Gabe was just thankful that he had changed the topic.

"All I can tell you is that we were on the news."

Gabe tried to think of what it could be. He imagined a party with hot girls, a keg of beer, and a swimming pool. "Come on—what?"

Rufus said, "Dude, if we told you, we'd have to kill you."

Zach added, "But maybe we'll let you join in sometime." He was still fidgeting, picking things up and putting them down.

Eldon gave Gabe a look he couldn't read.

Zach walked over to the door and opened the lock. Three stairs led up to the backyard, which was empty except for their old wooden play structure. The nearest neighbors were behind a tall hedge.

Rummaging in his pack, Zach came up with a small brown pipe, a lighter, and a baggie half full of gray-green crumbles. Rufus put down his weights.

Zach filled his pipe and fired it up. He took a long drag, held it, and then exhaled. He offered the pipe and lighter to Gabe. "Here you go."

Gabe waved it off. "That's okay."

"Come on, take a hit. It won't hurt you. All it will do is make you hungry, and that will help you put more weight on. And they don't ever drug test at our school."

Gabe tried to think of a reason to say no. "My mom's always hugging me. If she smelled that on me, she'd ground me for sure."

"Trust me," Zach said, "moms are clueless." He passed the pipe and lighter to Rufus, who lit up and sucked on it eagerly, while Eldon lay back on the weight bench and started doing chest presses.

Zach was taking his third hit on the pipe when there was the sound of a car stopping outside their house.

"My mom's home!" Gabe's heart felt like it would burst out of his chest. The basement reeked. He began to frantically fan the door open and closed, open and closed.

Eldon dropped the weights he was holding and they crashed to the floor. Rufus swore.

"We've got to get upstairs and pretend like we've been there the whole time. If my mom smells this, she's going to kill me!"

Zach calmly picked up a can of WD-40 from the workbench, shook it twice, and pressed the button. The metallic scent filled the air.

CHAPTER 21

In the driveway next to her Toyota was a maroon Forrester Mia didn't recognize. After parking the Suburban on the street, she hurried onto the porch. The door wasn't even locked, and when she went in, loud male voices were coming from the family room. Then Mia realized that they were laughing.

Gabe and three big teenagers she didn't recognize were sprawled on the couch and chairs. Brooke was sitting on the floor in front of the TV set. Her little face was only six inches from the screen, which was showing someone making an ill-advised effort to jump a bike over a wooden fence.

One of the boys turned and saw her. He jumped to his feet and came over with his hand outstretched.

"Hey, you must be Mrs. Quinn. Sorry if we surprised you. We're Gabe's friends from the football team. My name's Zachary Young, and that's Rufus Sledge and Eldon Reid." Eldon only nodded and gave her a sleepy smile, while Rufus slowly got to his feet. Rufus was a mountain of a boy, and even the other two made Gabe look small in comparison. Now the protein powder made more sense.

She felt uneasy that these boys she had never met before had been in her house. "It's nice to meet you guys," she said, smiling. "You can call me Mia."

"Mia." Zach nodded. "It's great to meet you. Gabe said you're a prosecutor, right? That must be a cool job, putting away the bad guys."

"It can be." Mia was impressed. Had any of Gabe's friends ever talked to her about her job before? She almost felt a little misty. If Gabe's friends were growing up, he must be too. She could only hope that with other adults, Gabe was able to rise to the occasion as this boy was.

"So I've always wondered—do you get to decide who to go after? Like, can you pick which bad guy you want to put away?"

And Mia had wondered if the kids on the football team would be less interested in academics. "My boss assigns cases, but there's still something called prosecutorial discretion." She tried to find the right words to explain it. "Sometimes what someone is charged with depends on the circumstances. Say the cops find a man standing over the body of his dead wife—and he has blood on his hands. Did he hit her over the head on purpose? Then he should be charged with murder. Did he get angry and push her, and she fell and hit her head? Then the charge should be manslaughter. But what if he'd just been talking to her when she slipped and hit her head and his hands got bloody when he tried to help her? In that case, he's not guilty of anything. That's where I come in. It's my job to review the evidence, determine what happened, and decide what the charge should be. I mean, sure, I have a boss, but he doesn't have time to go through all my cases. I get to make a lot of the decisions."

Eyes shining, Zach turned to Gabe. "You should definitely have your mom come talk for Career Day."

Gabe nodded. His cheeks were red, and he wouldn't make eye contact with Mia.

"Well, we should probably be going," Zach said, and Eldon heaved himself to his feet. They muttered good-byes as they passed her, and Eldon did some kind of fist bump thing with Gabe.

After the door closed, she turned to him. "Gabe, you need to be more careful about keeping the door locked and the curtains drawn when you're home. Don't ever let in anyone you don't know. And I know I haven't said anything about it before, but I really don't feel comfortable with you having friends over when I'm not home. Same thing with you being over at a friend's house. I don't want you to be there if there isn't an adult home."

Gabe snorted. "What—you don't trust me?"

"I do trust you. But kids take more chances when parents aren't around. Sometimes they get stuck in situations and don't know how to say no."

His face reddened. "I know what the issue really is. You just don't want me to have any friends. All you want me to do is watch Brooke. You already get home so late, and it's been even later recently. And most of the other parents work too. So with your rules, now I won't have any friends."

Mia's resolution to treat her son with kindness was forgotten. She gritted her teeth. "It's about keeping you safe, Gabe. You may feel like you're an adult, but you are not." She went into the kitchen.

Half the cupboard doors were standing open, and on the counter lay the orange plastic wrapper from a block of Tillamook, holding just a sliver of cheese.

Her anger found an outlet. "Gabe, did you guys eat all of this cheese? That was a two-pound block." She had been planning to make macaroni and cheese later in the week, the good, homemade kind, not the kind that came from a blue box.

"Sorry!" Gabe called.

She sniffed. "Come in here." When he did, he wouldn't meet her eyes. "What is that smell?" It was sweet, oily, metallic—and it seemed to be coming from the basement. She had caught a whiff of the same smell, only not as strong, in the family room.

"It's WD-40. Me and the guys were lifting weights in the basement. I need to bulk up and they were giving me tips. The leg extension piece was sticking, so we sprayed it."

How big of a mess was it down there? It was embarrassing to think of strangers seeing it. She definitely had to hold the garage sale soon, in case Gabe kept having friends over to lift weights—when she was home, of course.

"I'm going to run out to the store and get bread and cheese.

Is there anything else we need?" Maybe she would get a rotisserie chicken. That would save time making dinner.

"Can you pick me up some protein bars? All the guys say I need to eat more protein."

And how much would those cost? Still, she nodded and jotted it down.

The next few hours passed in a blur of shopping, pulling dinner together, cleaning, giving Brooke a bath and putting her to bed. Everything took longer than it should have.

Mia had enlarged a photo of Scott and put it by Brooke's bed, hoping that it would help him stay in her memory. Her chest ached when she thought of Brooke forgetting everything about her father. But tonight Brooke showed him a doll she liked, patted his face, and said good night, while Mia held back tears. When she bent over to kiss her daughter good night, she was sucking her thumb.

"Brooke—thumbs aren't for sucking." But they sure had been recently.

Obediently Brooke popped her thumb out of her mouth, but Mia was sure it would go right back in as soon as she left. She was a bad mother. She used to be a fairly good one, before Scott died, before Gabe stopped wanting to have anything to do with her. Now she needed to be mother and father both, and she was doing a poor job at both.

After she closed Brooke's door, she stuck her head in Gabe's room.

"Be sure to finish your history homework."

"That's what I'm working on."

Maybe. But his computer was open too. Was he writing a report or checking social media? She thought about nagging some more but then changed subjects. "And be careful on Facebook, okay? Don't ever say anything you wouldn't in person."

"I am careful, Mom." He made an irritated grimace. "It's like you don't trust me anymore."

"It's not that, honey. It's just that lately I've been seeing how much trouble someone can get into on Facebook. You have to realize that everything you do online, every place you go, every time you click on a link—it's all being recorded and stored on a server somewhere. Nothing you do is private."

"I *know* that, Mom." Gabe rolled his eyes at her, and she gave up.

Mia made sure the house was locked up tight, the curtains covering every inch of window. What if the same person *had* killed Stan and Colleen? Was it possible he might be out there, watching the house? She didn't want to give him any clues as to where she was. No one was going to shoot her through a window.

Finally she was in her bedroom with the printouts from Colleen's computer and a bag of Cool Ranch Doritos she had bought at the store and managed to sneak into the house under a pack of toilet paper.

She paged through Colleen's documents. Most were mundane. A food diary that lasted for eleven days and then stopped. Tax forms that showed no surprises. A budget, a packing list, a family tree. She hadn't kept a journal.

The most interesting were the notes from the dating site. Flirty, friendly, funny. Sometimes more R-rated than PG.

Mia fell asleep with her mouth tasting sour and spicy, her face pillowed on printouts.

At 12:13, Mia started awake.

Brooke was screaming again.

CHAPTER 22

Darin's room felt like the kid had just left to grab a snack. His math book was open on his desk and an uncapped pen lay across his notebook. Lined up at the back of the desk were a small, red wind-up robot, a jar filled with agates and other unusual rocks, and a tin can covered with blue felt that held pencils and paintbrushes. Intricate ink drawings of crows were tacked above the desk.

The desk itself was part of some sort of space-saving desk/dresser/storage unit combo made of blond wood, all of it topped with a bed. A shallow ladder led to the twin mattress, which was surrounded by a rail. The desk pulled out of a section of the middle, with a column of built-in drawers next to it.

Charlie didn't like heights. He told himself that's why he felt a little dizzy clambering up to Darin's bed on a ladder that offered only an inch of clearance for his toes. And it was a real trick to figure out how to look under the mattress when he could only reach the bottom end. He ended up perched precariously on Darin's desk chair. Pulling off the sheets and blankets released the kid's smell, a musky, slightly sour scent of sweat and feet. He could imagine Darin asleep, curled up in a ball. Hurting and afraid. Charlie knew what that was like.

In the closet the clothes were still pushed over to one side. His parents hadn't found a note, and so far Charlie hadn't either. It was possible Darin hadn't even meant to be successful. It was surprisingly easy to loop something around your neck and kill yourself. You didn't even need the noose to be tight or to get your feet off the ground. By the time you realized that maybe you didn't mean to be doing this after all, it could be too late. Death came fast.

It took Charlie a couple of hours to finish searching Darin's room. When he was done he had little to show for it except for three notes. Two were laced with expletives and threats. The first suggested Darin should do everyone a favor and die, and the second ended with *Watch out, gay boy, we're coming for you*. The third was something completely different. It read *I've been watching you and I like what I see. If you want to see if you'll like what you see, meet me by the south entrance to the track at 5 pm tomorrow.* All three notes had been crumpled and then smoothed out, as if Darin had thrown them away and then changed his mind before hiding them between some neatly folded T-shirts.

What intrigued Charlie was that all three notes appeared to have been written in the same hand.

He came out of the kid's bedroom and managed to close the door behind him while juggling Darin's computer, wrapped in a pink antistatic bag, and the three notes, which he had slipped into plastic sleeves.

Nate was sitting in the living room in the dark. The air seemed to be made up only of exhaled tobacco smoke. Laurie was nowhere in evidence.

"I found some notes in his room," Charlie said. "I'm gonna take them into evidence. As well as his computer."

He expected Nate to turn on a light, to ask to look at the notes, but instead he just grunted. Charlie heard more than saw him suck some more smoke into his lungs.

Charlie said good-bye and let himself out. Back at the office, he handed the computer off to the techs. When he left for home he took with him the printouts from Colleen's computer and Stan's murder book. Technically the murder book was supposed to stay at the office, but what other people didn't know didn't hurt them.

Technically you weren't supposed to work sixteen hours straight either.

At home Charlie checked the fridge, as if someone might have filled it while he was out. All he found was a half gallon of skim milk, packets of soy sauce, bottles of mixer—not much you could magically make a meal out of. In the freezer he discovered a microwave pizza, which turned out to taste as good as the circle of cardboard it came on. Chewing mechanically, Charlie flipped through the crime-scene photographs from Stan's murder. In them, Stan sprawled awkwardly, like someone had just shoved him to the floor. His glasses were askew, one lens resting on his forehead. The left side of his sweater was soaked with blood.

In the autopsy section, Charlie skipped over all the weights and measurements and descriptions of the actual procedure to the summary section and the corresponding photographs. There were no surprises. The bullet had hit Stan's heart first, and then bounced from rib to spinal column to rib again, chewing up his insides.

Carmen hadn't had much to go on in finding Stan's killer, with no evidence, no death threats, and Stan's personal life devoid of lovers and even close friends. Interestingly, she had also considered if Stan's activism in Safe Seattle might have made him a target, but hadn't been able to come up with much more than speculation.

Charlie read an interview with the neighbor who had first reported the shots and made a mental note to reinterview him. Other neighbors had reported that the streetlight had gone out the night before Stan was killed, and when the crime-scene investigators took a closer look, they found it had been shattered by a BB.

All the ballistics information interested him, and Charlie read it several times. The CSIs had theorized that the killer had stood across the street in the pool of shadow where the streetlight used to shine and used a scoped rifle. If that were true, the shot to the heart hadn't been lucky, but instead that of a skilled marksman.

Finally Charlie turned out the lights. He tried to sleep, but the dead kept parading through his head: Stan, Colleen, and the dozens of people he had only gotten to know after someone turned them into sacks of flesh. Every day he was given another reason not to get too close to people.

He thought of the pain he had seen in Mia's blue eyes when they spoke to Darin's parents. He imagined her turning her sorrowful eyes on him if she ever learned his story. But that story belonged to a much younger Charlie. A much weaker Charlie.

He liked his women uncomplicated and without baggage. Girls who said, "I like to work hard and play hard," and didn't think it was a cliché. Girls who didn't want a ring or kids or a guarantee that he would always be available. That holidays wouldn't be interrupted by someone calling in with news of a body dump. Girls who wouldn't ask any questions if the first thing he did after coming home from a particularly hairy scene was to put his shoes in the trash can before he even walked in the door.

Charlie was still thinking of Mia when he fell asleep. He dreamed she was saying something to him, but he couldn't make out the words, no matter how closely he watched her lips.

The next morning he met Mia at her office and brought her up-to-date. Charlie started by recapping what he had read in Stan's murder book, including the idea that the killer had used a rifle.

"But the brass was found in Colleen's yard, not across the street," Mia said. "Why didn't the shooter take the same approach?"

She had put her finger on what had bothered Charlie last night. He offered up the only explanation he had come up with. "Stan had motion-sensor lights the shooter may have been trying to avoid. Colleen didn't. And maybe there's not as clean a sight line for Colleen from the street."

Mia squeezed the bridge of her nose. "I got the IP address for the computer the jerk who called himself True Patriot used, but it came back to a Peet's Coffee wireless network. Peet's doesn't require users to sign on with a name or a credit card or anything. They could even have been sitting in a car in front of the coffee shop and using a laptop."

"I've got some better news. Martin Miller's agreed to come in. For some reason"—Charlie grinned a little, thinking of the panic in Martin's voice—"he didn't want a homicide detective coming to his workplace. How about if I have him come at one?"

"Okay. And let's end the day by talking to Darin's friends once they're out of school. I'll get in touch with the parents to get their permission."

A doughy-looking guy appeared in Mia's doorway, clutching a pile of files. "Hey, Mia, I've got those cases you asked for."

"Jonas, this is Charlie Carlson, a homicide detective. Charlie, this is Jonas Carvel."

"Hey," Jonas offered, not meeting Charlie's eyes. He put the files down on Mia's visitor's table. "I did as you requested and looked for defendants they've had in common. The number was not that large, even though I programmed it to consider nicknames, such as Bob for Robert, or spelling variations such as last names that end in s-e-n or s-o-n."

Some people didn't know how to cut to the chase. "So how many is it?" Charlie asked.

"Three. They both prosecuted the same guy, Eddie Shaughnessy, for assault, but he's been in prison for the last two years. And there's another man, Jonny Feather, who was prosecuted by both of them for domestic violence, but the victims were different women."

"When was Feather's most recent case?" Charlie asked.

"Eighteen months ago. And he was released from prison five months ago." Jonas picked up the top file in the pile. "And then there's Trumaine Lavender. His is the most interesting case. Six years ago, Trumaine was with someone who shot a third guy in the neck. According to Trumaine, he convinced his buddy not to pull the trigger a second time. Not that it did the victim much good. He still died. Trumaine never went to the police, and he helped the shooter dispose of the weapon. But when he was arrested as an accomplice, Trumaine offered to testify for the prosecution, and

Stan cut him a deal. Trumaine pleaded no contest to facilitation of murder. Stan recommended a five-year pretrial diversion."

That meant Trumaine's charges would have been dismissed if he had stayed out of trouble for five years. But if Stan and Colleen had shared him as a defendant . . .

"So what bad thing did Trumaine do next?" Charlie asked.

"Three years ago a drug deal went wrong, and the drug dealer ended up dead. Trumaine was the shooter. Colleen put him in prison for fifteen years."

"Three years ago," Mia echoed, and Charlie guessed they were thinking the same thing. None of these cases felt right. Two of the people involved were still in prison, and none of the cases seemed fresh enough to spark the need for brutal retribution.

Jonas frowned. "If you think of any other parameters you want me to search for, let me know."

"Thanks, Jonas," Mia said.

After the kid left, Charlie walked over to the flip chart, now tucked against the wall. "So where do we stand?"

Katrina stuck her head in. "How's it going?"

Charlie had never worked with her before, but now that he was spending so much time in the prosecutor's office, she was always finding excuses to engage him. She asked questions about the case, offered him snacks, even picked lint off his jacket. Katrina was another blonde, so not really his type. Although lately he was beginning to think he should be more flexible.

Mia sighed. "Lots of possibilities. No clear answers."

Katrina walked over to look at the flip chart. "What's 'gun rights' mean? You mean that Safe Seattle Colleen volunteered with?"

"It wasn't only Colleen," Mia said. "Stan too."

"Wow." Katrina took a step back. "So you think somebody decided to shut them up permanently?" She pressed her lips together. "The sick thing is that whoever shot them didn't have to worry that Stan or Colleen would return fire."

CHAPTER 23

NEW INFORMATION SOUGHT IN THE MURDER OF TWO KING COUNTY DISTRICT ATTORNEYS

King County Prosecutor Frank D'Amato announced today that he was devoting additional resources to solving the recent murder of King County District Attorney Colleen Miller. "The murder of Colleen Miller has understandably upset the community," D'Amato said. "But we believe that it was not a random act. In fact, we are currently exploring any connection it might have with the murder nearly five years ago of another King County prosecutor, Stan Slavich."

D'Amato said that was where the public's help was needed.

"Colleen's murder and the renewed media attention toward Stan's killing could prompt a reaction in anyone involved in one or both of these homicides," D'Amato said. "It's important for people around that person to make note of behaviors that may be unusual or out of the ordinary. The killer could make unexpected or inappropriate comments about either of the victims or their murders. The killer might be preoccupied with the cases and want to talk about them constantly. Or the very mention of either murder might make him or her shut down completely. Any stronger than normal reaction, any significant deviation from the norm, is what people should be looking for."

D'Amato added, "We know information about Stan's murder is

still out there. We know there are people who—because of fear, doubt, or other reasons—have not yet come forward. Regardless of the reasons, now is the time to come forward. Now is the time to tell us what you know. Now is the time to help us solve this crime. What you know may matter. Please call. What may seem to you to be a small, insignificant observation could be a critical clue for law enforcement."

Mia finished reading the press release aloud. Charlie was driving them to Second Amendment Seattle.

"Here come the crazies," he said succinctly.

"Exactly." Mia folded the paper and put it in her purse. "And the vengeful, the deluded, and the just plain lonely."

"Are you talking about me again?" Charlie said, and for a second they shared a smile.

The reception area for Second Amendment Seattle could have belonged to any business. On silvery-gray wall-to-wall carpeting, a Danish-style couch and chairs were grouped around a glass coffee table. But a closer look at the fan of magazines and what decorated the walls made it clear that this was not just a business. This was a cause. Instead of *People* or *Architectural Digest*, the magazines were *Gun Digest*, *Shooting*, and *Garden & Gun*. Instead of large framed photographs of flowers or landscapes, Second Amendment Seattle featured framed posters that were anything but soothing.

As they waited, Charlie sat on the couch with his eyes closed, looking like he would rather be asleep. Mia was so tired that she had decided it was safer to stay on her feet and keep the blood flowing. It had taken her nearly an hour to get Brooke back to sleep. After that Mia's own sleep had been choppy and full of nightmares in which Brooke had turned into a zombie.

She walked up to the posters to look at them more closely. One showed two men sporting long greasy hair, tattoos, and shirts with the sleeves torn off. The headline read, "Meet the new neighbors.

The government found them a nice house on your street." In smaller print it said, "Without your knowledge, sex offenders could be moved into a halfway house in your neighborhood. All while our right to keep and bear arms is under constant attack. The ultimate insult of gun control is that it leaves honest Americans at the mercy of those who will show no mercy."

The second poster featured a black-and-white photo of a frightened young woman wearing a camisole. She had her back pressed into a corner, and her wide eyes stared at something outside the camera's view. In one hand she held a shotgun, pointed up. The headline said, "A violent criminal is breaking through your front door. Can you afford to be unarmed?"

The receptionist called out, "Mr. Teller will see you now." Charlie gave himself a little shake and rose from the couch. Mia joined him, and together they followed the receptionist's pointing finger back to a corner office.

Mia had never met Gary Teller in person, although she had seen him often enough on the news. He shook hands with them before taking a seat behind his oak desk. It was big enough that the top could have doubled as a raft. Even though Gary appeared to be in his late fifties, there was something boyish about him. He was a slight man with a snub nose and thin lips. His twinkling blue eyes belied the thinning crop of hair that was a little too uniformly auburn to be real.

"So what did you want to talk to me about today?" He gave them a pleasant smile.

"We wanted to ask you some questions about Safe Seattle," Charlie said.

"Oh please." He rolled his eyes. "They call themselves Safe Seattle. I would ask: safe for whom? In their version of utopia, the only people who own guns would be criminals, leaving the law-abiding citizen with no way to protect himself or his family. They have a laundry list of ridiculous demands. For example, they want handguns to be sold with trigger locks. But you can *only* safely deploy a trigger lock on a weapon that's already unloaded. At that point, the gun is nothing but a lump of useless steel with a lock on it." He looked at Mia. "Imagine that you wake up in the middle of the night with a rapist at the foot of your bed. Will you have time to unlock and load your weapon?"

Before she could think of an answer, he shook his head. "They also want to require handgun owners to take an eight-hour safety course before they can even legally possess a gun—or risk a felony charge." He threw his hands in the air. "If guns are criminalized, then only criminals will own guns. The right to own a gun is enshrined in our constitution just below freedom of religion and freedom of the press. Our civil rights should be sacred. Yet Safe Seattle constantly seeks to infringe on those rights—and sometimes they even succeed."

Mia said, "Are you talking about the measure that prevented anyone who has been involuntarily committed to a mental hospital for two or more weeks from purchasing a gun?"

He pressed his hands into his desk. "What I'm talking about are the five thousand Washingtonians who each and every year are now deprived of their Second Amendment right to keep and bear arms."

She refrained from pointing out that the reason they had been hospitalized was that they posed a risk to themselves or those around them.

"The truth," Gary continued, "is that Safe Seattle as well as the mainstream media would be happy to have us all weapons-free. The gun control groups spend millions of dollars buying influence. We're just trying to inject a note of sanity into the process."

"And what we're trying to do is investigate two murders," Charlie said. "One occurred over four years ago, the other on Sunday. Both victims were King County prosecutors: Stan Slavich and Colleen Miller. Both of them shot at night, at home, through a window, with a .22."

"So you're thinking that whoever shot Mr. Slavich almost five years ago has struck again with the same firearm?" Gary sounded amused. "Crooks aren't generally smart, but most of them aren't stupid enough to hold on to a gun used in a crime for five years and then use it again."

"There's one other thing Stan and Colleen had in common," Mia said. "Both of them were active in Safe Seattle. And we're considering whether that was really a coincidence."

Gary furrowed his brow, managing to look both confused and amused. "So your theory is—what? That we were so threatened by these people in this ineffectual organization that has only managed to pass one law—one—in years, that we sent someone out to kill two of their members? And how would that do our cause any good? All it would do would be to play into the stereotype that people who support the right to keep and bear arms are trigger-happy."

"Look," Charlie said soothingly, "we all know that any movement attracts a fringe element, a tiny minority of people who might be passionate to the point of being unbalanced. Your organization has always been open about its contempt for Safe Seattle. What if someone drawn to your cause decided to take that a little too far?"

Gary heaved a sigh and folded his hands. "It's true that you're always going to get a few people so attracted to a cause that they would be willing to do anything if they thought it would serve the greater good."

Mia leaned forward. "So help us out. Who are the people with that kind of mind-set that Second Amendment Seattle has attracted?"

He gave them a sly smile. "Actually, I was talking about the other side."

"Other side?" Mia asked.

"Safe Seattle."

"What?" Mia wasn't following.

"Ask yourself: who would benefit from Mr. Slavich's and Ms. Miller's deaths? Not the gun rights cause. No sir. In fact, whoever killed them just made martyrs of them. And since Washington State is squarely behind the Second Amendment, who needs a martyr more than those pro–gun control nuts? No, whoever did this was only helping our enemy's cause, not ours."

"So you're saying," Charlie said slowly, "that if Ms. Miller and Mr. Slavich were murdered by someone advocating for this issue, it would have been by someone on their *own* side?"

"Yes." Gary nodded happily. "That is exactly what I'm saying. Safe Seattle is not getting any traction in this state. They haven't passed a ballot measure in years. People in Washington grow up with firearms. This is a largely rural state where guns are simply useful tools. The only hope our opponents have is to manipulate the residents of Seattle—city dwellers who haven't grown up with a tradition of safe firearm usage—into believing the lie that people who support the Second Amendment are unstable gun crazies. To do that, what they need most are martyrs. And now they've got them."

For a second Gary reminded Mia of Gabe, who sometimes argued circles around her until she simply gave up. There was no point in disagreeing with his convoluted argument. Instead, she passed over the printout of True Patriot's call for more deaths. Gary's expression didn't change as he read it. Then he looked back up at them.

"So?"

"Are you telling me he's not part of *your* fringe element?"

He shrugged. "It's possible. But these are words, not deeds. All kinds of people love to go to these websites that accept anonymous postings, set off verbal bombs, and then sit back and enjoy the fallout. This same person is probably making racist comments on stories about immigrants, or anti-gay slurs if a news story talks about a same-sex couple."

"But what if True Patriot or one of your members decided to use more than words?" Mia asked.

"I can assure you that our members are law-abiding citizens who use the legal system to effect change. Let me repeat that these crimes are horrible, and that whoever committed them does our cause no good. It only plays into the hands of our enemies. Plays so well that one has to wonder if it's really a dirty trick." He raised an eyebrow. "Besides, the shooter was clearly not an experienced gun user. I understand they recovered a shell casing at the scene of Ms. Miller's murder. Someone who knew firearms wouldn't have used a revolver that would expel shells, leaving them and maybe even fingerprints behind. Or they would have picked up the shell."

Mia stiffened. How did Gary know about the brass? That hadn't been released in the media. Did he know because he had friends on the force?

Or was it because he knew far more about Colleen's murder than he was admitting?

CHAPTER 24

On the monitor, Mia watched Charlie as he waited for Martin, Colleen's ex-husband. Although waiting wasn't exactly the word for what Charlie was doing. The man simply couldn't sit still. He tapped his feet, shifted in his seat, drummed his fingers on the table. He had either drunk too much coffee, had ADHD, or simply couldn't handle downtime. Or maybe all three.

The interview room offered Charlie no distractions. It was plain, with bare walls. No point in providing a suspect a place to focus other than the face of his questioner and his own guilty thoughts.

Mia looked at her watch. Martin was five minutes late. She tried to recall the last time she had seen him. Before he and Colleen divorced, the four of them had gone out to dinner a few times, and sometimes Martin would drop by the office to take Colleen out to lunch. Mia had chiefly known him as a good dresser, a good conversationalist, and a good-looking man. He had thick straight hair so black that sometimes walking down the street she had glimpsed a Japanese man from behind and briefly mistaken him for Martin.

Fourteen years ago Colleen had been blindsided when Martin told her that there was someone else, that he was moving out, and that there was nothing she could do to change his mind, because their marriage was dead. The next day Colleen had hidden in her office, crying, while Mia handed her tissue after tissue.

In between bouts of blowing her nose, Colleen had choked out, "He had the gall to tell me, 'The heart wants what the heart wants.' That's actually what he said." Her face was red, her eyes nearly swollen shut from crying, but her voice had been as sharp as acid. "And I told him, 'You know, Martin, I don't believe it's actually your *heart* doing all this wanting.'"

Martin was a liar, a philanderer—but could he also be a killer? Of all the things Colleen had said about him, she had never hinted he was abusive. Still, that was a secret many women hid.

When a uniformed police officer ushered Martin into the interview room, Mia was startled by how much he had changed. His hair was now sparse and mostly white. While his hair had thinned, Martin himself had grown. He had a belly now. Still, his well-tailored charcoal suit and butter-colored shirt were what the old Martin would have worn back in the day. When he shook hands with Charlie, Mia caught a glimpse of a silver cuff link.

Charlie had buttoned his jacket so that it hid the police badge on his belt and the gun on his hip. This was supposed to be just an informal chat.

"I really appreciate you coming down here today," Charlie said easily as the two men sat down. He had brought some papers in with him and now shuffled through them, letting his eyes skim over them as if refreshing his memory. It was always good to make suspects think you knew far more than you did. "I just want to ask you some questions about Colleen's death. Fill in some of the missing pieces."

"Have you caught the guy who did it yet?" There were bags under Martin's eyes.

"We're looking at a number of potential suspects," Charlie said. "What do you think happened?"

Martin pushed his lips out and sighed. "Colleen's in a dangerous line of work. Every day she deals with lowlifes. Look at the people she's prosecuted: killers, rapists, drug dealers, guys who are in motorcycle gangs. I think one of them got mad and took it out on her."

He used the present tense, as if Colleen were still alive. Could a killer do that?

"We argued about it when we were married," Martin went on. "I thought she should go into private practice. Do corporate law. She could have made more money, and I wouldn't have had to listen to her war stories. Who wants to hear about murder and rape and setting people on fire over the dinner table?"

In his words Mia heard echoes of Scott's objections. Maybe that was why Colleen had never talked about her cases to Violet. After Martin left, she might have seen the virtue of silence.

"What was her response to your suggestion?" Charlie asked.

"She said it would be boring. I mean, I put her through law school, but I always thought the idea was for her to get a high-paying job. Not to work for the county."

"And what is it you do exactly, Martin?"

"I work at Washington Health. The HMO?"

"Are you a doctor?"

Martin raised his eyebrows for a millisecond before saying, "No. No, just an administrator. I do database management. Everything is outcomes-based these days. The purchasers all want statistics. And they want those statistics to be good."

"Same here," Charlie said. "All the rates for the different types of crimes are tracked, and heaven help you if the rate isn't going down, or if the percentage that are unsolved is going up."

This was true, but Mia knew Charlie wouldn't be above lying if he thought it might build rapport.

"When was the last time you talked to Colleen?"

"About a week ago." Martin didn't elaborate.

"Did the two of you keep in close contact?"

Martin waved a hand. "Our marriage was over a long time ago, but Colleen is still the mother of my child. I certainly wouldn't wish her any harm."

"Do you know if anything has been bothering her?"

He shrugged. "We don't talk that much, unless it's about Violet, and now that Violet's older she's straightened up. It's not like when she was a teenager and there was always some issue with her skipping school or partying."

"What did you talk about when you spoke last?"

He began to pick at his cuticles. "I've been trying to help pay for Violet's college, but I was explaining to Colleen that things are a little tight these days. Frankly, we're maxed out. See, my wife, Gina, and I have spent years trying to get pregnant. First the old-fashioned way and then through IVF. Each IVF cycle cost thirteen thousand dollars. We went through all our savings, and Gina got pregnant twice, but the pregnancies never lasted long enough to even hear a heartbeat. And then we decided to adopt. I mean, Gina deserves to be a mom. We took money out of our retirement to pay for the adoption, and then the first one fell through when the birth mother changed her mind. But now we finally have a baby." He smiled briefly, keeping his lips together. "But we are flat broke, and Colleen seems to just expect us to shell out year after year for Violet, who only worked about twelve hours a week this summer. I asked Colleen if maybe she could take out a line of credit or something, but she wouldn't even talk about it."

"Tell me about it," Charlie said. "My buddy has to pay alimony and child support every month. By the thirty-first, if he wants to go to Subway for a sandwich, he has to dig in the couch cushions."

Now it was Martin who couldn't keep still. People who were nervous—or who had something to hide—often invented little grooming tasks for themselves during an interview, like Martin's ragged cuticle that now sported a bright spot of blood.

Charlie stretched, then made a show of checking his watch. "I'm gonna go get a bag of Fritos from the vending machine. I'll be back in a second. Do you want anything?"

Martin shook his head. "No, I'm good."

Charlie got up. Martin glanced up at the one-way glass and then away. The room had been designed well, with the glass beginning five feet up, so that it was not in the direct line of sight of a seated suspect. You didn't want to remind them they were probably being watched.

Even with Charlie gone, Martin still seemed jittery. But that didn't necessarily mean anything. After all, Charlie had been the same waiting for Martin. And Mia had also seen murderers who steadfastly denied all involvement and then fell asleep as soon as they were alone in the interrogation room, exhausted from keeping their lies straight.

Martin was checking his phone when Charlie walked into the observation room carrying a bag of Chili Cheese Fritos.

"How do you think it's going?" he asked Mia.

"It's interesting that he owned up right away to their arguing about money."

"He probably figured Violet would tell us about it."

"He's nervous about something," Mia said, checking the monitor again.

"He's in a police station and his ex-wife is dead. A lot of men would be." Charlie raised one shoulder. "But you're right, he is. Text me if you think there's something I'm missing. I can tell him I've got a call I have to take and then come back in here."

"Sounds good," Mia said.

In the interview room, Charlie opened the Fritos bag so that it split down the middle and set it between himself and Martin. Despite what the other man had said, he immediately picked up a handful.

"So, Martin, can you just walk me through what you did on Sunday?"

"Sunday. Um, sure. Gina and I got up around seven." Martin's smile seemed private. "Having Wyatt is forcing us to be morning people whether we like it or not. We ate breakfast, and then we went to the coffee shop and then the park. Then we came home, had lunch, and then I have to admit all three of us took a nap. After that we went to the grocery store together. We grilled salmon for dinner, and I played with Wyatt while Gina cleaned up. Then Gina gave him a bath and we put him to bed and watched a little TV."

Mia listened to his words, but it was his posture, eye contact, gestures, hesitations, and facial expressions that interested her. A good liar could control some of those things. A sociopath might be able to control all of them, might even believe the lies he spun.

She didn't think Martin was a sociopath. But she also didn't think he was telling the whole truth. His gestures were abrupt and choppy.

"And where were you around eight thirty?"

Martin swiped at what Mia was pretty sure were nonexistent crumbs on his jacket. "Watching a movie Gina had gotten from Netflix. It was called *Must Love Dogs*. It's got that John Cusack in it. My wife loves him. Absolutely loves him." It struck Mia that Martin had once looked something like John Cusack.

"Let me ask you something, Martin. Do you own a gun?"

Martin reared back as if Charlie had slapped him.

"A gun?" It sounded like he was stalling for time.

"Yes. Do you own a gun?"

"We have a gun that we keep in our bedroom closet, yes." He nodded a little too vigorously. "Gina needs it for protection when I have to travel."

"What caliber is it?"

"I think it's a .22."

Mia straightened up, but Charlie's body posture didn't change.

"Why are you asking me these things? Am I under arrest?" With every word, Martin's voice rose. He sounded eerily like Gabe when he was under stress.

"Of course not," Charlie said easily. "You're not under arrest, and you can leave at any time." The courts had ruled that it was being in custody that triggered the need for the Miranda warning. As long as Martin was freely talking and didn't think he was in custody, there was no need to remind him that any information he gave could be used against him in court.

"Let me tell you something. Colleen and I may have had our disagreements, but I honestly did not harm her in any way."

Mia stiffened at the sound of the *-ly* word. *Truthfully, honestly, absolutely*—sometimes those were the words of a liar desperate to reinforce falsehoods.

Charlie finished the interview and ushered Martin out of the room. Mia watched him go, trying to look past the well-fed, well-clothed exterior to the man inside. Could Martin have been so angry over Violet's tuition that he had killed Colleen?

CHAPTER 25

To Charlie, Shiloh Arnold's living room did not seem to be meant for living at all. Instead it looked like a furniture showroom display. The two couches sitting at right angles were cream colored, without a single spot or even strand of hair to mar their perfection. Each was decorated with three mustard-colored throw pillows set at precise angles. Even the accent rug was cream colored, with a mustard yellow border. The blond coffee table was centered in the middle of the rug, far out of reach of either couch.

And in Charlie's hand was a delicate cup filled to the brim with black coffee that Shiloh's mom had offered them. Feeling the weight of the long day, Charlie had said yes. Even though he knew Mia was exhausted too—she had told him that her daughter had had another one of those attacks—she had declined. Maybe she had glimpsed the room.

Rainy Sibley and Shiloh Arnold lived next door to each other, only a block and a half from Darin Dane's house. Their parents had agreed to let Charlie and Mia interview the two girls together at Shiloh's, and they hadn't protested when Charlie had asked them not to sit in on the interviews. Afterward he and Mia planned to repeat the process at Jeremy Donaldson's.

Mia was already sitting on one couch, with Shiloh and Rainy on the other. "So how long have you two known Darin?" she asked.

As he held the thin loop of the cup's handle, Charlie decided that if he tried to take a seat he would manage to slop the dark liquid on the carpet or the couch. Or both. It was too big a risk, so he stayed where he was and waited for the girls to answer.

After looking at Shiloh, Rainy said, "I don't know. Since first grade, maybe?" Rainy had high cheekbones, light brown skin, and stick-straight hair that fell past her shoulders.

Charlie raised the cup to his lips and sucked, too afraid to risk tilting it. The coffee was only a few degrees below boiling, but he ignored the pain.

Shiloh said decisively, "We all met in kindergarten. I remember us sitting on the mat for story time." She was a little bit plump, with blond corkscrew curls springing out from her head.

Charlie forced himself to take another sip and managed to lower the coffee to a half inch below the rim. He raised his head, walked five careful steps forward, and sat down next to Mia. As he did, hot coffee splashed his thigh. He bit his scalded lip and didn't make a sound. Better his pants than the couch.

"I still can't believe Darin's dead, you know?" Rainy nibbled on her thumbnail. "I've never known anyone who was dead before."

Had Charlie ever been this young? By now, it seemed that the dead he knew outnumbered the living.

"At school everyone's been asking about him." Shiloh shook her head. "They all looked the other way when those boys were picking on him, but now Darin's a lot more interesting because he's dead."

"They had an assembly and talked about him for, like, an hour, even though none of the teachers at school really knew him yet," Rainy said. "And they had this room full of grief counselors? And we all got a list of warning signs to watch for, you know, to tell if people were suicidal?"

"Did you ever see any of those signs in Darin?" Mia asked gently.

"No!" Shiloh leaned forward. "He never talked about wanting to kill himself or how he would do it or anything!"

"Darin was just, you know, all unicorns and rainbows?" Rainy said. "He was almost always happy. Except for, like, the last six months."

"Tell us more about Darin." Charlie took another sip. "What was he like?"

"He's really sweet," Shiloh said. She touched her dangling earrings, gold and ruby red. "He bought me these earrings at a flea market."

"He makes cupcakes all the time and hands them out to people at the bus stop." A smile lit up Rainy's face. "One time he bought me hot cocoa at Starbucks? And because he knew I like it with marshmallows, he brought a little plastic bag full from home. Just for me."

"In fifth grade we started our own *Sisterhood of the Traveling Pants* club," Shiloh said. "It was Darin's idea."

"What's that?" Charlie asked.

"There's this book?" Rainy said. "And in it these four friends find, like, a magic pair of jeans at a vintage store? And the jeans fit all of them. So Darin went to Value Village and got this pair of jeans and said they would be just like in the book. Except they really didn't fit him? He was already too tall. But when it was his day to wear them, he did anyway. And he didn't care if people made fun of him. He said those pants were magic and good things always happened to him when he wore them."

Shiloh blinked and tears ran down her face. She made no move to wipe them away.

Mia had brought along a photocopy of one of the notes, and she offered it to the girls now. "Do you recognize this handwriting?"

Shiloh and Rainy bent their heads over it, but when they looked up there was no recognition.

"It kind of looks familiar," Rainy offered. "Maybe."

"It looks like a boy's handwriting," Shiloh said. "All square and blocky. But I don't know which boy." She exhaled sharply and turned to Rainy. "Rain—remember when Darin got beat up after school last spring? I wonder if that's what happened. Maybe some jerk sent him a note, and then when he came they jumped him." She turned back to Charlie and Mia. "He would never say how, but somehow he ended up with bruised ribs and a split lip."

Charlie had heard that chickens would peck at an injured

chicken, peck and peck until it stopped moving. Were human beings any better?

"What happened to Darin's Facebook page?" he asked.

"Kids are always doing stupid stuff on Facebook," Rainy said. "But this was the worst."

"What kind of stuff do they do?" Mia asked.

"You know, people will post something mean? And then just say, 'Oh, I was joking around.'" Rainy bit the end of her finger, thought better of it, took it out. "Or one of the really popular girls might put down that she's married to another girl, you know, to show that they're friends? And then the next day she will, like, unfriend her and start talking trash about her."

Shiloh said, "Whoever hacked into Darin's Facebook page unfriended me and Rainy so we couldn't tell him. I heard the kids at school talking about some crazy kid, but I didn't realize they were talking about Darin. And Darin hasn't been going on Facebook that much lately, so he didn't know at first." Her eyes shone with fresh tears. "Darin would never hurt anyone, so why did those boys want to hurt him? It's only because of those terrible boys that he's dead."

Mia said softly, "What else did they do besides alter his Facebook page?"

Rainy rolled her eyes. "What didn't they do? In the hall, kids would walk right behind him and pretend they were him, you know? They would walk like him, but, like, all exaggerated, swinging their hips." She swayed from side to side, arms raised, loose hands flapping at the end of limp wrists.

Shiloh ticked things off on her fingers. "They shoved him into lockers. They kicked his books down the hall. They left him these terrible notes. They squirted maple syrup and ketchup through the vents in his locker. They called him names."

"They talked about him, like, right in front of him?" Rainy contributed.

Their words were setting off echoes in Charlie. His hand was starting to shake, but he told himself it was simply a reaction to a long day and little sleep. He rested the coffee cup on his knee.

Bright red spots of color had appeared on Shiloh's cheeks. "And I've seen people push him and trip him, but I know when I wasn't around it was worse. I already told you about that one time last spring. And I heard it was really bad in PE, that they even punched him. I've seen bruises on his arms when he forgot and pushed up his sleeves."

"And this all happened in school?" Mia sounded horrified.

"It wasn't in class so much," Rainy said. "It was, like, you know, in PE or hallways or in the bathrooms, or waiting at school for the bus."

"Who do you think the main offenders were?" Charlie asked in a colorless, just-the-facts voice.

Rainy and Shiloh looked at each other, and then Shiloh said, "Two of the guys on the football team were always going after Darin. It was bad in eighth grade, but it's gotten a lot worse since school started. It's like they figured that now they're in high school they had something to prove. Brandon Shiller and Reece Jones. I'll get my yearbook and show you their pictures." She jumped to her feet.

"Reece is just, like, really bad?" Rainy said. "He likes to beat people up and call them Reece's Pieces."

Shiloh came back with the yearbook and handed it to Mia. Charlie looked over her shoulder as she found the two boys. Brandon had wide-spaced eyes and light brown hair that had been gelled straight up so that he looked like the cartoon character Tintin. Reece Jones had blue eyes, dark hair, and a smile that hovered on the border of a smirk.

Charlie winced. That smile brought back memories. Looking away from the yearbook, he caught sight of his reflection in the flat-screen TV. He looked like a ghost, a shadow, a frightened boy. As if the specter of who he used to be had been summoned back to this room.

Abruptly he got to his feet, desperate to get some distance from his old self. Only then did he remember the half-empty cup of coffee—just as it splashed on the formerly pristine rug.

Charlie had offered to scrub the rug clean, but Shiloh's mom had insisted it was fine, fine, fine. When it was clearly not, not, not.

Twenty minutes after their very awkward exit, they were sitting in Jeremy Donaldson's living room with a tray of Ritz crackers topped with cheddar cheese. Jeremy's mother had offered it to them before scurrying from the room.

Jeremy had close-cropped, dirty-blond hair that emphasized his high forehead and long face. He looked unfinished, like modeling clay that needed some sharp edges cut into it.

"So we understand you and Darin used to be close?" Mia slipped a Ritz cracker into her mouth.

He looked down at his oversized feet. "Yeah, we were friends in grade school, but in middle school we kind of grew apart. I mean, you can't really base a friendship on your last names starting with the same letter of the alphabet."

"Were you aware of Darin being harassed at school?" Mia asked.

After a moment he nodded. "I tried to tell him if he just changed a few things it would get better. Like you don't show up on the first day of high school wearing a rainbow-striped scarf. I mean, didn't he want to have a life?" His knees began to bounce. "To do that, you've got to fit in. You don't want to be noticed, at least not for something like that. But Darin wouldn't listen."

Everything was rawer when you were a kid. Your terrors, your joys, your humiliations. You hadn't learned how to put a good face on things. You hadn't learned the importance of plodding forward, of ignoring even the deepest wounds. You hadn't learned that no one was paying as much attention as you thought. Not even you.

"What kinds of things did they do to him?" Charlie asked.

"Once they locked him in the supply closet with a girl and said he couldn't come out until he'd gotten to second base. That was last year. This year from day one they've been going after him in PE, you know, teasing and pushing him in the showers. Pinching his chest and twisting. The PE teacher just stays in his office, so he doesn't see what happens. But then he heard Darin wasn't taking showers, and Darin got in trouble."

Jeremy took a shaky breath. "The day before he died, I saw Darin at the end of a hallway after school. He was down on his knees and crying, and blood was coming out of his nose and dripping onto the floor. Two guys were standing in front of him. They had their backs to me."

"Who were they?" Charlie asked.

His eyes swung from Mia's face to Charlie's.

"Jeremy, we need you to help us," Mia said. "Do you know the kids who did these things to Darin?"

He bit his lip.

She added, "We also heard that someone might have beaten up Darin after school on the track last year. Do you know who that was?"

Jeremy swallowed. His knees were still going.

After a long moment Mia said, "We heard it might be some boys named Brandon and Reece."

She gave Jeremy a long look. Charlie wondered if it had been practiced on her own son. It would be hard to hide much from those blue eyes.

"Maybe . . . ," Jeremy said slowly. "If I say anything, will you tell them who said it?"

"Don't worry," Charlie said. "We can keep your name out of this." They certainly didn't need another victim.

"But how much trouble can they really get in?" Jeremy twisted his hands together. "It's not like they killed Darin. What if it was like a joke?"

"It's a joke to hurt people? To mock them and hit them and say those terrible things on Facebook? It's not a joke," Mia said fiercely. "What it is, is harassment and cyberstalking and assault, and Washington State has clear laws about it. Don't you worry, Jeremy, we can take care of these bullies so that no one will ever be tempted to do what they did."

With every word of Jeremy's, Charlie had felt his muscles getting tenser. He could picture what had happened to Darin so well.

He could picture it because he had lived it.

CHAPTER 26

"Today I'm going to bring you two cases," Mia told the grand jurors, who were seated at three long tables set up in a U-shape. As she spoke, she caught sight of a spot on her navy blue skirt. "The first is that of a fourteen-year-old boy named Darin Dane who committed suicide last Thursday. We want to find out if cyberstalking, harassment, and/or a violation of his civil rights contributed to his death. The second is the murder of a King County prosecutor, Colleen Miller. She was shot to death at her home on Monday night."

Tomorrow the grand jurors might hear about a burglary ring or domestic violence. Their purpose was solely to indict—or decline to indict—suspects. Because they weren't asked to determine guilt or innocence, their standards were looser than those of a trial jury. Their decision didn't even need to be unanimous.

When she said Colleen's name, Mia saw a few nods of recognition. Grand jurors weren't banned from watching the media in general, which meant they often had a passing familiarity with any headline cases. But now that they knew they would be considering Colleen's case, they would have to stay away from any fresh news. And no matter how high-profile the case, they were sworn to keep secret what went on inside the grand jury room.

"First, I'd like to present King County homicide detective Charlie Carlson."

While the bailiff brought Charlie in from the anteroom and swore him in, Mia took a quick second look at the stain on her skirt. It was a long flaky trail just above her knee. And then she realized what it was. Snot. This morning Brooke had hugged her knees goodbye while Mia was leaving her at daycare. Only she hadn't been hugging or even clinging. She had been wiping.

Mia wondered how many people had noticed it today. If so, she hoped none of them had identified it. She tried to brush it off while she asked Charlie to explain to the grand jurors who Darin was and how he had taken his own life.

While not allowed in a trial jury, hearsay was permitted before a grand jury, so Charlie could talk about what he had learned through their interviews. Once more Mia was amazed at Charlie's ability to remember conversations almost verbatim.

Last night she issued target letters to Brandon Shiller and Reece Jones, ordering them to appear next week in front of the grand jury as hostile witnesses. While they had no choice but to appear, they could still refuse to answer any question if the answer might tend to incriminate them. The boys could also bring lawyers with them and even leave the grand jury room to consult them, but in this room it would only be Mia, the jurors, the court reporter, and the witness.

Mia said, "What might have tipped Darin over the edge was when his Facebook account was hacked." She asked Charlie to read some of the printouts aloud. While he did, she watched the jurors' faces, not his. She saw revulsion, embarrassment, and pity.

When he finished, she asked, "So do you have any questions for Detective Carlson?" She liked to hear what regular people were thinking. The grand jurors' questions could help shape her approach to any future trial. And sometimes jurors even thought of angles she had missed.

"What about the school?" a plump woman in a red cardigan asked. "Did they know about what was happening?"

"Some of the harassment occurred at Darin's middle school," Charlie said. "Some continued over the summer. And some seems to have taken place at his new high school. While the middle school knew there was an issue and tried to intervene, the high school was unaware of the problem until it was too late."

"What's the dividing line between cruel behavior and criminal behavior?" asked a middle-aged man in a pin-striped suit.

"Sometimes that can be difficult. Cruel behavior can be despicable without being criminal. However, in Darin's case, we are talking about more than simple cruelty. I told you that Jeremy Donaldson saw Darin on his hands and knees with a bloody face and with Mr. Shiller and Mr. Jones standing over him. All of Darin's friends and his father reported seeing bruises that appeared to be the result of physical contact. In other words, assaults." When Charlie took a breath, there was a slight hitch to it. He added, "And the hacking into Darin's Facebook account is clearly covered by Washington's cyberstalking law."

Something seemed to have shifted in Charlie as they interviewed Darin's friends. Mia had found herself wondering just what memories had been stirred up.

A frail-looking man with white hair said, "Can we really hold a teenager criminally liable for the suicide of another teenager?" Each word was pronounced with precision. "These kids didn't put the scarf around his neck, after all. They were nowhere near when it happened."

Mia said, "That's why we're here in front of you. We need your help in deciding whether the cruelty rises to the level of criminal behavior." She waited a moment, but no one else spoke. She took a deep breath. "Okay, if there are no other questions, I'm going to turn to the death of my colleague, Colleen Miller. And again I'm going to ask Detective Carlson to go through some of the facts we've already learned about her death. I'm also going to have him tell you about the death of Stan Slavich, another King County prosecutor who was also shot at home over four years ago, and whose killer has not yet been found."

After summarizing the basic facts of Colleen's and Stan's deaths, Charlie said, "We don't know if their deaths are linked, but we can't overlook the similarities. You may already be familiar with this idea, but when we investigate a murder, we try to figure out who had the motive, means, and opportunity. One problem with Ms. Miller's death is that we have not been able to ascertain the motive. If the motive was her work as a prosecutor, then it may be no coincidence that she was killed in the same manner as her co-worker. However, just because they were both shot to death may not prove anything. After all, guns are involved in nearly thirteen thousand homicides in America each year. However, one thing Ms. Miller and Mr. Slavich did have in common was they were both active in Safe Seattle." Charlie summarized their efforts to find True Patriot and their visit to Second Amendment Seattle, including Gary Teller's contention that a pro–gun control vigilante might have tried to make martyrs of Colleen and Stan.

"Do you believe that last theory is possible?" Mia asked.

"Possible?" Charlie echoed. "Anything's possible. Likely? No. There's a saying: when you hear hoofbeats, don't look for zebras. With Ms. Miller's death, I think we need to consider some of the more common reasons for murder. Normally those are jealousy, revenge, profit, or to conceal another crime."

"Can you tell the jury about Ms. Miller's romantic relationships?" Mia asked.

"As far as we know, there was only one recent one. Ms. Miller had an online relationship with a man named Vincent. We're getting his contact information."

"What about the profit motive? Was there anyone who would have benefited financially from Ms. Miller's death?"

Charlie nodded. "I also interviewed Ms. Miller's ex-husband, Martin Miller. He admitted arguing with Colleen about paying for their daughter's college tuition. He also has a .22 caliber handgun, which is the same caliber as the bullet that killed both Ms. Miller and Mr. Slavich. His alibi is that he was with his current wife. We have submitted a warrant to his phone carrier for his cell site location information."

Mia said, "Can you explain what that is?"

"Sure," Charlie said. "Even when someone isn't making or receiving a call, their cell phone still automatically registers with the nearest cell tower. And it continues to reregister as they move around. In a city like Seattle, that means we can pin down a user's location within a few blocks."

When Charlie was finished, they broke for lunch. Mia scraped off the worst of the stain, and then instead of going back to her office she went out to the Suburban. The Suburban that she had listed on a site for people who wanted to take over someone else's lease payment. The car was the only place she could be alone, without anyone overhearing her. And at least during lunch she wasn't driving and talking, the way she had been this morning.

Mia knew that hands-free wasn't really safe. She'd seen the studies. Their office had even prosecuted egregious cases of distracted driving. And those studies had probably been of people having normal conversations. Not trying to work out repayment plans for thousands and thousands of dollars.

She picked up the next bill in the pile. It was for a Visa card. Squinting at the tiny print, she called the number for customer service. "My husband died and left me with some large credit card bills that I was unaware of. I need to work out a repayment plan that I can afford."

Mia spent the next half hour being transferred, explaining her situation, and laying out the hard numbers that still shocked her. At the end of her lunch break, she had achieved a reduced interest rate and gotten the late fees and penalties waived.

Three down. Nine to go.

CHAPTER 27

When Mia went back to her office, she was surprised to find Charlie waiting for her. On his face was an expression she hadn't seen there before, a kind of glee. "I just got the cell site location information for Martin."

"And?" Mia waited for the other shoe to drop.

"And it matched what he said. He was at home all evening."

For how indispensable cell phones had become, they could still be dispensed with. "Or at least his cell phone was," Mia pointed out, wondering why Charlie seemed so happy. Had he found a witness or footage from a nearby security cam that had showed Martin near Colleen's house that night?

He gave her a Cheshire grin. "I didn't just run Martin's phone. I ran all the phones on his account."

Comprehension dawned. Not Martin. His wife. "Gina."

"Exactly." Charlie got to his feet. "Gina's cell phone was within a two-block radius of Colleen's house around the time of the murder."

"So either Martin was there with Gina's phone or Gina herself was there. Either way, Martin lied."

"Yup." Charlie pulled his car keys from his pocket. "Now we've got motive, means, and opportunity." In two quick strides he was at her door. "Let's go talk to her."

As they hurried down the hall, Jonas came up to them.

"Mia, there's something I need to talk to you about."

"Um . . ." She looked at Charlie, who was shifting from foot to foot. "Can it wait?"

"I'm not sure that it can. I believe there's some facet of the data regarding Colleen and Stan that I'm overlooking. I looked for common defendants. I looked for affiliations with fringe groups. But I fear there's something's missing. With your permission, I'd like to ask an outside computer expert for help. She specializes in database searches."

Mia flashed back to Frank's talk about money. "Unfortunately, Jonas, I don't think there's room for that in the budget."

"That won't be an issue," Jonas said. "If she's interested, she doesn't charge."

That was certainly unusual, but Mia didn't have time to ask more. Charlie was jingling his keys impatiently. "Okay, sure," she said, waving her hand. "We'll talk about it more later."

Martin and Gina lived in a thirty-story silver-and-glass condo building layered with jutting balconies that made it resemble a giant electric razor.

"It looks like a giant piece of medical equipment," Charlie said, craning his neck.

"I think it looks great," Mia said. "All those clean lines. And just think—no lawn to mow, no gutters to clean, no roofs to keep the moss off of."

"Yeah, just you and your thousands of neighbors living in the hive."

The open lobby had a floor made of large squares of white marble set off by smaller strips of black marble. The silver doors of the elevator slid open, and Charlie pressed the button for the twenty-third floor.

Even before he knocked on the door of the Millers' condo, they could hear a baby crying inside. After a moment a woman opened the door.

Colleen had once shown Mia a picture of Martin with his new wife. In the photo Gina had had shiny dark hair that fell past her shoulders. Now, her gray-threaded hair, pulled back in a sloppy ponytail, looked like it needed to be washed. She was still slender and petite, only now there were hard lines around her mouth. She looked almost brittle.

"Gina Miller?" Mia had to raise her voice to be heard over the baby's crying. The sound was monotonous and oddly devoid of emotion.

"Yes?" She stiffened slightly.

"I'm Mia Quinn with the King County District Attorney's Office. And this is Charlie Carlson with the Seattle police."

Her expression didn't change. "Yes?"

"Can we come in?" Charlie asked. "We'd like to ask you a few questions. We're gathering information on Colleen Miller. Your husband's"—he lowered his voice, as if there were neighbors around who might hear—"first wife."

Gina stepped back and let them in.

At one point the condo must have had a modern, stripped-down feel, with its recessed lighting, pale trim, and squared-off furniture floating on stainless steel legs. But all of that was now covered with a layer of baby paraphernalia: bottles, sippy cups, stuffed animals, a package of diapers, and receiving blankets in various pastel hues. An empty blue playpen was set up in a corner of the living room.

In the dining room a baby who looked about a year old was strapped into a blue-and-white plastic high chair. He put one hand in his mouth and began to flick his tongue with the tips of his fingers. On the smeared glass tabletop was a jar of bright orange baby food. A tiny blue spoon sat next to it. Suddenly Mia felt nostalgic for Pack 'n Plays and miniature rubber-coated spoons.

The overheated space had the sharp, sweet stink of diapers. Charlie sniffed and winced, and Mia hoped Gina didn't notice.

"So what did you want to know?" Gina asked as she walked toward the baby.

"You do know that Colleen Miller is dead, right?" Charlie said to her back.

"Do you want me to pretend that I'm grief-stricken?" Gina leaned over to unbuckle her son from his high chair. "Colleen had everything, and she wanted us to have nothing. Violet wasn't even planned, but here Colleen just goes and has this accidental baby and everything turns out fine. Then she got to raise her daughter while keeping a huge chunk of Martin's salary. Meanwhile we had to spend twenty-six thousand dollars from our retirement fund on IVF. And all that got us was two pregnancies that lasted a few weeks each." She hoisted the baby to her hip. He put his fingertips back to his tongue. "Sometimes she'd even call up Martin and ask him to come by the house to help her fix something. Say her pipes were leaking or whatever and she didn't know how to fix it. When we've been married years longer than they ever were. I knew what she was doing. She was trying to get him back." With an exasperated huff, Gina tugged her son's hand from his mouth.

Mia tried to see Colleen through Gina's eyes. She didn't even recognize the person Gina was describing.

"So you felt the financial situation was unfair," Charlie observed mildly.

"Do you know how expensive it is to adopt? It cost us sixteen thousand to adopt Wyatt after he had already spent the first twelve months of his life, the formative years of his infancy, living with his eighteen-year-old mom. His *stripper* mom. Who has a problem with meth, and more than likely used during her pregnancy. If we had tried to get a healthy newborn, we would have paid at least double. But we didn't have that."

"He's certainly a cutie," Mia said. "Do you mind if I hold him?"

Suddenly she remembered her dream from the night before. She had been in an empty house, walking long stretches of polished wood floor with sunlight streaming in through uncurtained windows, when she heard a baby crying. She could tell it was hungry. No problem, Mia had thought. She would find the baby and nurse it. But when she finally located the baby and picked it up, she realized she had no milk to give it. She was all dried up.

"Sure." Gina handed him over, swamping Mia in memories. Brooke was only four, but she didn't have the same warmth a baby did, the same smell. She held Wyatt so that they were eye to eye, and smiled. Wyatt's face didn't change. It was as if Mia wasn't there.

Two kids didn't make Mia an expert on anything, except knowing that every kid was different. But something about Wyatt felt . . . off. He seemed oddly heavy and floppy. She perched him on her hip, but his heels didn't dig into either side as her own kids' heels had done, some mammalian reflex that told a baby to hang on.

Mia did the math based on their earlier conversation with Martin. Wyatt was probably around fifteen months old. "So is he walking yet?"

"No." Gina didn't elaborate. Instead she said, "You said you were from the District Attorney's Office. That's where Colleen worked."

"Yes."

"So you knew her?"

"Yes." Mia didn't know where this was heading, so she kept her answers short.

"What did she say about me?"

"She really didn't talk about you very much." That was true, at least recently. In the beginning Colleen had despised Gina, obsessed about her looks, her age, the lies she must have used to lure Martin in.

Wyatt held his hand out in front of his face and began to turn it back and forth, back and forth, his eyes fixated on the rhythmic movement.

Gina said in a rush, "He never makes eye contact. He repeats the same sounds over and over. He flaps his hands for hours. He's constantly flicking his ears and tongue. The doctors say it's too soon to know for sure, but they think he's autistic."

"I'm so sorry," Mia said, and Charlie mumbled his apologies. She looked down at the baby's face again, his blank blue eyes. Her heart broke for Gina. For Martin. And for Wyatt.

And a little for herself. She had made a doctor's appointment for Brooke, but she hadn't been able to get in until next Tuesday. What if Brooke's nighttime screaming fits were caused by something awful?

A brain tumor? Epilepsy? Childhood schizophrenia? Bad things happened. Happened even to kids. Wyatt was proof of that.

How long would it be before she was just like Gina—irrational, sleep-deprived, angry, and broke?

"He needs play therapy, speech therapy, all kinds of therapies," Gina said. "He's going to need a lot, and we can't afford to give it to him. But we have to. He's our son. We can't turn our back on him. This is our life now. Even if it's not at all what we planned on."

"So you went over to Colleen's house on Sunday night," Charlie said in a soothing voice. "To make her understand."

Gina nodded, then scrubbed her face with her palms.

Mia froze. Gina had done it. She had really done it.

"I just wanted to ask her to think of our poor boy. Her own child's as healthy as a horse, and Violet is now an adult for all intents and purposes. And Wyatt's just a baby. But they're both Martin's children."

"You just wanted her to listen," Charlie said.

Gina's expression was anguished, her lips trembling, the whites showing around her eyes. "Have you ever made a mistake? Made a mistake and then realized it was too late and there was no way to undo it and your life was ruined forever?"

"So you took the gun with you?" Charlie said, still in the same soothing voice.

Gina's eyes widened as if the full import of what she had done had finally sunk in.

CHAPTER 28

Eli Hall was early for his first day as an adjunct professor at the University of Washington—he still felt a bit funny saying "UDub"—School of Law. Ten students—the maximum number—were registered for his session, but he felt as nervous as if he were about to address a crowd of thousands.

He was in the faculty lounge pouring a cup of burnt-smelling coffee when Mia Quinn walked in. "Want some?" he said, holding it out to her.

Her smile seemed distracted. "I probably should say no." But she still held out her hand.

He noticed it was trembling. If Eli hadn't already been a little off balance himself, he wouldn't have said what he did next.

"So are you nervous too?"

"What?" She tilted her head. "Oh no, it's not the teaching that's getting to me. I just came here from listening to what I thought was going to be a murder confession."

Eli took a step back. "Murder?"

Mia leaned against the counter, which was cluttered with torn sugar packets and discarded sections of the *Seattle Times*. "I'm investigating the murder of one of my colleagues, Colleen Miller. I was just with the homicide detective at the home of a suspect. The second wife of Colleen's ex-husband, if you can follow that. Anyway, we thought she was going to confess to murdering Colleen, but it turned out that she was really confessing to not wanting to be a mom anymore."

"That must have been hard on both of you," Eli said. "Does she by any chance have a teenager?" He thought of Rachel. She was sixteen and had figured out how to push every button he had. As he spoke, he poured another cup of coffee for himself.

"No." Mia's lips turned down, and he realized that his joking response was not quite in step with what she was feeling. "A baby they adopted three months ago when he was a year old. Only he hasn't started to walk or talk, and now the doctors think he's probably autistic. This woman's looking at thousands of dollars of bills in early intervention therapy that may or may not work."

Eli was getting a little lost. "So what does that have to do with Colleen's murder?"

"As I said, this is Colleen's ex-husband's second wife. And her cell phone records showed that she was near Colleen's house around the time of the murder. But she says she was just planning to talk to her about adjusting how much her husband pays in child support. And that when she saw the cop cars roaring up to Colleen's house, she turned around and left."

Eli cut to the heart of the story. "Do you believe her?"

"Maybe. I'm not sure." Mia took a tentative sip of her coffee and grimaced at its bitterness. "She didn't try to hide that she disliked Colleen. It was not liking her baby that she had trouble admitting. I think for her it would almost be easier to confess to murder than to confess to not loving her child. They sacrificed everything to have a child, and now she's feeling stuck with it. Like it wasn't worth it."

"Yeah, well, it's not exactly like you can give them back." For all the trouble she could get into, Rachel was healthy and smart. Eli sometimes lost sight of those blessings. And he had the hope that she would gain maturity, learn to make better decisions. A disabled child might never grow up, never leave home. "Having a kid is more permanent than anything. You can abandon your pet, you can get a divorce"—a touch of bitterness entered Eli's voice at the thought of how Lydia had just walked out of their lives—"but unless you do something so bad the court takes them away, a kid is yours forever."

"I've got two. It's one of the reasons I'm so tired." Mia took a deep breath and drank the rest of her coffee in one gulp. By the time she finished, her nose was wrinkled in disgust. Eli couldn't help noticing it was a cute nose, straight and slightly snub. "I think she might be telling the truth, but the homicide detective isn't too sure. This lady clearly had the motive and opportunity. And she and her husband even own the same caliber of gun as the one that killed Colleen. But she flatly denied taking it with her that night."

"Too bad it's way too late now to check for gun residue on her hands," Eli said. There was also no way to figure out if a gun had been fired recently, despite what some TV shows would have you believe. "And wasn't another King County prosecutor murdered the same way a few years ago? Wouldn't that rule this lady out? After all, she wouldn't have had any motive to kill *him*, would she? What's your working theory on that case?"

"That's the problem. We don't have one. Or rather, we have too many." Mia threw her cup in the trash. "Did I hear you just moved from Portland? What made you come up here?"

Mia's honesty brought out his own. "I wanted to give my daughter a fresh start. She'd fallen in with the wrong crowd in Portland."

Eli had felt they had to get away. Away from the kids Rachel was hanging around with. Away from Lydia. Maybe then it wouldn't be so obvious that his ex-wife didn't want to spend time with their daughter. After all, a sixteen-year-old did not exactly fit with Lydia's new image.

"How old is she?"

"Rachel's sixteen."

"I have a fourteen-year-old myself. It's an . . . interesting . . . age. It's probably more challenging for Gabe because"—she began to turn her wedding ring with her thumb—"my husband was killed in a car accident a few months ago."

"Oh. I'm sorry." Eli was kind of surprised that Mia was teaching with all that on her plate. Although maybe she had to, now that her husband had died. His own caseload was already overwhelming, but he needed the extra cash. The flip side was that it gave Rachel a couple of hours where he couldn't even stay in touch by text.

"So are you settling in?" Mia asked after the silence had stretched out too long.

"Kind of. Tami's files are a bit disorganized."

Calling them files was generous. Tami Gordon seemed to have kept much of what she knew in her head. And what little was in her files hadn't been entered into a computer, but jotted down in her scrawled handwriting that seemed to substitute whole strings of letters for a single curvy line.

Still, she had been a good defense attorney. Not good in any way Mia would think of as good. But she had succeeded in striking plea deals for many of her clients, people who would otherwise have had to throw themselves on the mercy of a judge or a jury. People with track records and track marks. People with very few redeeming characteristics.

"I need to stop by and speak to one of your colleagues," Eli said. "I think her name is Kristina?"

"Katrina?"

"That's it. The morning of what turned out to be Tami's last day, she offered a pretty generous plea deal for one of Tami's—now my—clients. I'm just hoping she hasn't changed her mind." He realized he was probably saying too much. "I guess I probably shouldn't be discussing that with you."

"I'm just glad it wasn't my case. I didn't like dealing with Tami. She could be . . ."

"Very persuasive?"

"More like a pit bull. Her only priority was her client. She would bend any rule, make any wild accusation—for her the end always justified the means." Mia sighed and looked at her watch. "I guess I had better get moving."

Eli thought about how dark it would be when they finished. "Want me to walk you to your car after class?"

"That's okay. I'll be fine."

Eli didn't press it, even though he knew rapists liked college campuses. Lots of girls who were engrossed in their texts and Tweets and Facebook updates, headphones in their ears, or girls who had had a little too much to drink, girls who believed they didn't even need to worry about being safe, that bad things only happened to other people.

"Then I'll see you next Thursday. And I'll bring some good coffee for both of us."

She brightened at that. "Sounds like a plan." She gave him a little wave as she left.

Mia Quinn. There would probably come a time when they were on the opposite sides of the courtroom. Eli didn't know whether he was looking forward to it or dreading it.

"Welcome to Trial Advocacy," Eli said a few minutes later in the miniature courtroom that was actually a classroom. "In this course you are going to be on your feet for most class sessions. This is the one place where you really get to practice what we have taught you over the last three years. By the end of the semester you'll have practical experience in jury selection, opening statements, direct and cross-examination, introduction of exhibits, use of expert testimony, and closing arguments. And we'll be ending the course with a full-scale trial for which we bring in a real judge and a jury of laypeople."

Eli looked from face to face as he spoke, almost in the way he would examine jurors. They represented a range of ages, races, and levels of attentiveness. This one seemed fully engaged, that one seemed distracted, this one nodded a little too eagerly.

He passed out white index cards. "I want you to write down the personality traits you believe you have that will help you be a successful trial attorney. When you're done, put it in your pocket or purse. When class is over, I want you to check what you wrote to see if your self-image matches up with what we do tonight. I'll give you two minutes to write your traits down."

As they bent over their index cards, he wondered what traits Mia Quinn brought to her job as a prosecutor. Forthrightness, he guessed. Intelligence. Compassion.

And for himself? He was methodical and stubborn. Maybe those were great traits for a public defense attorney. But maybe not so good for his personal life. He needed to act on his gut more.

When they were finished, Eli said, "Now, when you think of the typical trial attorney, you might imagine some silver-haired, silver-tongued guy in a fancy suit who can quote you the law chapter and verse. But in point of fact, there are a hundred different ways to be an excellent attorney. I want you to pair up with someone you don't know well. One of you will be the presenter, the other the subject. The presenter's job is to interview the subject and figure out what personality traits he or she has that will bring them success in the courtroom. You need to uncover facts, examples, and stories, because the rest of the class is going to be sitting in the jury box. It's not enough to say that Susan relates well to people; you need to be able to show the jury through a story that this is true.

"You'll have five minutes to make your presentation. There are only two rules. One is to both address the jury and examine the witness—in this case, the subject. And the other is to make it interesting."

Interesting, Eli thought as the students began to pair up. Well, if there's one thing his life was right now, it was interesting. And he found himself wondering if the presence of Mia Quinn might make it even more interesting.

Eli was walking back to his car when he heard a commotion at the other end of the parking lot. A woman was shouting, "Get away from me. Get away!"

And he knew that voice.

CHAPTER 29

"Are you okay?" Eli asked Mia between ragged gasps of breath. She had heard him yell out, "I'm coming!" before he had sprinted across the parking lot to her. Now he leaned over and put his hands on his knees, but his eyes never left Mia's face.

"I'm fine," she said, and then burst into tears as the reality of what had just happened—or almost happened—hit her.

He snapped straight up and put one hand on her shoulder. "Did he hurt you?"

"No, no. He was just following me. At first I thought I was imagining it, but he kept walking faster and faster. That's when I realized I was really in trouble." She had turned and yelled at the man to go away. He hadn't done that, but had stopped about fifty feet from her, standing in a pool of shadow. The night had been quiet except for the sounds of his harsh breathing. Then Eli had shouted from the far parking lot. After a second's hesitation the man had turned and run the other way.

"We should report this to security," Eli said decisively.

"And tell them what? Some guy in a baseball cap and hoodie was following me? That's how half the kids on this campus dress. I didn't hear his voice or even see his face." She would make a terrible witness. She hadn't noticed the colors of his clothes or any logos. She had noticed nothing. It was like part of her had shut down when she realized she was in danger.

"What do you think he wanted?"

"Probably my purse." At least Mia hoped it was that.

"You'd make a better target than most of these girls," Eli said thoughtfully. "They probably don't have much cash, let alone credit cards."

Eli looked surprised when Mia started laughing.

The next day Mia stood beside Charlie in front of the gray two-story Dutch Colonial that belonged to Vincent Riester, a.k.a. Tall, Dark, and Handsome. All of his e-mails to Colleen, no matter what time of day, had come from the same IP address, which matched up with Vincent's home address. Mia and Charlie had decided it would be better to show up unannounced.

In the car on the way over they had argued over suspects. Charlie favored Gina and wanted to take a closer look at Violet. Mia didn't feel either woman could have done it. She still thought it was likely either a disgruntled defendant or someone connected with Second Amendment Seattle. About the only thing she and Charlie had agreed on was that it was simply too convoluted to think that a gun control advocate had murdered one of their own.

Foregoing the bell, Charlie knocked three times on the heavy wooden door.

Footsteps echoed across a hardwood floor. Then a blue eye stared out at them through the peephole.

"Vincent Riester?" When there was no answer, Charlie held up his ID. "Seattle Police. We'd like to talk to you."

After a long moment, a lock turned and the door swung back.

Mia let out an involuntary gasp.

The man in front of them barely looked human. His face could have belonged to an alien or a monster. His left eye was an empty red slant of flesh. The tip of his nose was missing, revealing two dark tunnels. The scars from skin grafts crisscrossed his face like lines on a map. His odd, flesh-colored lips appeared to be melting off his face.

"A fire?" Charlie asked in a conversational tone. He appeared completely unruffled.

The other man nodded. "Three years ago a drunk driver hit the car I was in and crushed it against a building. I was trapped. Then the car caught on fire."

Mia shuddered. What had it been like to be unable to move away from the flames?

"I've had thirty-seven surgeries," he continued, "but all the king's horses and all the king's men can't put Vincent Riester back together again."

His words were clear, so the damage hadn't gotten deep enough to damage his tongue or teeth. Mia wondered, a little giddy with horror, if it could be termed cosmetic, but then she caught sight of his hands. His right arm was now nothing but a stub ending midway between his elbow and nonexistent wrist, and his left hand was missing the tips of the ring and pinky fingers.

It was this hand that he held out. "And yes, I'm Vincent Riester."

"Charlie Carlson," Charlie said, shaking it. "And this is Mia Quinn." She pressed his fingers awkwardly and then released them. "Can we come in?"

"Of course." Stepping back, Riester opened the door wider. The living room was decorated with heavy oak furniture and old brass floor lamps. One long wall held built-in bookshelves that stretched from floor to ceiling. Even with that much space, books were still stacked sideways and layered on top of rows. In the background classical music played softly. Mia thought it was Rachmaninoff.

Like Darin Dane's house, here all the blinds and curtains were closed. Was it to keep the outside world from seeing Riester—or him from observing their reaction when they did? Mia's skin was hot with shame at her unmuffled gasp.

"So what is this regarding?" Riester asked as they sat down. If he was anxious about their visit, his voice didn't show it.

"You're a member of eHeartMatch?" Charlie asked.

"Yes. Why?" He sounded genuinely puzzled.

"And you use the screen name Tall, Dark, and Handsome?"

"That's my real photo on the profile. What I really looked like before. And I guess I'm still tall and dark." His voice held a little more bite.

"We want to talk to you about a woman named Colleen Miller. You may have known her as Irish Red."

"'Known her'?" Riester echoed, his voice sharpening, and it seemed to Mia that some of his carefully maintained composure crumbled. "Why are you using the past tense? What's happened? Is something wrong with Colleen?"

His concern sounded genuine, but his face was so scarred and stretched there was no way to read his expressions. But Mia realized she could still observe how he positioned his body, how he moved, whether his gestures matched his words or seemed out of sync.

Right now Riester was facing them head-on, without turning away or slumping, as people who were lying or planning on lying might. He wasn't leaning back in an unconscious effort to put more distance between them. As she watched, he crossed his arms over his belly, his hand and his stub pressed against his sides. That could indicate defensiveness but could also be self-soothing, filling an unconscious need to give himself a hug. Or maybe, Mia thought, mocking herself for overanalyzing, Riester was in the habit of tucking what remained of his hands out of sight so that he didn't have to endure stares like hers.

While she was thinking this, Charlie said bluntly, "Colleen's been found dead."

Riester flinched as if Charlie had stuck him. "Dead? Colleen?"

"Yes."

He let his head drop and put his hand over his eyes. Finally he took a ragged breath and straightened up. "You mean she was murdered?"

Mia leaned forward. "Why do you ask that?"

A snort came out of his wreck of a nose. "You don't need to be a genius to realize that the police are only going to be asking questions if it wasn't a natural death." He pressed his pale lips together. "What happened?"

"Someone killed her Sunday night around eight o'clock at her house. She was shot through a window and died a few minutes later."

Riester closed his eyes. The three of them sat in silence for a long moment. Finally he looked back up at them with his one good eye. "Do you have any suspects?"

"Not yet," Charlie said. "But we need to ask you—where were you on Sunday evening around eight p.m.?"

"What?" His jaw dropped. "You actually think I could have killed her?"

"We're talking to a lot of people," Mia said.

"I was here. I'm always here. I don't ever go out."

"Never?" Charlie asked.

"I'm just lucky I live at this time in history. I can do pretty much everything I want on the Internet. I work on it—I'm a freelance writer. I'm actually pretty fast for a three-fourths-handed typist. On the Internet I can order groceries, watch movies, make new friends . . ."

"When was the last time you were in contact with Colleen?" Charlie asked.

"We've never actually met. Our . . . relationship was carried out solely over the Internet and the phone. We were e-mailing that night. It can't have been that long before she"—he hesitated—"died."

"We found your correspondence with her," Mia said. "You were trying to break things off. Why?"

His skin-colored lips—which Mia now realized must be the product of another skin graft—twisted. "It's been fun. It's been more than fun. But I couldn't let it go to the next level, the way Colleen wanted me to. And if she wouldn't accept that, then I had to end things. It was better for both of us."

"The next level?" Mia asked.

"She's been insisting that we meet."

"And that's a bad thing?"

"Colleen isn't the only woman I know online. But since the accident, I've only been out on a date once. It wasn't that long after it happened. The woman excused herself to go to the bathroom and never came back." Riester sucked in a breath. "I can still see with one eye. And do you know what I see? I see people's horror. Their pity. Their disgust." His gaze pierced Mia. "I saw it on your face today when I opened the door. And you know what? I feel the same way. I took all the mirrors down in the house. I shave by touch. I don't ever want to be reminded of what I look like now. Of how I'm a monster."

"But you're not a monster inside," Mia protested. Charlie cut her a look, reminding her that they were there to find Colleen's killer, not offer absolution.

"Human beings are hardwired to think certain things," Riester said. "They see a baby's snub nose and big eyes, and they think, *Ooh, how cute.* And when they see someone who looks like me, they think, *Monster.* And they are also hardwired to think that the inside matches the outside." He was quiet for a moment, and then looked at Mia with his one good eye. "I know about you from her e-mails. She said you were her friend."

"That's true." Mia wondered where he was going with this.

"Then why don't you know about me? If she really was serious about me, why didn't she tell her best friend?"

It was the same question Mia had asked herself earlier, when she had doubted her friendship with Colleen. But now Riester was drawing his own painful conclusions.

"I don't know," she said simply. "Maybe she wondered if it was real."

Mia remembered what Colleen had said about not liking what you might find when you lifted up a rock. When you worked in the legal system, it wasn't hard to find out someone's home address, even if it wasn't for a strictly law enforcement–related reason. Colleen could have grown suspicious about why Riester was pushing her away. If she had seen Riester's real face, would she still have wanted him?

"She might have reacted differently than you think." Mia spoke almost to herself.

"Okay," Riester said in an uninflected voice, "say that Colleen had really grown to love the real me, the me I still am inside. Could she have gone out with me in public and felt comfortable? Even when I wear a hooded sweatshirt and a baseball cap and sunglasses, everyone still stares. Some even point. Could she have introduced me to her friends and family and co-workers and been prepared for their reactions? She would have tried to find ways not to look at my face. And would she ever have wanted to kiss these lips? Have me touch her with this hand?" He held it up. "Online, I usually tell women that I'm a trauma surgeon and that I work crazy hours. That keeps the pressure off, for a while."

The words burst out of Mia: "Is it just a game to you?"

He regarded her calmly. "I told you I was hit by a drunk driver. But he wasn't the only person who was drunk that night. We all were. Me, my girlfriend, him. My girlfriend had decided that she was the least drunk of the two of us, so she was driving my car when we got hit. Her arm was broken, and she got some cuts and bruises, but otherwise she wasn't too badly hurt. The important thing was that she was still able to get out. But she didn't come back to help me even when I screamed at her that my leg was caught. She didn't come back even when I told her that I could see flames and begged her to help me. She didn't come back, even when I started screaming." His voice dropped to a whisper. "She just stood there and watched me burn."

CHAPTER 30

Mia couldn't get Riester's terrible story out of her head. Like she needed anything else to feel bad about, anyone else to fret over.

At least after today, Mia wouldn't have to worry about how to make the Suburban's payments. And that was a good thing, she told herself as she sat at the car dealership, signing again and again each time the notary pointed.

Sitting next to her was Craig Silverman, the man who had seen her listing on the website that paired up people who needed to get out of a lease with people who were willing to take over the car and payments. Under his bristling mustache Craig had a wide, white smile.

And he should be smiling. He was getting a good deal. Mia had just seen the paperwork Scott had originally signed, and he had paid a hefty deposit for the Suburban. That money was gone now.

Mia signed her name one last time. Craig smiled even more broadly and shook her hand. Then she handed over the two sets of car keys and fobs.

Blinking back tears, she walked out to the dealer's parking lot where her dad was waiting in the waning afternoon sunlight. She opened the door and climbed in without speaking.

"Ready to go?" he asked.

Mia managed a nod. They drove in silence for five minutes. Then Mia let out a shaky sigh.

"You okay?" Her dad shot her a concerned look. He didn't know how bad things were, but she thought he was beginning to guess.

"It's been a tough week. And tomorrow's going to be a long day. I've got two funerals to go to."

"Two? One must be for your friend Colleen, but who's the other one for?"

"Darin Dane. A boy who committed suicide after being harassed in high school."

Her dad's eyes widened. "Oh no. Is he a friend of Gabe's?"

"No, thank goodness. They're the same age, but they go to different schools. We're investigating Darin's death to see if we can charge the bullies with something."

He nodded. "What are Brooke and Gabe doing while you're at the funerals?"

"I'm taking them to Colleen's funeral, since they both knew her pretty well." Mia hadn't told her dad about how she had asked Gabe to listen to what turned out to be Colleen's last breaths. "And I'll have Gabe watch Brooke while I'm at Darin's funeral in the morning and then during Colleen's wake."

"Why don't you let me do that? In fact, I can watch Brooke all day. She's really too young to understand a funeral."

Was he judging her? "She'll be fine. And Gabe can watch her before and after."

"I want to do it. And I know it's really none of my business, Mia, but sometimes I think that since Scott died you've been too hard on the boy."

And what did her dad know about being a single parent? When he left their mom, he had also left her and Peter.

"The truth is, Dad, I was too easy on him before. Scott and I were both too easy. Gabe basically didn't have any responsibilities. If he left his homework at home, he knew I would drop it off at the school. I never asked him to help cook or clean. The only chore we consistently said he was responsible for was putting out the garbage and the recycling. And half the time I was the one who ended up taking it out to the curb. But Gabe's fourteen now. He's got to learn responsibility sometime."

At least Mia hoped he was getting better about taking responsibility. Sometimes it seemed like Gabe was just getting better at whining. At being resentful. At being secretive.

"Lately he's got this idea that he needs to be bigger," she said. "I think it's from football. He says he wants muscles." She thought of Darin, of how the other kids had picked on him. At fourteen, maybe the only important thing in your life was to fit in. "When I came home on Wednesday, he and some friends from the team had been lifting Scott's weights in the basement. That and basically eating anything that wasn't nailed down. But when I came in, one of those guys stood up, shook my hand, looked me straight in the eye, and asked me about my job." She exhaled sharply. "I have a feeling that if Gabe met some adult he didn't know, he would just stand there all slouched with his hair hanging in his eyes and barely rouse himself to say hi."

"You never know," her dad said. "Your kids are sometimes different with other people than they are with you." He took a deep breath, and she saw his hands tighten on the steering wheel. "I know I wasn't that good of a dad when you were growing up, but now I want to be around more for you, Mia."

The admission must have cost him. The dad she knew—or used to know—hadn't needed anyone, but now he seemed to need her. But this wasn't what *she* needed, her dad wanting more of her time. Not now, when she barely had time to turn around. When Mia was twelve she would have given anything to hang out with her dad. Instead she had gone weeks, even months, without seeing him.

Why did you always get what you wanted, only far too late for it to do you any good?

When she didn't say anything, her dad continued, "What I mean is, I want to help you. I know I can't make up for not having been much of a father to you, but I can do a better job at being a grandparent. Let me help out with the kids more. Or do more around the house and yard. Things Scott probably did."

Had her dad really changed? Or was he just getting older, feeling frail, feeling regrets? If he hadn't been pushed out of his old job, would he be talking like this?

"You worked hard all your life, Dad. You deserve to take it easy."

"Frankly, I'm bored." He shifted in his seat. "I've been thinking about taking a mission trip with my church down to Guatemala. They're going to build a school."

A mission trip? Dad? Now Mia really had walked through the fun-house mirror.

Somehow it seemed easier to talk to him when they were both staring at the black pavement and the cars in front of and around them. When he signaled a lane change, they turned together to check the blind spot.

Mia found herself asking, "So why did you and Mom get a divorce anyway?"

He was silent for a minute. "Looking back, it's hard to say. One thing is that we grew apart. It was my fault, I can see that now. I let it happen. I didn't like to talk about work when I was at home, and I was always at work, so what was there left to talk about?"

In his words Mia heard an echo of her relationship with Scott.

"I don't think you knew this, but things were hard with Scott before he died. I always said I would never get a divorce. Never do to my kids what you guys did to Peter and me. But when Scott and I started growing apart, I didn't know how to pull things back together. I thought if I acted like things were okay, then maybe they would be." She sighed. "Since Scott died, I've realized there was a lot he wasn't telling me. He would just drive off to his office space every day. I thought he was working, but he must have spent a lot of the time worrying. Maybe he didn't want to burden me. Maybe he thought the way we had split things up meant he couldn't ask for help. He died trying to carry everything himself. I let him down, Dad. I left him all alone." Tears closed her throat.

He reached over and squeezed her knee. "If there's anything I've learned, honey, it's that we are all imperfect. We can't change the past. We can say we're sorry, we can try to make amends, we can know that God forgives us if we ask Him, but it's really about what we can do now as we go forward."

He put his hand back on the wheel. Mia had a sudden flashback to him teaching her to drive—"hands at ten and two"—one of the few ways he had been involved in her life after the divorce.

About the only other memories she had of her dad from her teenage years were of the few times when he'd had them for the weekend and had invariably wanted help with some fix-it project. Peter, who was two years older, usually managed to get invited to a friend's house or otherwise get himself off the hook. Even though her dad always billed it as learning experience, Mia was usually reduced to being the mute helper: handing him the wrench, holding the light. She could almost hear his impatient voice in her head: *"No, right there. Can't you see where you need to point it? Oh, good grief, give it to me! It would be easier if I just did it myself. I don't know why I even asked you for help!"*

And suddenly she wondered if that was how she seemed to Gabe sometimes. Impatient. Critical.

"Just how bad are things, honey?" her dad said, interrupting her train of thought.

What could she say to him? That she was holding on by her fingernails? "Pretty bad, but I'm working on it." It would be way too embarrassing to spell out just how bad, like owning up to eating two gallons of ice cream and an entire cake by yourself. Although in this case, Scott had bought the cake and ice cream, and she had only eaten part of it. "Scott's business wasn't doing well. But instead of telling me, he just started putting everything on credit. Now I'm going to have a hard time even paying the minimums."

"Why'd he lease that big SUV, then?"

"When he got it, I think he thought things were turning around. He'd just landed this new client. Plus, he thought a big car would be safer for the kids. And he wanted to look successful. By the time his new client decided to file for bankruptcy, it must have been too late."

"You know if I had any money I'd give it to you, honey."

"Yeah, Dad, I know." She could imagine how Peter would react if their dad actually had any to give her. But it was a moot question. "We'll make it. We'll be okay. I'm just glad Frank D'Amato took me back at King County and I still have that gig as an adjunct professor."

"How are things going in catching whoever killed Colleen and that Stan guy?" her dad said as he turned onto the street where Brooke's preschool was.

"We've got more than enough suspects, but no one that's a slam dunk. Frank's been appealing to the public for help. The problem is, I don't think the public knows anything. Whoever did this is not going around running their mouth about it. These killings were planned. But what the police are getting are folks calling about their dreams or saying it's probably the neighbor they're having a beef with."

He parked and she went in to get Brooke. After Mia came back and buckled Brooke into the car seat in the back, she got into the front passenger seat and briefly rested her head on her dad's shoulder. When was the last time she had done that? Had she ever?

They made one more stop before going home, at Pagliacci's for pizza to go. That made two times in one week. Mia promised herself that soon she would start planning and shopping for real meals. But tonight they had to hurry so they could make Gabe's game. She was back to life in the fast lane as soon as she walked in the door—trying to pick up the house, sort through the mail, check the answering machine and her personal e-mail. Her dad coaxed Brooke into eating some strawberries as well as nibbling on a slice of pizza. Mia poured her a glass of milk, then reached for one of the beers she had bought at the store a week earlier.

"Want a beer, Dad?"

"I'm not drinking anymore."

Mia stood up too fast and hit her head on the ceiling of the refrigerator. She turned toward him. "Really?"

He drew an X on his chest with his index finger. "Cross my heart and hope to die."

Mia thought of what she had found in the basement underneath Scott's old ski clothes the night Colleen was killed. A bottle of whiskey. Scott had told her he had stopped drinking years ago. Well, just another thing that he hadn't quite been truthful about. Or maybe it had been true when he said it and then it had become not so true.

And today her dad was claiming to be a changed man.

But tomorrow? Why, tomorrow he might go back to being the same old dad.

CHAPTER 31

The stadium was packed. Mia turned and waved at where Brooke was sitting with her grandpa about halfway up the bleachers. The powerful lights stole the stars from the sky. It looked like the type of daylight Mia had lately been experiencing in her dreams. Surreal. Metallic. Unforgiving.

Gabe, so bulked up by his uniform and pads that he was identifiable only by his number—79—sat on the end of the bench. This was the third game his team had played, and the coach hadn't put him in once. And if Gabe wasn't playing, Mia didn't care much about what was happening on the field. She recognized one of the boys who had been at her house on Wednesday, plowing his way through a pack of opposing players like a moving mountain. As she waited for Charlie, Mia stared at the orange gravel track that outlined the field without really seeing it. The crisp air smelled of dirt and torn grass.

"The klieg lights remind me of a nighttime crime scene," Charlie said, coming up behind her. "Now all we need is a body."

Trust Charlie to paint such a peaceful picture. "Not like the football games of your youth?"

It was a guess, but by the way he flinched it seemed to have struck home.

"I was only on the team for a few games, but then we came to a mutual parting of the ways."

"I've never actually been to a football game before," Mia admitted.

Charlie did a double take. "What—did you go to an all-girls Catholic school or something?"

"Or something. I knew the only way I could afford to go to college was to work, so I worked every weekend." She looked across the field. "So have you heard anything over on the other side?" Trying to pass as a parent, Charlie was moving around on the fringes of the crowd, trying to overhear anyone talking about Darin's death.

Charlie followed her gaze. The kids from the opposing high school were no different from the kids on this side. The girls were bundled up in down jackets, wearing matching hats and scarves. Some of the boys wore just flannel shirts and jeans and pretended they weren't freezing. Everyone was chanting, clapping, yelling. No different at all, except that one side wore green and yellow and the other orange and black. Yet Mia knew that some of those kids had watched Darin being tormented and done nothing. Maybe some had done much more than that.

A shiver danced across her skin. The air had a bite to it. Winter was coming. Long dark nights with no one to hold her. And if a pipe froze or the heat went out or they had to get someplace over icy roads, it would all be on her shoulders.

Charlie spoke, pulling her back to the here and now, to a crisp fall instead of a bone-chilling winter. "I've heard Brandon's and Reece's names mentioned several times. And a couple of others—some kid named Conrad, another named Zane or Zen." Since this was Seattle, either name was possible. "But from what I'm hearing, Brandon and Reece were the ringleaders." He looked up at the stands. "I think your daughter wants you." Brooke was beckoning Mia with white-mittened hands.

"Okay. I'll see you tomorrow at the funerals. But if you hear anything really juicy before that, let me know."

She picked her way back up the stadium steps. The crowd was on its feet, clapping in rhythm and calling, "Let's go, de-fense! Let's go, de-fense!"

As soon as she found her way back to her daughter's side, Brooke asked, "Can we go to the snack stand?" She had picked at her pizza and strawberries, but her appetite had returned at the thought of snacks.

Mia realized she could say no. She could lecture. If she were a really good mom, she would now pull a healthy snack from her purse. Instead she said, "Sure."

Brooke turned around. "Hold our seats, okay, Grampa?"

"Will do, honey." He smiled and patted the top of Brooke's hat, which was made of felt and looked like a cat's face. "And if they have any of those Payday bars, get me one."

The snack stand was the one place where both sides gathered. The air was redolent with the smell of hamburgers, hot dogs, and brats grilling on a smoky fire, tended by a man in a long dirty apron. But despite the mouthwatering smell, Brooke had no interest in meat. If she had her way, she would live on only white or tan food. Mia was bent over her, discussing the merits of a soft pretzel versus a muffin, when a man spoke behind her.

"Beautiful night, isn't it?"

Mia straightened up, surprised. "Eli! What are you doing here?"

"My daughter's a cheerleader. For the opposing school, I take it." Sometimes Seattle was a small town on a big scale.

When Eli had talked about his daughter needing to get away from Portland, Mia had developed a mental image of the girl, but cheerleader certainly hadn't been part of it. Now she looked at the girls dancing in front of the other team's crowd:

Patriots got the power,
Patriots got the heat,
Patriots got the spirit,
to knock you off your feet!

"Which one's yours?" she asked.

"Rachel's second from the left."

Mia glimpsed strawberry blond hair, the tip of a snub nose.

"So does your son play?" Eli turned toward the field. "What position?"

"Right now what he's playing is the bench. So far the coach hasn't put him in."

"We've still got awhile to go before the game's over."

"No, I mean this season," Mia said. "It's a sore spot for him."

Eli winced in sympathy. "And who's this kitty you have with you?"

"Oh, I'm sorry. This is my daughter, Brooke. Brooke, this is Mr. Hall."

Brooke pressed her face into Mia's thigh.

"She's a little tired."

"She looks like you." Eli half turned toward the snack stand. "What are you getting?"

"A muffin for Brooke and a Payday bar for my dad, if they have any. Maybe a cup of cocoa for me."

"I saw you eyeing those bratwurst."

They did look good—and they smelled even better. "I probably shouldn't." She had gobbled a slice of pizza at home. But only one.

"Any calories you eat in a stadium don't count," Eli said with a smile. "Hasn't anyone told you that?"

He ended up buying Mia a bratwurst and a cup of cocoa, Brooke a muffin, and her dad a Snickers, the closest thing the snack bar had to a Payday. Eli also ordered two brats for himself. After Mia thanked him, they went their separate ways. The brat plus the cocoa and the candy bar meant she had both hands full when she really needed one to guide Brooke, who was preoccupied with her muffin. But they finally made it back to their spot. Mia hoped she wasn't alienating the five people who had to keep standing every time she needed to get by.

"Here you go, Dad," she said, handing him the Snickers. "Hope that's acceptable."

"Sure." He took it from her but didn't open the wrapper. "Who was that you were talking to? Another cop?"

"No. Eli is one of the other law professors at UDub. And the rest of the time he's a public defender." Mia took a sip of her cocoa. It tasted like what it was, various artificial powders mixed with water. Clumps of powder burst between her teeth. You shouldn't be able to chew hot cocoa. That made her think of Rainy's story about Darin bringing her marshmallows.

After Mia finished her bratwurst, the rest of the game dragged. Around her, parents cheered and clapped, but many also chatted or sneaked occasional glances at a smartphone.

Brooke clambered onto Mia's lap and almost immediately fell asleep. It was technically past her bedtime, but keeping to a regular schedule had gone out the window when Scott died. Mia welcomed her warmth, savoring the contact. Since going back to work, she had had little time to just cuddle.

Her lower back ached. Her rear end was both painful and numb. Some of the other parents were smart; they had brought blankets or cushions.

"Which one's yours?" asked the mom next to her.

"That one," Mia said, pointing. "Number 79. The one on the bench."

Four minutes left, and Gabe's team was up by twelve. Mia silently begged, *Please, Coach, let him play. Let him show what he can do*. He kept clapping his hands, yelling encouragement, but she knew he was in agony.

Then the game was over and his team, victorious, stormed off the field, leaping, yelling, and bumping fists.

Stiffly, Gabe followed.

Her dad leaned over. "Tell Gabe I'm sure he'll get in next time." He pulled his keys from his pocket. "I'm going to head on home. I'll see you tomorrow."

"Okay," Mia said. She gently shook Brooke awake, and they slowly made their way down the stairs. Before Mia finished buckling her into the car seat, her daughter was asleep again.

She listened to the radio while she waited for Gabe to finish showering. After about ten minutes she turned to look for him. The parking lot was emptying out. Then she saw something that made her freeze.

A few rows back stood a man with a hoodie pulled over his baseball cap. Did he look like the man who had chased her in the university's parking lot? Her heart started to beat faster. If it was the same man, then he must be after more than her purse.

He must be after her.

She had to do something. But what? Should she honk the horn, yell at other people for help, drive away even if Gabe wasn't yet in the car?

Just as Mia's panic was reaching a peak, the man in the hoodie turned and got into a small black car and started it. She realized she had been holding her breath and let it out in a whoosh of air. She was getting paranoid. Seeing killers in every passerby.

Her heart was still beating fast when Gabe climbed in the car. "Why me?" he yelled. "I'm the only one who never goes in." He slapped the dash.

She tried not to flinch. "Do you want me to talk to the coach?"

"No! Then I'll be the kid who plays because his mom complains."

"But we need to know what the coach is thinking."

"I know what he's thinking," Gabe said shortly. "He doesn't like me."

"Gabe!" Mia turned the ignition key all the way over. It clicked, but the engine didn't catch. She tried again. The radio dwindled to nothing. She turned the key a third time.

This time there wasn't even a click.

"What's wrong?" Gabe asked.

"I don't know." Cars were Scott's area, not hers.

She pulled the release, got out, and, after some fumbling, managed to prop up the hood.

It was dark underneath. By now Gabe was looking too. Mia got the flashlight from the glove compartment, but when she turned it on, all it made was a fuzzy circle of light so small and soft it was useless.

"Is there a problem, Mia?"

She twisted her head. It was Eli, calling out to her from a small brown Honda.

"My car won't start."

He pulled his car over and got out. His daughter followed, hanging back. She wore a cropped jacket over her tiny orange cheerleading skirt. Mia said, "Gabe, this is another one of the professors,

Eli Hall, and his daughter, Rachel. Oh, and, Rachel, I'm Mia. Mia Quinn." Gabe, who was a half head shorter than Rachel, looked up at her like she was a cross between a goddess and a lioness. Rachel appeared supremely disinterested.

Eli touched a few buttons on his smartphone and turned it into a flashlight. He leaned over the engine compartment.

"Do you mind if I ask your daughter something?" Mia asked Eli.

"Go right ahead."

The girl was leaning against the Honda while Gabe made halting small talk with her. "Rachel, I was wondering, did you know Darin Dane?"

"That boy who killed himself?" When Mia nodded, Rachel said, "I'm not even sure I ever saw him. When they put his picture up at assembly it didn't look familiar at all. School hasn't been going on that long."

"How about the football team? Have you heard anything about any of the players being involved in bothering Darin?"

"There're always rumors." Her eyes slid sideways. "It's kind of cold out here. I think I'm going to get back in the car."

Well, it had been worth a try. Mia went back to Eli. They both bent over the engine compartment, which was full of shadows, recesses, protuberances, belts, and miscellaneous parts she didn't know the names of.

"What are we looking for?" she asked Eli.

He turned his head toward her but was silent for a long moment. Finally he said, "To be honest, I have no idea."

They both started to laugh. Mia lost her balance a little. For a second, Eli's lips grazed her cheek, and then she moved her head back.

It had been an accident. Hadn't it?

Charlie's voice boomed behind them. "You got a problem, Mia?" They pulled apart and straightened up. Mia's palms were sweaty. What had just happened?

"Hey, Charlie," she said, wiping her palms on her coat. "This is Eli Hall, another law professor. He's trying to help me because my car won't start."

The two men shook hands. Charlie was broader and messier-looking than Eli.

"Tell me what happened." After she did, Charlie said, "Sounds like you ran down your battery listening to the radio."

In five minutes he had his car nose to nose with hers and the two batteries hooked up. When her car started, both Eli and Charlie left her to her own devices.

On the drive home, Mia took a deep breath. "We've been hearing that the kids who were the worst to that Darin Dane were on the football team. Does anything like that happen on your team?"

"No, Mom." He snorted. "I can't believe you asked me that."

"But football is kind of a macho culture, isn't it? So there's no horseplay or roughness on the team?"

"Stop it. Stop cross-examining me."

"I'm not."

"Yes, you are. You're not accusing me, exactly, but you sound like a prosecutor. Like I'm a bad guy and you've got me on the stand. But I'm your kid." Gabe took a shaky breath and repeated more strongly, "I'm your kid."

CHAPTER 32

"In closing, let us pray," the minister said in his soft, quavery voice that probably didn't even reach to the last pew at this small chapel inside a funeral home. Mia obediently closed her eyes. She was sitting a few rows behind Darin's parents. Charlie was on the other side of the room. Jeremy, Shiloh, and Rainy were here, as well as about thirty other people, most of them adults. How long had it been since Mia had been to a service? When they were newlyweds, she and Scott had attended church regularly, but as they got busier they had fallen out of the habit. And when Scott died, she had found no comfort in their pastor's murmured platitudes.

"God our Father," the minister began, "we thank You that You have made each of us in Your own image, and given us gifts and talents with which to serve You. We thank You for Darin. We thank You for the years we shared with him, the good we saw in him, and the love we received from him. Now we ask You to give us the strength and courage to leave Darin in Your care, confident in Your promise of eternal life through Jesus Christ our Lord. Amen."

"Amen," Mia murmured and then opened her eyes. Charlie was looking at her. Correction. Charlie was staring at her. She had the feeling that he had been staring at her throughout the prayer. Had he seen Eli almost kiss her last night?

And why did she care?

"The family has asked that you join them in the lobby for some refreshments," the minister said. He looked like he was at least seventy, and from the way he had spoken about Darin during the service, Mia had gotten the feeling he had never known the boy in life.

In the small T-shaped lobby, people clustered around the food set out on a table—cheese, crackers, a vegetable platter from the supermarket, a pitcher of punch, some lumpy-looking homemade cookies. Before Mia had come here, she had gone to Colleen's house to help Violet prepare for the gathering that would take place after her mother's funeral. They had set up rented folding chairs and tables, shaken out pressed white tablecloths, and dispensed various nibbles, dips, and snacks from Trader Joe's into white serving ware, which had also been rented. Then she had driven to Darin's funeral.

Now, from a large photo propped on an easel, Darin watched his family and friends, neighbors and teachers. He was smiling without showing any teeth. The photo had the gray background that Mia associated with school portraits.

"Darin had a fantastic sense of color," said a woman with a French accent and dyed black hair. "He was phenomenal." She took a sip of the punch and made a face.

"He helped me in the library nearly every day at lunch last year," a woman wearing a black chenille cardigan said. "I should have asked why he was in the library instead of with the other kids. I just thought he liked to read." Tears began to roll down her red, blotchy face, and she snatched up a napkin.

Standing a few feet away from the adults and with their faces showing evidence of their own recent tears, Shiloh and Rainy were talking quietly to Jeremy. His suit was too small, with the pants ending above his enormous-looking shoes. On the other side of the room, Nate Dane was also wearing a suit that didn't fit, only his was too small at the waist. He pushed past Mia, his mouth twisted around an unlit cigarette. One hand was already pulling a lighter from his pocket as he went out a side door.

A second after he left, a loud voice broke through the quiet conversations.

"Hey, Jeremy, what are you doing here?" All heads turned toward the front door. Electricity shot up Mia's spine. It was Reece Jones, one of the two boys Shiloh and Rainy had said tormented Darin. Reece laughed, a showy, humorless laugh that sounded like he had practiced it.

But he hadn't practiced what happened next. Jeremy let out a roar while putting his head down and running straight toward Reece. He head-butted the other boy in the chest.

With an "Oof!" Reece landed hard on his backside as women screamed and people backed away.

Reece was up faster than Mia would have thought possible, swearing, fists jabbing the air. Jeremy swung back at him with wide, wild punches.

A man shouted, "I'm calling 911," but his words didn't seem to reach either boy.

Reece easily dodged Jeremy's blows, dancing out of range on his tiptoes. While Jeremy was nearly as tall as Reece, Reece was at least fifty pounds heavier.

"You don't belong here," Jeremy panted.

"It's a free country," Reece said, not even sounding out of breath. "I've got as much right to be here as you do. Maybe more, if you think about it."

The two boys circled each other. Tears and snot were now running down Jeremy's face, but Reece just looked intent, like he was in his element. Mia wondered if that was what he had looked like when he beat up Darin. Not angry, but nearly peaceful.

Mia moved forward with her hands up and out, as if she could calm them with a gesture.

"You were never his friend!" Jeremy yelled. "Never!"

At that moment Charlie darted in between them, his arms outstretched to keep them apart, one hand resting on each boy's chest.

"Okay," Charlie started to say, then his head snapped to one side as Reece caught him with a big roundhouse to the temple.

Mia gasped.

Charlie dropped his hands and gave his head a little shake, a strange smile lighting his face. Something about his expression scared Mia. Turning his back on Jeremy, Charlie cocked one fist and drew it back.

"That's it," Nate yelled as he burst in through the side door, a cigarette still in the corner of his mouth. "Out. Now." His chest was puffed out, his fisted hands ready, his shoulders hunched like a boxer's. "Both of you get out of here."

He shoved Reece forward so hard that he almost fell. Charlie grabbed the back of Jeremy's jacket like a mother cat picking a kitten up by the scruff of the neck. Both boys were quickly hustled outside. Before the doors closed Mia saw Jeremy, red-faced, racing down the sidewalk. But Reece wasn't in hot pursuit. Instead, he slowly sauntered away in the other direction. And he seemed to be smiling.

Mia could not wait to get him in front of the grand jury.

Two funerals in one day. Once, the summer between college and law school, Mia had gone to two weddings in one day, one in the afternoon and the other in the evening. But never two funerals. Before leaving Darin's funeral, Mia tried to talk to Charlie about what had just happened, but she couldn't find him before she had to leave. She would barely have enough time to pick up Gabe and get to Colleen's service.

At home Mia found Gabe in the middle of a wardrobe crisis while her dad looked on helplessly. She had bought Gabe a suit to wear to Scott's funeral, but in the intervening three months he must have grown.

"It doesn't fit anymore!" He looked up at her, his hair falling into his eyes. In length the pants were borderline acceptable, but the waist was another matter. Even though Gabe was tugging at either end of the waistband, there was still a gap of at least two inches between the button and the buttonhole.

"Gabe's fat!" Brooke shouted, capering around, high on the

energy buzzing through the room, even if it was negative energy. "Gabe's fat!"

Everyone ignored her. Mia had taught her kids not to use the "F word"—*fat*—or the "S word"—*stupid*—but she would deal with this lapse later. Right now she had to get them out the door and to Colleen's funeral.

"Can you still button your jacket?"

The suit jacket was tight through the biceps, but looser through the waist. Gabe buttoned it. "Yeah."

"Okay, there's a trick I used when I was pregnant." She rummaged through the junk drawer until she found a rubber band. "Loop this through your button hole and pull one end through the other." He unbuttoned his jacket and did as she said. "Okay, now take that loop and put it around your button."

"That doesn't really fix it," he complained.

After watching the scuffle at Darin's funeral, Mia's adrenaline was still running high. She bit her lip so she wouldn't yell. What did Gabe think she could do, buy him a new pair of pants in the next five minutes? "Just button your jacket and it will fix it long enough for the funeral. I'm bringing you back here after the service, so it only needs to last for an hour or so. Come on, we have to go." She hustled him out to the Toyota. The first time she turned the key in the ignition, it just clicked, but the second time it caught just fine. On her never-ending mental to-do list, Mia underlined the words *Get battery checked.*

The church parking lot was full. Mia finally found street parking two blocks away. When they arrived at the church, a little out of breath, the contrast with Darin's funeral was staggering. At least three hundred people were crowded inside. Every King County prosecutor was here, as well as cops, judges, parole officers. Mia also recognized victims and even a few people she was pretty sure had once been defendants.

When Mia had first started working for King County, Colleen had told her, "In this job you work with gangbangers, doctors, drug users, rape victims, and little old ladies. And you have to find common ground with each of them. It's compassion first and litigation second. The unsuccessful attorneys forget compassion."

Colleen had never forgotten compassion. And now all the people who had been the recipients of that kindness sat shoulder to shoulder, ready to celebrate Colleen's life and condemn her death. Scattered among them, Mia knew, were cops who were also looking for clues, looking for suspects, looking for answers. Outside, more police officers would be photographing license plates and videotaping people as they walked through the church's doors.

In the family pew Violet was sitting next to Colleen's mother, Sue. And on the other side of Violet was Martin. Just Martin. Well, it probably wouldn't do to bring your current wife to your ex-wife's funeral. Especially when she was a suspect. He had his hand on Violet's shoulder, and she was leaning into him. Whatever tension there had been between them because of the missed tuition seemed to be gone.

Katrina was sitting near the back, with some free seats next to her. "Are you saving these for anyone?" Mia asked.

"No." Katrina patted them. "Why don't you guys sit with me?"

"Thanks. Oh, and this is my son, Gabe. Gabe, this is Katrina Nowell from my office."

He reached out his hand and shook Katrina's. "It's nice to meet you." Gabe even looked her in the eye.

Dressed in his suit, he looked nearly as grown up as Zach had when Mia met him. She felt a flash of pride. Maybe he was more adult than she thought.

Mia scanned the room as an older couple she didn't recognize settled on the other side of Gabe. She sucked in her breath when she saw what seemed to be a graying Stan Slavich seated not far away. He had Stan's thick mustache, wire-framed glasses, and standard short-sleeved shirt.

Katrina leaned over, looking concerned. "What's the matter?"

"That guy"—she pointed—"looks just like Stan Slavich." The answer came to her. "It must be his older brother. I didn't meet him because I was on bed rest with Brooke when Stan was killed."

The woman sitting on the other side of Mia spoke to her husband. "Why would anyone dress like that to go a funeral?" She was staring in the direction of a man who had just entered the chapel. "It's disrespectful."

Her husband grunted. "He looks like the Unabomber."

Mia followed their stares. The man they were looking at wore the hood of a dark sweatshirt pulled over a baseball cap. She froze. That was what the man who had chased her through the university's parking lot had been wearing. And the same hoodie and baseball cap combo had been worn by the guy who had watched her while she waited for Gabe at the football game.

She looked more closely. Dark glasses obscured most of his face. But not all. The bright light of daytime revealed patches of red, scarred skin. Vincent Riester. He found a spot in a back corner of the room and leaned against the wall. She looked for the empty sleeve that should mark his missing arm. But even though it hung limp, it still had been plumped up with something. Mia imagined Vincent stuffing it with a rolled-up hand towel, something that would help him pass if a viewer wasn't looking too closely.

But Mia had been chased through UDub's parking lot the night *before* she and Charlie met Riester. Although he had already known about her because of his relationship with Colleen. If it had been Riester, then why? Did he think that Mia knew more than she did? Was he the killer? With just one hand—and a damaged one at that—it would have been difficult for him to shoot Colleen. But not impossible.

Or to shoot Mia, if it came to that.

CHAPTER 33

Mia checked her watch. She still had a few minutes before the service began. "I'll be right back," she told Katrina and Gabe, then threaded through the crowd to Charlie. Like Vincent, he was also standing in the back of the room, but on the other side of the chapel.

"What's up?" he asked.

Leaning close, she dropped her voice to a whisper. "See what Riester is wearing?"

Charlie cut his eyes to the right and then back to her. "Yeah? So?"

"Thursday night I was followed by a man dressed like that. Maybe last night too."

He pulled back to look at her. "What do you mean?"

"Thursday night after I was done teaching, a guy in a hoodie and a baseball cap followed me through the parking lot. I thought he was after my purse. When I yelled at him to go away, he took off. And last night after the football game, a guy dressed like that seemed to be watching me."

Charlie's mouth twisted. "Why didn't you say anything last night?"

"I thought it was a coincidence. Or that I was being paranoid. A baseball cap and a hoodie—that's like Seattle's version of an umbrella."

He shot a second quick glance in Riester's direction, but the other man didn't seem to be paying them any attention, just looking at the program for the service. "Did you see the guy's face either time?"

"No. He didn't get that close, it was night, and with the cap, his face was in shadow. All I can say for sure is that the guy—or it could have been guys—I saw weren't wearing dark glasses."

"I'll talk to Riester again after the service."

"Thanks." Mia touched his sleeve.

He gave her a long look. "If it was him, he must think you know something."

"I only wish I did." The organ began to play, and she returned to her seat.

"What was that about?" Katrina whispered, looking intrigued.

"I had an idea that I wanted Charlie to check out."

"About whoever did this?" Katrina nodded at the shiny wooden casket at the front of the room.

"Yes." The plain hard fact of the casket brought it home to Mia: no one was truly safe. If Colleen could be killed, so could she. Scott had asked her to stay home for two reasons. One was to be there for their kids. The other was that he felt her job was too dangerous. Until today, Mia had thought he'd been wrong to believe that.

But maybe Mia had been wrong to believe that she was safe.

If only Scott were still here, she could ask his forgiveness. Maybe if he hadn't felt so shut out he wouldn't have started drinking again, after swearing on the lives of their children that he had stopped. He would have shared the money problems with her, and together they could have found a way to solve them.

But instead he had pulled away. By the time he died, the gulf between them had seemed unbridgeable.

And now Mia had to run in place just to keep up, work longer and longer hours while her kids were either in daycare or raising themselves. But she couldn't keep pretending that it was all right, that she was coping just fine, that she had worked through her grief and anger and fear. She couldn't even make sure Gabe had clothes that fit. And what if there was something seriously wrong with Brooke?

Scott was dead, and Mia could never fix what had broken between them. And now Colleen was gone too. Her husband and her best friend.

As the service began, Mia bowed her head and wept.

"If somebody killed Colleen, and killed that guy Stan, then why are you still working there?" Gabe hissed as Mia drove home after the funeral. "Quit and go do some other kind of law. Boring law. Not prosecuting killers and crazy people and drug dealers."

After the service he had overheard enough to realize that Colleen wasn't the first King County prosecutor to have been murdered. He had stormed out to the car ahead of her, barely waiting until she had gotten behind the wheel before he started fuming.

Mia tried to speak calmly. "We don't know that the same person killed both Colleen and Stan. And we don't know that their deaths had anything to do with their jobs." She was gripping the steering wheel so hard it hurt. "Besides, I'm working with Detective Carlson. He'll make sure I stay safe." Charlie could do no such thing, but she didn't want Gabe to be consumed by fear for her. "Of course, if you ever see someone acting suspiciously or think something is wrong, call me or call 911."

"Like that would have done Colleen any good," Gabe retorted. "She was on the phone with you when she was shot."

There was no way she was going to win this argument, so Mia kept silent. Her eyes ached like fresh bruises. In the past few hours, every negative emotion had coursed through her: fear, anxiety, anger, sadness, hopelessness. Now she just felt empty, like a big hand had reached down and scooped out her heart, leaving a hollow space in her chest.

Once they got back to the house, Gabe stomped inside without saying anything. Mia walked into the family room, where her dad was watching some history show. "Where's Brooke?"

"Oh, she's taking a nap." He muted the sound. "How was the service?"

She had to press her lips together and take a deep breath before she could answer. "It was tough." How could she put into words the despair that had gripped her? "It all just started feeling so useless, Dad. I mean, I know this sounds melodramatic, but we're all just going to die. We run around and try to keep busy and try to fool ourselves, but in the end doesn't it basically all add up to nothing?" She was aware that she sounded like a teenager, some kid who had just taken his first philosophy class and felt himself enlightened, but what she was saying still felt true and real. "I mean, what's the point?"

Her dad met her gaze with unshadowed eyes. "It feels like that sometimes, doesn't it?"

She waited, but he didn't say anything more. "You're not going to talk to me about our reward being in heaven?"

"Nope."

Mia surprised herself by laughing and then plopping on the couch next to him. "I kind of wish you would. So we could have a big knock-down, drag-out fight."

"Sometimes it feels really good to yell, doesn't it?" Her dad had done plenty of yelling back in the day. "It's great stress relief, at least as long as you're not the person being yelled at." He put his arm around her.

After a moment, Mia melted against him. "It just feels so empty. *I* feel so empty."

"I don't think you can fill yourself up with big things, big concepts, big philosophies. What matters are the little things. What we do today. How we treat each other this very minute. It's how we live our ordinary days that matters. Because today is all we have." He gave her a hug. "Now go over to Colleen's and I'll hold down the fort."

In the car Mia thought about what her dad had said. *Something* had definitely changed him, because the dad she knew would never have thought about how he treated others.

At Colleen's, Mia parked across the street in front of the house with its listing For Sale sign. It looked sad and closed off, with all the blinds closed tight.

There was a much smaller group here than at the funeral, but still the house felt crowded. She said hello to Frank, who was busy shaking hands and promising that they were making progress finding Colleen's killer. She had been giving him daily briefings, so he knew exactly how much progress they were—or weren't—making, but he appeared to be in full campaign mode. She nodded at a handful of her co-workers who were looking at a series of framed watercolors that Colleen had painted a few years ago.

In the kitchen she poured herself a glass of red wine from one of the many freshly opened bottles. When she went back out into the living room, Anne gave her a sideways hug. They hadn't talked since Anne had given her the advice about keeping her heart where her shoes were.

"Doing okay?" Anne looked at her. Really looked. And for a second Mia felt less alone.

"It's not easy," she said, and decided to leave it at that.

Katrina came up carrying a plate filled with snacks. "How's the list on that flip chart of yours going?"

"It keeps getting longer, not shorter." Mia drained the last of the wine from her glass, then held it up. "If you guys will excuse me, I'm going to go get some more wine."

Back in the kitchen she poured herself another glass, her hand shaking ever so slightly. She didn't know much about wine, but this one tasted of oak and fruit. And it was making everything pleasantly distant. Making it so she could stand to think about how she would never see Colleen again, or Scott, or even Stan.

Mia snagged an unopened bag of Trader Joe's sesame seed honey cashews, an irresistible mix of sweet, salt, fat, and crunch, and then picked up an untouched bottle of wine. She slipped out the back door and went out into the side yard. She settled back against a maple tree, out of sight of the house. It was warm, nearly seventy degrees. If she didn't look up at the scarlet leaves, she might not know it was fall. If she didn't turn and look back at the house, she wouldn't know she was at the wake for her best friend. Instead, Mia alternated sips of wine with handfuls of cashews. The two flavors didn't really go together, but after a few swigs, she didn't notice it as much.

"I was wondering where you got to." Charlie stood over her. She couldn't see his expression because the sun was behind his head like a halo. Charlie an angel? She didn't think so.

"I'm still here," Mia said, trying to enunciate her words. "Still here even if no one else is."

CHAPTER 34

Mia Quinn. Tipsy. Well, Charlie supposed he couldn't blame her. What with everyone she loved being dead and all.

Taking off his jacket, he settled on the grass next to her. The ground was cool and slightly damp, but the air was warm enough to offset it. Warm enough that he could pretend summer wasn't over. Mia's short-sleeved black dress set off her golden skin. Earlier, her blond hair had been pinned up in a tight bun, but some of it must have snagged on the bark of the tree she was leaning against. Pieces now curled softly around her throat.

"I talked to Vincent," Charlie said. "He said that he was at home Thursday and Friday nights."

"Did you believe him?"

"I'm leaning that way." Which was about as good as it got for him. "I'm still gonna pull his cell site location records and look for any cameras that might have caught the guy you saw at the university or at the football game. The thing is, I can't see why Vincent would have wanted to attack you before we even talked to him. And then there's the matter of the locations. If I wanted to harm someone, the UDub parking lot after dark wouldn't be a bad place. At a high school football game, though, doesn't make much sense. Which makes me wonder if it was even the same guy, or if we're putting the wrong spin on things, seeing patterns that aren't really there."

"Don't you mean me?" Mia narrowed her eyes. "That *I'm* putting the wrong spin on things?"

"I didn't say that," Charlie said mildly, although he had thought it. "And it would be natural for you to be a bit jumpy. A lot's been going on in your life." He looked around. "Where are Gabe and Brooke?"

"My dad's watching them." She lifted the glass to her lips and took another sip. "I'm thirty-seven years old and I'm still relying on my dad to do things for me."

"Yeah, but you're also lucky that you still have him in your life and that he wants to help you out." Both of Charlie's parents had been dead for years.

"Oh yeah, Charlie, I feel lucky. Real lucky." Her eyes skewered him. "My best friend is dead and my husband is dead and I'm broke. Scott was always promising me that we would spend more time together. But it turns out the reason he was so busy was that he was juggling our finances. And then when he died, all the balls got dropped. I'm just trying to pick up the pieces."

He pointed at the bottle. "Mind if I share that with you?" Mia certainly didn't need any more.

She shrugged. "I don't have another glass."

"That's okay, I don't need one." Charlie picked the bottle off the grass and took a swig. Shifting his weight, he tugged his shirttail free, then wiped the neck before passing the bottle back to her.

Mia gave him a cockeyed smile, then raised the bottle to her own lips, forgoing her glass, and took a long swallow. *So much for keeping some of it out of her system,* Charlie thought. Now she seemed bent on competing with him. But she didn't have his leathery liver to protect her.

"And meanwhile"—she raised the bottle toward him in a mock toast—"I'm teamed up with this homicide detective who wants to go riding off like some cowboy. And I've got to keep reining him in."

"So you're saying I'm really the horse?"

"All right, I'm mixing my metaphors." She poured a handful of sesame cashews into her palm. "I'm just saying he's just not interested in doing everything by the book. Like almost getting in a fistfight with a suspect at the victim's funeral is probably not on anyone's list of proper investigative techniques."

"I was breaking up that fight, not starting it." Charlie pushed away the memory of how his vision had narrowed until all he could focus on was Reece's face. And how all he had wanted to do was see it bleed.

"And didn't you tell me you took home Stan's murder book? I'm pretty sure those aren't supposed to leave the office."

"Every homicide detective would be in trouble if we really got dinged for that."

Mia finally cut to the chase. "Okay, then what about the last time we worked together? When you screwed up my case?" Grabbing another handful of cashews, she began to chew furiously.

Charlie had wondered when she would bring this up. Before answering, he tossed a cashew in the air and caught it in his mouth. "That was a long time ago. Donny Jackson has been dead for years." Donny had died from an overdose after making a career, if you could call it that, of burglarizing small businesses. "Things have a way of taking care of themselves."

"Taking care of themselves?" Mia sat up, eyes narrowed, jaw clenched. She didn't look so soft and pretty—or even so tipsy—anymore. "What, so you thought it didn't matter that you screwed up my case, because eventually karma would take care of it?"

"Why don't you tell me what you think I did that was so awful?"

"You know what you did." She gritted her teeth and exhaled. "We knew Donny was behind the burglary of that computer repair place. We got a search warrant for his house, and we found the computers he had stolen. And then Donny said he had seen you take something, and you wouldn't say what it was, only admit that you had taken it. And of course the case was thrown out. Everyone always said you must have helped yourself to a laptop or two. If the union hadn't stood behind you, you would have been out of the force. But no, pretty soon all was forgiven and forgotten. But I never forgot." Mia spit the words at him. "When I saw you eating Colleen's candy the other day, I was reminded of that all over again. About how you never think about the consequences of your actions. You just think about yourself."

Her misplaced anger slipped past his guard. "Is that what you really believe? That I'm some petty thief no better than Donny? Okay, Mia Quinn, you want to know so badly, I'll tell you. Not that you need to know. Not that you deserve to know. When we went through Donny's house, I found the computers he'd taken in the robbery. I also found a bunch of pictures of a girl. Let's call her Liz," Charlie said, which was actually the girl's name, although she went by Elizabeth now. "You can imagine the kind of pictures they were. But since those pictures had been taken, Liz had gotten off the street and out of the life. She was respectable, and no one in her new life knew about her past. She had a responsible job at a bank, a husband, and a new baby girl. And I knew if those photos got entered into evidence, the cops would track her down, and it was possible she might lose everything. So I took them. And then when Donny said what he did, I told the truth. I said I had taken something from his home that wasn't directly related to the case. I didn't do it knowing the case would be dismissed. But I figured tomorrow was another day, and Donny was for sure gonna steal again, but that girl, when was she ever gonna get another chance?"

Mia bowed her head, put her hand over her eyes, and was silent for a long time. When she spoke, all the anger had leached from her voice. "Why didn't you tell me what was really going on?"

"I was trying to keep it a secret, Mia. The more people who know something, the less chance it will stay a secret."

Mia shook her head. "But then secrets just come back around to bite you, Charlie. Look at Scott. He thought he was protecting us by not telling me how bad things were. But he wasn't protecting us at all. He let his life insurance lapse, and he didn't tell me. He didn't tell me much of anything those last few months. He didn't have enough clients, and some of them were starting to look like they were never going to pay, but instead of talking with me about it, he just pulled away from me."

"He probably didn't want to worry you," Charlie said. "He probably hoped he could fix things and you would never know."

"I feel like the last year of our marriage was nothing but a big lie. He betrayed me in so many ways. He'd supposedly been sober for three years, and yet last weekend, when I was on the phone with Colleen, I found a bottle of whiskey hidden in the basement."

Charlie didn't point out the irony of Mia's wine bottle. "Was the seal broken?"

"What?" She wrinkled her nose. "No."

"Look, people who are alcoholics hide liquor all the time. With my second wife, I used to find bottles hidden in the back of the bathroom cabinet, in her laundry hamper, in the bag of birdseed. Just because you found a bottle doesn't mean your husband was still drinking. It might just have been one of his old backup cache bottles he'd forgotten about."

Mia's shoulders relaxed a bit. Then she must have run back over his words in her mind. "Second wife?" She raised one perfectly arched eyebrow. "How many times have you been married?"

"Three." Charlie let his head hang down a little, as if he were embarrassed. But it seemed to him that each marriage had had good reasons for beginning and good reasons for ending. Too young for the first one. They'd both been nineteen, and it had lasted five months. The second had gone three years, three years of Charlie trying to save her, and her not loving herself enough to want to be saved. The third one had foundered when she realized that Charlie's job came first and probably always would.

"Three?" A little laugh spurted from Mia. "Scott and I were together for sixteen years. Things were rocky between us this last year, but I just figured things would come back around, because they always do. But I guess you never waited long enough to know that."

"None of the divorces were my idea," Charlie said, which wasn't exactly true. He hadn't fought any of them. He would never make a woman stay if she didn't want to. He had seen what happened when a man did that.

And here Mia was acting like her relationship with Scott had been one for the ages, when just last night he was pretty sure he had caught her kissing that new public defender, Eli Somebody, under the hood of her car.

Mia picked up the wine bottle and tipped it over her glass. Only a drop came out. "Looks like it's time for a refill," she announced and stood up. Charlie caught a quick glimpse of her thighs and looked away. Maybe a little slower than he should have.

But Mia hadn't noticed. Instead she was staring at something. Something across the street. He followed her gaze.

It was the white house that was for sale. On the top floor, one of the blinds was pulled halfway up.

CHAPTER 35

"Mia? What's wrong?" Charlie asked. "Mia?" He swung his gaze back to the house across the street, the house that was for sale and obviously had been for some time. What was she seeing?

Without answering him, Mia ran through Colleen's yard to the front of her house. Charlie hurried after her until they both were standing in front of the boarded-up window, staring at the house across the street.

"When I came here this morning to help set up, the blinds were all down." Mia pointed. "Now that one's half up. And I'm pretty sure I just saw a person's face in the window." She now sounded completely sober. "Charlie, I think someone is in that house."

He turned to look at the plywood and then back up at the window across the street. If anyone had been up there Sunday night, they would have had a clear view of Colleen's murder. Then another thought occurred to him. Could whoever had killed Colleen have holed up just a few yards from where the murder had occurred?

Unbuttoning his coat, Charlie put his hand on the butt of his gun and hurried across the street. Mia followed.

"Don't come any farther," he told her as they reached the edge of the wild lawn. She started to protest, but he cut her off, keeping his voice down. He didn't have time for this. "Somebody could be lying low here. Maybe even the person who killed Colleen. Empty houses attract all kinds of bad people." Addicts broke in to steal appliances, fixtures, or any copper wire or pipes they could pry out of the walls. Vacant houses were magnets for vandalism, drug dealers, or even prostitutes looking for an out-of-the-way place to service a client.

He pointed at the sagging For Sale sign. "Call the real estate agent and ask when she last showed the house, or if anyone has permission to be inside. And if things don't add up, tell her to meet us down here ASAP to open the house. While you do that, I'm gonna call it in and check the perimeter."

Charlie notified dispatch, then went up onto the front porch, gun in his hand. He knocked on the door, then tried the handle. Locked. Holding his breath, he listened intently for the sound of footsteps or movement but heard nothing. He went back to the driveway and began to make his way around one side of the house, checking the windows as he went along. Everything was closed and locked.

But then he got to the back door. At his touch, it swung open with a faint squeal, revealing an empty kitchen with shadowy corners.

Protocol called for Charlie to back off and wait for backup. He hesitated for a second. If things got really hairy, there were probably two or three cops still at the wake, cops who could be over here in a second. Mia might even be alerting them now.

Taking his gun out of its holster, Charlie stepped inside.

"Seattle Police," he called out. His voice echoed through the empty space. The air was cool and stale. He sniffed. No stench of cat urine, which was what meth smelled like when it was being cooked. Still, his gut told him that someone had been here recently.

Was maybe even still here.

The question was, who was it? Colleen's killer? Someone mentally ill? Homeless? On the lam? Dealing drugs?

A new thought occurred to him. Had someone killed Colleen because of what she had witnessed happening in this supposedly empty house? Or had the killer decided to hide out here—hide out in plain sight—after killing Colleen for a different reason?

With his Glock leading the way, Charlie moved at a half crouch through the kitchen, past the stainless steel refrigerator and the matching range. The cupboards were too small to hold a person, so he ignored them. It was so quiet he could hear his heartbeat in his ears.

At the end of the kitchen there were doors to the left and right. Taking a deep breath, he opened the one on the left, keeping well out of the doorway. He heard nothing. He stuck first his gun and then his head past the door frame.

A laundry room. Empty, except for a washer, dryer, and utility sink.

He turned his attention to the door on the other side, which had a metal pull instead of a knob. He pulled the handle back with his free hand.

Too hard. The lightweight door banged into the wall, making him jump. His heart was hammering in his chest. The doorway framed only darkness, then his eyes adjusted and he dimly made out steps leading down to a basement. With him backlit at the top. There was a reason cops called doorways vertical coffins. Stepping back, he spotted a double light switch and flicked both of them up. One light came on over his head and another in the basement. The stairs ended in one corner, and even with the light on he couldn't see much past them. But the basement seemed as empty as the kitchen.

Holding his breath, Charlie listened for movement or even just breathing. Nothing.

Now he had a decision to make. He was in the middle of a house sandwich. There could be bad guys above him and/or bad guys below. There might even be bad guys on this floor. Whatever he did, he was taking his chances that someone from another floor might decide to ambush him.

He had been trained to start a search at the bottom of a house and then work his way up, which meant he should start in the basement. But Mia had seen a face at the window on the second floor.

His eyes caught the brass gleam of a bolt on the basement door. He closed the door, then pushed the bolt home. It wasn't much of a bolt—maybe one-third of an inch thick. But even if someone managed to shoulder or kick it open, it would make some noise before they succeeded.

Charlie still hadn't heard a sound. He moved through the small dining room on tiptoe and then into the living room, where he opened the closet door. Empty.

But then he turned back and saw a white face peering in through the windowpane on the front porch. His heart jumped. And then he realized who it was.

Mia! Hadn't she just been lecturing *him* about playing by the rules?

Gritting his teeth, he made a shooing motion, but he didn't wait to see if she obeyed. Instead he circled back to the far side of the house. Here a hallway connected two bedrooms and a small bathroom, as well as a set of stairs leading up to the second floor. Everything empty, including the closets. Everything quiet.

Standing at the bottom of the stairs, he saw the first sign that someone had been in this house since it went on the market. Someone who didn't belong here.

A silver can of Coke sat on the top step. Taking a deep breath, Charlie went up the carpeted stairs on tiptoe.

CHAPTER 36

"What's shaking, dude?" Zach said in Gabe's ear. "Ready to have some fun?"

Gabe had been getting out of his stupid funeral suit with its pregnancy rubber band when his cell phone rang. So far the day had been filled with one bad thing after another:

A. Having to wear this suit that reminded him so much of his dad's death.
B. Having the suit not fit anymore—but not because he was taller, or his biceps had bulked up, but because his gut was bigger.
C. Having to sit in a crowded, too-quiet church next to his mom while she couldn't stop crying.
D. Trying not to remember what it had been like hearing the harsh, wet-sounding breaths that had been the last sounds Colleen had ever made.
E. Learning that some crazy person in Seattle was targeting prosecutors.
F. And that, hello, his mom didn't even care.

Now Gabe told Zach, "I'm more than ready."

Three minutes later he was standing in front of Grandpa, who was in the family room watching a black-and-white documentary about World War II. Brooke was still asleep upstairs.

Grandpa tilted his head. "So your mom said you could go out with your friends?"

Gabe had this feeling like he was hovering above himself. If he said he hadn't asked her, then his grandpa might say no. Or Grandpa might call his mom, who would probably still say no.

But if he just went out for a couple of hours and then came back, his mom might not ever find out. She would probably stay a long time at Colleen's, maybe until the end so she could help clean up.

"Yeah." Gabe nodded briskly, focusing on a spot on his grandpa's forehead just above his eyes. He was fourteen. Old enough that he didn't need to check in with his mommy every minute. Young enough that he should be allowed to be a kid, at least every now and then. Since his mom went back to work, it was like he had a job too, only no one ever paid him.

"So are you in?" Zach asked. The four of them—Zach, Gabe, Rufus, and Eldon—were sitting on the steps in front of a real estate office that was closed on weekends. It was just a couple of blocks from their high school. Around his neck Zach was wearing a blue bandanna, which looked a little weird.

"In for what?" Gabe asked. Rufus and Eldon looked at each other.

Zach punched him in the arm. "You know. The fun."

"Sure." Gabe felt the first brush of uneasiness.

"Good. I'll alert the troops." Zach pulled out his phone and began to send a series of texts. Gabe tried to follow what he was typing with his thumbs, but it was too fast. And the screen was upside down, so he couldn't read it.

"Your T-shirt's tight, dude," Rufus said, pointing.

Gabe looked down at his chest. "My friend Sadie made it for me last year." It was the one his mom hated, with the impossibly cute kitten and the words *I hate everyone*. She said it sent the wrong message. Which was one reason he had pulled it on as soon as he heard her car back out of the driveway.

"I've seen that girl around. She's hot," Eldon offered. "Even if she is just a freshman."

Gabe shrugged. He and Sadie had known each other since kindergarten, and for Gabe there was no mystery.

Instead he said, "What about that blond cheerleader, the one with the curly hair? She's all kinds of sexy. Ellie Something." Gabe wanted to find out her last name so he could Facebook-stalk her.

"Wallace, I think." Rufus rolled his big head around as if his thick neck was tired of holding it up. His baseball cap started to fall off, but he caught it in time.

Zach was still typing. Surreptitiously Gabe looked from him to Rufus to Eldon. The other three guys looked more like men, with muscled chests and thick arms, and here Gabe was wearing a T-shirt he'd gotten in eighth grade. And it was still loose across his skinny chest and arms, despite the peanut butter sandwiches and the cans of tuna and the protein drinks and the reps and everything else he was doing.

Yesterday Gabe had bought three magazines on weight lifting. The guys on the covers were oiled and tan, and it looked like someone had stuffed whole plucked chickens under the orange skin of their thighs. Although Zach, Eldon, and even Rufus looked nothing like the men in those magazines, they could still lift way more weight than he could. And Coach Harper played all three of them regularly. Gabe was beginning to wonder if he would ever get off the bench.

Zach slid his phone back into his pocket.

"So exactly what is it we're going to do?" Gabe asked.

"You know what a flash mob is?" Zach's eyes were bright.

Gabe thought of stuff he'd seen on YouTube. "You mean like when those groups of people suddenly start singing or dancing?" He'd seen videos of people at a shopping mall singing Handel's *Messiah*, and pedestrians on a city sidewalk suddenly breaking into the dance from *Thriller*.

"That's one kind, right," Rufus said with a grin that made him look like he had a secret.

Gabe hoped they wouldn't make him do something he couldn't, like break-dance or sing in a high-pitched voice. If it was a bunch of people doing the same thing at the same time, he could probably manage that.

"Just follow our lead," Zach said.

In the next five minutes a dozen more kids gathered on the steps. They nodded, and a few said "hey," but nothing more than that. All guys except for two girls. A couple were from the football team. Gabe thought he'd seen most of the rest at school, but he wasn't sure. He saw another guy with a bandanna around his neck, which again struck him as weird. His stomach was starting to feel queasy.

"Okay," Zach said, getting to his feet. "Let's go."

All of a sudden Gabe got the reason for the bandannas, as Zach and the other dude pulled theirs up over their noses. Other kids tugged down the bills of their hats or pulled up sweatshirt hoods. And then the mass of people moved across the street as one.

Gabe was reminded of ants or bees. Wasps. Using their hive mind, making a single decision. Only instead of stinging someone to death, he realized, with growing horror, they were about to swarm the convenience store across the street. The Sunshine Mart wasn't part of any chain, just one of those stores with some Asian guy behind the counter. One of those stores that catered to people who bought snacks and cigarettes and the occasional half gallon of milk two days away from its expiration date.

They poured inside and began to stream up and down the aisles. Just before Gabe walked in the door, he ducked his chin and pulled his T-shirt over his mouth and nose. He didn't like what he thought was about to happen, but even more than that, he didn't want to get caught. At some signal that he must have missed, the other kids began to laugh and whoop, snatching and grabbing what they could. A bag of Cheetos fell to the floor, and then someone stepped on it with a loud *pop* and an explosion of orange powder. Ahead of him, some dude was laughing as if it was all really funny.

Gabe met the eyes of a guy on the other side of the aisle and saw that he didn't look like he was having a good time. He looked terrified. And then Gabe realized he was looking into a strip of mirror, mounted at the top of the shelf and running the length of the aisle.

He was looking at himself.

A girl skipped past him with a giant bag of Cool Ranch Doritos clutched to her chest. She wore a green hat shaped like a frog. Brooke had a hat like that, but it was a cat hat. She called it her Cat in the Hat hat.

Gabe's mind was filled with nonsense and his hands were empty.

The store owner had his own hands in the air and was yelling, "Stop! Stop!" while he turned in circles, shaking his head in disbelief. A tiny woman that Gabe assumed was his wife grabbed the back of his green polo shirt and pulled him back behind the counter.

They were afraid of the kids. Of what they could do.

But Gabe didn't feel powerful.

He felt scared.

Zach tossed him a Mars bar and he caught it. He didn't even like Mars bars. He stared at it for a long moment and then let it drop on a shelf that still held a few Hostess pies. An arm reached around from behind him and grabbed the candy bar and the pies. In the distance sirens began to wail. Kids grabbed up more things, then pushed and ran. Gabe followed.

In less than ninety seconds it was all over. Gabe looked behind him as he ran out the door. The shelves were stripped bare of candy bars, jerky, and bags of chips.

He sprinted outside and around the corner. His teeth were chattering even though it was warm outside.

What had he just done?

CHAPTER 37

It wasn't even the well-loved stuffed brown bear that broke Mia's heart. Instead it was the algebra textbook.

The textbook lay next to the sleeping bag in the master bedroom of the supposedly empty house across the street from Colleen's. The carpet still had dents marking where a bed, a dresser, and two night tables had once stood. But now there was just this twisted blue sleeping bag and a teddy bear with patches of missing fur. Two white plastic garbage bags lay like deflated balloons next to the clothes that had filled them until the officers had emptied them out, looking for weapons or drugs and finding nothing. A fat pink candle and a box of matches rested on a metal pie tin. Next to a box of saltines sat an open jar of peanut butter that still held a spoon.

This poor girl had been eating peanut butter and crackers, while across the street people snacked on stuffed mushroom caps, mini quiches, and pot stickers. Not to mention sesame seed honey cashews.

Charlie had finally allowed Mia upstairs after they had determined whoever was living in the house must have left in a hurry, probably after Mia had spotted the face in the window. The other officers had left once they realized the house was unoccupied.

"Judging by the clothes, whoever is squatting here is a girl," Mia observed now. "Who did Violet say used to live here?"

"A mom with two kids," Charlie answered. "I'm wondering if one of them never left." He picked up the textbook and flipped through it.

In the bathroom Mia found a toothbrush and paste, a towel, a washcloth, and a scrap of soap. In the shower stall, plastic hangers held clothes that had been hung up to dry. She touched a sleeve. Still damp. The lights didn't come on when she flipped the switch, but when she tried the faucet, a stream of cold water ran out.

The adrenaline that had surged through her when she realized the blinds had been raised seemed to have flushed the wine from her system. She felt completely alert. And embarrassed by how she had chattered away to Charlie.

"It must get awfully cold and dark," she said, walking back into the bedroom, which smelled dusty and slightly sour. "I wonder how long she's been living here."

"Do you remember how long the house has been for sale?"

"Since sometime this summer. But I guess that doesn't mean she's lived here that whole time. I guess it doesn't even have to be the same girl who used to live here. It could be just someone who was looking for a safe place to live."

"No sign of forced entry, though," Charlie pointed out. "Which means she probably has a key."

Mia went to the window. It directly overlooked Colleen's yard, and the plywood tacked over the shattered basement window. "From here she would have had a clear view of Colleen when she was shot."

Charlie joined her. "But why would she be looking out the window at night? It's an interesting theory, Mia, but I don't think it's likely that she saw anything."

"Even if she didn't see anything, the poor thing's got to be pretty freaked out. First she's been trying to hide from everyone and keep it a secret that she's living in a supposedly empty house. And now she's got to worry that there's a murderer loose in the neighborhood."

"Hello?" a woman's voice called from downstairs. "Hello?"

Charlie went to the head of the stairs. "Yes?"

"It's Linda Langston," the woman called up. "The real estate agent."

"Come on up."

The real estate agent was tall and thin and dressed in a navy blue suit. She started shaking her head the minute she saw the girl's belongings. With the toe of one high-heeled pump she nudged the teddy bear. Her lip curled back as if it were roadkill.

Mia's stomach cramped as she wondered how much further she would have to fall before her own house would be foreclosed. She was still making the mortgage payments, but barely. The more she tried to untangle the mess Scott had left, the more she wondered how long she could keep juggling everything. In another few months, would Linda Langston be demanding her keys, impatiently tapping her high-heeled foot, while all of their worldly possessions sat inside a U-Haul truck in the driveway?

"I called a locksmith to come out and change the locks." She made an exasperated noise. "That woman swore she had given me all the keys when the bank took possession. Obviously she was lying." Picking up one of the garbage bags, she shoved the bear inside and then grabbed a handful of clothes.

"Hold on a minute," Charlie said. "What are you doing?"

"Well, I certainly can't show the house when it looks like a homeless encampment. It's going to be hard enough attracting buyers when someone was murdered across the street."

"I can only imagine," he said drily.

"With Google, there're no secrets anymore." She pursed her lips in disapproval.

"What are you going to do with the girl's things?" Mia asked.

"Do with them? I'm going to throw all of this out." She leaned over to grab the textbook.

"I'll take care of it." Mia grabbed the textbook and the bag from the other woman's hands. She tried to imagine Gabe alone, homeless, living in an empty house with nothing but peanut butter and crackers to fill his stomach. And yet this girl was still making it a priority to go to school.

The real estate agent shrugged, clearly unmoved. Maybe with today's down market, you had to harden your heart. If the girl was over eighteen she could be charged with illegal entry, but Mia wasn't going to mention that possibility if the other woman didn't bring it up. And if she was under eighteen, once they found her she would go to a foster home until her mother could be located to pick her up.

Charlie helped Mia bring the girl's belongings downstairs. While they were carrying them to her car, Violet came outside to meet them.

"So you didn't find anybody?" Violet asked.

"No." Mia shifted the bundles so she could press the button to unlock the car's trunk. "But judging by the belongings she left behind, it looks like it was a high school girl. I think she saw me notice her and took off."

"If she could see you looking up at her from our yard, do you think she saw what happened to my mom?"

Mia didn't want to raise false hope. "It's a long shot, but that's why we want to talk to her." Leaning in, she set the bag next to her spare tire.

Violet shivered and crossed her arms. "It would suck to be a girl on the streets alone."

"Assuming this was the kid of your old neighbor, what's her name?" Charlie asked.

"Veronica Slate. But she went by Ronni. I heard the family moved out to eastern Washington to live with her mom's brother. It sounded like it was going to be pretty crowded. Maybe that's why Ronni decided to stay here."

"Do you know the uncle's last name?" Charlie added the sleeping bag and the second bag full of clothes to the car trunk.

Violet shook her head. "Sorry. All I know is that Ronni was going to be a senior this year. She was always asking me questions about college."

"We found a math textbook." Mia closed the trunk. "So maybe she's still taking classes."

Charlie said, "On Monday I'll go to the high school, see if they have anyone registered as living here. Maybe she'll even be in school. And if she's not, once we figure out for sure who she is, we'll put out a BOLO on her." BOLO stood for "be on the lookout."

"Can't you have someone watching the house to see if she comes back?" Violet asked.

Charlie shook his head. "We can't put someone here 24-7. After all, if Ronni sees the cops, she's not gonna come back. I'll ask for some random patrols, but even still, the real estate agent is changing the locks, so she wouldn't be able to get back in unless she broke in."

"Which she might be tempted to do," Mia said, thinking out loud. "After all, what's in my trunk is probably everything she owns in the world. Call us if you see her, Violet. And I'm going to tuck one of my cards into the back door with a note on the back saying I have her stuff and that I can help her."

"Can you?" Violet asked. "Help her?"

"Well," Mia said, realizing how little she could actually do, "I could try."

"Won't she just end up in foster care or out in eastern Washington?"

"That's still better than being homeless," Charlie said.

Violet didn't look convinced. "Ronni didn't think so."

"There aren't a lot of alternatives." As she pressed the lock button on her fob, Mia realized that the street was now empty of cars. While they had been busy searching the house, the wake must have broken up. "Hey, Violet, can I help you clean up?"

"It's mostly just folding up the chairs and tables," Violet said. "And loading the dishwasher."

"Loading the dishwasher?" Charlie echoed. "Why didn't you say so? That's my favorite thing to do in the whole world!"

Suppressing a smile, Mia walked with Charlie and Violet across the street.

The next morning Mia woke up craving French toast. It had been Scott's favorite breakfast. The last time she made it, though, had been months before he died. But today the guilt didn't weigh on her as much. She remembered what her dad had said. She couldn't change what she had done. She couldn't change anything about the past. All she could do was do better in the future.

She went downstairs and mixed eggs, vanilla, and a dash of cinnamon in a shallow dish, and started melting butter in a pan.

"That smells good," Gabe said as he came into the kitchen. He leaned in the doorway, looking like he wanted to say something more. Mia waited, but after a few seconds he dropped his gaze and began combing his hair with his fingers.

"I was thinking how much your dad liked to eat this, and I decided I should make it." Mia picked up a spatula and flipped one of the pieces. Just the perfect amount of golden brown.

Gabe took the syrup from the fridge and began to set the table.

"Did you have a good time yesterday? Dad said you went out with your friends."

"Oh, yeah, sure," Gabe said, concentrating on lining up the silverware. "How was the wake thing?"

"It was a little bit strange. When I was there we figured out that someone has been living in the foreclosed house across the street. We think it's a high school girl."

His startled eyes flashed up to hers. "Living in an empty house?"

"She had a sleeping bag and some clothes and a little bit of food. It looks as though it might be the same girl who lived there before the bank took the house."

"That's sad, Mom." Gabe's face changed. "Are we going to be okay? You know, since Dad died?"

She should never have mentioned Ronni to him. "Of course we are. I mean, I'm working now, and I wasn't before. We should be fine."

"I miss him."

"I know." Mia sighed. "I do too. And I know it's been hard on you. I've asked you to grow up so fast."

He looked away. "I don't think I've been doing a very good job of it."

"Of course you have. What are you saying?"

"Sometimes . . ." Gabe hesitated. "Sometimes I screw up."

He must be thinking of how much she had to nag him to get him to do his chores. "We all make mistakes. But you've really stepped up. You're watching Brooke after school, you're starting to pick up the house and help with dinner. You're doing a lot. You're growing up before my eyes."

Mia felt a pang of pride. She had been so worried about how Scott's death would change Gabe, but it had clearly been an overreaction. Sure, he had been faced with challenges, but he seemed to be taking them in stride. Looking at her son this morning, so polite and pleasant and humble, Mia was sure she was doing something right as a parent.

CHAPTER 38

On her way to the office kitchen to get a cup of coffee, Mia passed a conference room where a half dozen of her co-workers crowded around a monitor.

Curious, she stepped inside. Someone hit the button on the remote and started whatever they were watching over again. It was silent black-and-white footage from a security camera mounted above the door of a small convenience store.

Young people began to pour in through the door. Since the camera was looking at their backs, it took Mia a moment to figure out there was something different about their appearance. They seemed blank, anonymous, and then she realized it was because they all had their hoods pulled up or their hats pulled down. Then she saw a kid with a bandanna obscuring the lower part of his face, like he had stepped out of one of the old Western movies Mia's grandpa used to love.

She was looking at a crime.

More kids poured in. A few wore no disguises, just T-shirts pulled up over their noses. And one or two were even barefaced, as if their sheer number made them invisible. At first they just milled through the aisles, their fast strides and swinging arms betraying their nervous energy. Then at some sound or signal they began to snatch and grab—cans of soda, candy bars, bags of chips, packets of miniature donuts.

An Asian man came out from behind the counter with his hands raised, his mouth moving in a silent yell. The kids began to run out. Someone threw a can of soda at the man, and he ducked. One of the kids knocked into a circular card rack, which wobbled back and forth, spinning. A second kid crashed into it and it fell. The man spread his arms and tried to block the thieves from leaving, but the kids just pushed past him, sometimes shoving him. A tiny woman ran up and grabbed the back of his shirt and pulled him back behind the safety of the counter.

And then the kids were gone, leaving the floor covered with trampled cards, spilled soda, and squashed snacks.

And it had all happened in ninety seconds.

Mia was rooted to the floor. Her first, incongruous thought was, *I thought I told him not to wear that shirt.*

Gabe had been in the middle of the mob, with his *I hate everyone* T-shirt pulled up over the bottom of his face.

"That's crazy!" DeShauna said. "They were like . . . like locusts."

"It's called a flash mob," Tracy said. She worked in the Juvenile Unit. This had to be her case.

"I thought flash mobs were those people who got together in public someplace to sing or dance." DeShauna did a jazz hands motion. "Like that big group of people that got together at Westlake Park a couple of years ago and danced a routine from *Glee*."

"That's what flash mobs *used* to be." Tracy tapped the end of the remote into her open palm, reminding Mia of a cop with an old-fashioned nightstick. "People alerting each other by text or Facebook to get together to do something spontaneous and fun. Now it's more like a flash *rob*. It's gone from fun to felony."

It sounded like hyperbole. Until Mia looked at the tape, frozen on the last frame of the trashed store.

"But those are just kids on that tape," Jesse said. "Don't you remember how it was when you were a kid? One person started something, maybe dared everyone else, and you would just follow along. A crowd mentality takes over. I bet in their normal lives these kids wouldn't think of stealing."

"So you think these kids are blameless? Harmless?" Tracy asked, her jaw tight. "Three weeks ago there was another convenience store robbery just like this, only they didn't have a security camera. In that robbery, a customer was pushed to the ground and sprained her wrist. If these incidents continue, it's only a matter of time until they become violent." With one long red fingernail she pointed at the frozen image of the shop owner and his wife. "We all know what those mom-and-pop places are like. Half the time there's a baseball bat under the counter. Maybe even a shotgun. What happens when a clerk pulls that out? Or a customer tries to stop someone?"

Jesse looked torn. "I'm not saying we don't need to do something about it. But those are just kids, and people's brains don't fully develop until they are like twenty-five or something. Teens are just more into thrill-seeking and risk-taking. They simply don't recognize the consequences."

In Jesse's words Mia heard an echo of Frank's "kids will be kids" argument. But she hadn't let Darin Dane's tormentors off for that. How could she even be thinking of letting Gabe off the hook for this?

Or not off the hook exactly. But part of her was saying that she could keep this private, between her and Gabe. And she would make sure he never did anything like this again.

Tracy said, "On the East Coast they've been having a huge problem with flash mobs. They've had groups of kids who gather and then just randomly attack whoever walks by. Or they pour into high-end clothing stores and make off with stacks of expensive jeans. This"—she pointed at the screen—"is penny-ante stuff. Literally. But we need to nip it in the bud before it gets worse. We don't need kids thinking that they control the streets, making it so people are afraid to go out. This is our chance to teach these kids a lesson."

"So you don't know who they are?" Mia asked. "Nobody was caught?"

"The owner pressed a silent alarm when he realized there was a robbery in progress. A cruiser was on-site less than two minutes later, but by then they were gone." Tracy pointed at the screen again. "Luckily, the quality of this surveillance tape is very clear. We've counted at least twenty-one individuals. We're going to be working with officials from neighboring schools to see if they can help us put a name to any suspects. If we can identify the ringleaders, they are going to face some serious charges."

Tracy ran the tape again. This time Mia only had eyes for Gabe. At one moment, someone tossed him a candy bar, but then he let it fall onto a shelf. When he left the store, as far as she could tell he left empty-handed.

Could he be charged? He hadn't even stolen anything.

But then she argued with herself. He had clearly been part of the mob that terrorized the poor shop owners. He hadn't tried to stop them. He hadn't even said no and walked away. Instead he had pulled his T-shirt over his nose and walked inside.

Mia checked the time in the upper left-hand corner of the tape. It was not long after she had left for Colleen's wake.

What should she do? She had taught her kids that it was important to tell the truth, to accept the consequences of their actions.

But it would be easy to say nothing. It might not ever come out that he was part of the mob. And then she would punish him herself. Ground him for weeks. Months.

But there were so many kids in this video they were sure to catch up with some of them. And those kids would rat out the others.

Although what was she thinking? It wasn't "rat out." It was "tell the truth." It was "cooperate with law enforcement." It was what in her line of work they called a CI—confidential informant.

And if she didn't make Gabe come forward? Then Tracy might come for him first.

She went into the bathroom and splashed cold water on her face, then stared into her own eyes. Just below the left one, a tiny muscle was twitching.

Katrina came out of one of the stalls. "So did you see that video? Pretty horrifying, isn't it?"

Mia swallowed. "Yes. Yes. It was."

"Are you all right?" The other woman's face creased with concern.

"I think . . ." She forced herself to say the truth. "My son, Gabe, was one of them."

"Oh no." Katrina looked around, even though they were the only two in the bathroom. "Are you going to tell Tracy?"

"The sad part is that I thought about just keeping quiet. But it won't do him any good. The thing is—it feels like it's partly my fault."

"Just because you're his mom doesn't mean you are responsible for his behavior."

"I don't know about that." Mia took a deep breath. "Remember how I was on the phone with Colleen when she was shot?"

Katrina tilted her head. "Yeah?"

"I wanted to keep listening to see if she said anything. I also wanted to get over there as fast as I could, and I was talking to her on a landline. So I handed it to Gabe and asked him to listen in case she said anything."

"Oh no." Katrina's eyes widened. She put her hand over her heart. "And *did* Colleen say anything?"

"No. That's why I'm keeping it kind of quiet. The only thing Gabe heard was the sound of her dying. But I can't imagine how terrible that must have been. And I think it hurt him."

"Then don't tell Tracy," Katrina said decisively. "It's not worth ruining his life. Certainly not over a bag of chips or whatever."

"But even if I don't say anything, it will still come out." Mia could feel the muscle twitching faster. "They're going to figure out who is on that video."

"Then you should talk to her. Nip it in the bud before it gets any worse."

Mia nodded, but she couldn't help thinking that it might well get worse no matter what she did.

CHAPTER 39

Online in the Mystical Realms of Everland, Ophelia wasn't Ophelia Moyer, but Eric the Mage, an elf wizard who had amassed a fortune in griffin's gold with his famed Worstalk, the magic wand that could both save and destroy.

And Jonas Carvel was Mercenweaver, a cyclops who possessed a mirror shield that could reflect back any spell onto the person casting it.

Ophelia didn't know about Jonas, but there were many days when she would have preferred being Eric the Mage to being Ophelia.

Eric the Mage and Mercenweaver had begun a tentative friendship, still online but not within the main arena of the game. Gradually they talked a little bit about their real lives and the parallels they shared. Both of them worked daily with crimes, he with computers at the King County District Attorney's Office, she as a Portland private investigator who specialized in solving crimes against women.

A few weeks ago Ophelia had slipped and revealed that she was actually a girl, an idea that seemed to fascinate Jonas.

When Jonas's name showed up in a chat bubble a few days ago, Ophelia almost clicked the X to close it. But then she read that he was seeking her help—not as Eric the Mage, but as a PI. A woman he worked with had been murdered, and he was trying to figure out if her death was related to the earlier murder of another co-worker. So far, his search of the office's database had come up with nothing.

The problem sounded interesting. Ophelia had long wielded her magic, not just in Everland, but also with the Dow Jones. Her uncanny ability to see patterns had made her rich—in money, at least. It had also given her the ability to take on cases solely on the basis of whether they piqued her interest. She told Jonas she would drive up the next day to see if she could help deduce the answer. Just after lunch she met him outside the King County Courthouse.

Jonas turned out not to look anything like his avatar, other than that they were both blond. On the computer his alter ego, Mercenweaver, had biceps as big as barrels and high, chiseled cheekbones. Jonas was altogether softer and rounder, without a single hard edge.

The look he gave her made it clear he was not at all disappointed that she bore no resemblance to Eric the Mage, with his pointed ears and velvet robes. Objectively, Ophelia didn't believe she was attractive. Yes, she was height-weight proportionate and her face was symmetrical, but those qualities weren't unusual. She had blond hair, but it was what was known as dishwater blond.

At the main desk Jonas flashed his ID at the security guard. Ophelia had to show her driver's license and sign her name. "Folks in your office are sure working long hours these days," the guard said to Jonas as they went through the metal detector. "People are even coming in on weekends."

"We're trying to figure out who killed Colleen Miller," Jonas said, straightening his shoulders. To Ophelia, he seemed to be placing himself in the center of the investigation.

He led her down the hall to what he had called his office, but turned out to be a cubicle. He sat in front of his computer while she leaned down to look over his shoulder.

"I was asked to look for any defendants that Colleen Miller and Stan Slavich had in common," he said. "I wrote the program so that it checked for misspellings, as well as common nicknames."

She guessed he was looking for approval, so she nodded. But she was really focused on the code on his screen.

"I also checked for defendants who had connections to the same groups, like the Mob or neo-Nazis. The thinking was that Stan and Colleen had both prosecuted the same defendant or group, which resulted in revenge killings. But I only came up with a handful of matches, and they're either dead or seem unlikely to be behind this."

"Well, that's where you probably made your mistake," Ophelia said. "Do you mind if I . . . ?" She leaned into his space until he got the hint, got up, and gave her his seat.

Regular people—or neurotypicals, as they were called on the websites Ophelia liked to visit—craved variety. They thought two hundred flavors of ice cream were better than two. They would happily buy something that served the same purpose as an item they already owned, just because it differed in some nonessential way, such as color.

But when it came to computers and databases and information, neurotypicals wanted everything simplified and dumbed down. Ophelia could wear the same thing every day, just as long as it was more or less clean, but when it came to data, the trick was to throw your focus as wide as possible. The people who had asked Jonas to search had done the opposite.

"The program needs to be rewritten to check all the variables. Maybe it's not the same defendant," she said, as her fingers flew over the keyboard. "Maybe it's the same witness. Or the same judge. You had all these factors to work with, but you limited yourself to just one."

Two hours later Ophelia found a hint. And the more she looked, the more she found.

It wasn't the same defendant. It wasn't even the same judge or the same witness.

Jonas brought Ophelia in to meet Mia Quinn, the prosecutor working on the murdered woman's case, and Charlie Carlson, the homicide detective. Mia had to borrow an extra chair from a co-worker's office before the four of them could sit around her small round table.

They hadn't even sat down when Jonas burst out with the answer. "It was the same victim."

"The same victim?" Charlie echoed.

"Let me explain," Ophelia said. "I widened the search to look for anything the cases of Colleen Miller and Stan Slavich had in common. Not just the defendant. Anything. Witnesses, judges, charges. There was a lot of overlap, as you can imagine. But eventually this is what I—we"—she corrected herself, mindful that this was important to Jonas—"found. Stan Slavich and Colleen Miller both prosecuted murder cases involving the same victim."

"So there were co-defendants with separate trials?" Mia asked.

"No." The words crowded into Ophelia's brain. She resisted the urge to jiggle her leg. Recently she had learned that this behavior was distracting to others. "Two men charged with the same crime, but the first one was actually innocent. Five years and seven months ago, six-year-old Laura Lynn Childers was found in a park two blocks from her home. Beaten to death. Probably sexually assaulted. Nearly five years ago Stan Slavich prosecuted the girl's neighbor, eighteen-year-old William—Willy—Mercer for the crime."

A kid who had dropped out of school in ninth grade, Willy had been considered a weird loner. Ophelia's mouth had twisted when she read that. If you didn't fit in, if you weren't in lockstep, then neurotypicals thought there was something wrong with you.

"No DNA evidence linked him to the crime. All they had to go on was a single witness ID. At night. A block away. But that witness picked Willy out of a lineup." Ophelia gave in to the need to lecture. Her college professors hadn't appreciated her tendency to answer other students' questions before they could. For Ophelia, information could be like a fire hose. Once she opened it, it sprayed out full force. "However, one problem with a lineup is that if the witness doesn't see the person who was actually there, they will still pick the person who looks most like him. Another is that the cop in charge of this lineup had had a past run-in with Willy, when Willy was charged with being a Peeping Tom. His parents always claimed he had been drawn to the Christmas lights on a tree, but the home owner was convinced that he had been peeping at her. While that case was ultimately dismissed, it still left room for bias when Willy was put into the lineup."

Ophelia bit her lip so she would stop lecturing, wouldn't point out that the gold standard was a double-blind lineup, one where the detective conducting the lineup didn't know who the suspect was or where they were in the lineup so they couldn't even inadvertently suggest who it was through a micro-expression, tone of voice, or even the way he held his body.

"After his arrest, Willy was interviewed for nearly twelve hours. During that time he did not request a lawyer. He asked several times if he could go home, but the police convinced him he needed to stay to help them."

Neurotypicals were hardwired to want answers, to see patterns even if they didn't really exist. But in many cases, evidence never pointed in one direction. There was no clear pattern, no obvious answer. Ophelia was sure that the cops had been convinced that they were right about Willy. Once they believed he was guilty, then they had only recognized evidence that served to confirm this unconscious bias. Evidence that didn't had been discarded—again unconsciously.

Sometimes people missed details because they weren't paying attention, but sometimes it was because they were concentrating too hard on something else. In a Harvard experiment that Ophelia found fascinating, neurotypical participants had watched a video of people dressed in either black or white passing a basketball. The subjects were told to count the number of passes made by players in white. During the test, a woman wearing a gorilla suit strolled through the players. About half the people who took the test never even noticed her.

Ophelia had spotted the woman in the gorilla suit the moment she stepped onto the court.

"Look," Mia said, "you know that in the majority of cases, there's no DNA. There are no fingerprints. In the real world, the bad guy wears gloves and throws the gun in a river. Yet justice demands that all crimes be prosecuted, not just the easy ones."

"Does it?" Ophelia asked. "Should Willy really have been charged with kidnapping, rape, and murder if the only evidence linking him to the crime was a single witness?"

"But if there was nothing to contradict the ID, then you could argue that justice for the victim, her family, and the community demanded that Willy be charged," Mia said. "And I remember a little bit about that case. Didn't Willy confess?"

Ophelia's mouth twisted. "If you can call it that."

Questioned by people who were already half convinced of his guilt, Willy had finally agreed that he must have done it, that he must have gotten angry with Laura Lynn and hurt her without meaning to. One of the officers had hinted that it would all be over if Willy simply agreed. That they could let him go home.

So Willy had said yes. And then obligingly added details. But to an impartial observer, it was clear that the details he used were the same ones the police had inadvertently supplied to him during the long hours of questioning.

"You said Colleen also prosecuted someone for this girl's murder," Charlie said. "How is that possible?"

"Two years ago Laura Lynn's mother divorced her second husband, the girl's stepfather, and came forward with new evidence implicating him. Colleen then prosecuted him for the same crime Willy had already been convicted of. He's now serving a life sentence."

Mia's mouth opened. "Wait. What happened to Willy?"

"He's dead." Ophelia didn't try to sugarcoat it. In prison, a chi-mo—slang for child molester—was the lowest of the low. "Three weeks after he went to prison he was killed in the yard by a lifer. And less than two days after Willy died, Stan Slavich was murdered."

"Why didn't anyone figure that out back then?" Charlie asked.

"At the time no one realized Willy had been wrongfully convicted. They also limited themselves by looking at people who had recently gotten out of prison." Ophelia pushed her fingernails into her palm so she wouldn't blurt out that the error was not that different from the one they had made. They both stemmed from looking at a limited data set.

She reminded herself that it was now their turn to talk. Neurotypicals had so many unspoken rules. You weren't supposed to monopolize the conversation. You weren't supposed to stand too close. You weren't supposed to stare. Ophelia worried she might have violated all of those since she entered this room. You also weren't supposed to talk about death, sex, blood, or anything that happened in the bathroom. Taboos made no logical sense, but neurotypicals were oddly sensitive to them.

"We've got to take a look at Willy's friends and relatives," Charlie said. "Maybe one of them went after Stan because they thought he was responsible for Willy's death. And then when Colleen prosecuted the real killer, they may have wondered where she was when Willy was being wrongfully convicted."

Mia pressed her palms flat on the table. "They could have even believed Colleen was part of a cover-up."

CHAPTER 40

In the hours since she had seen the videotape of the flash mob robbery, Mia had been a wreck. Useless. Her head throbbed. Her stomach roiled.

They had made a breakthrough in figuring out the link between Colleen's and Stan's murders, or at least this Ophelia woman had, but all Mia could think about was her son.

Gabe was a thief, or an almost-thief. She had thought she had raised him to stand up to peer pressure, but she had thought wrong. Instead he had gone along, joined a faceless mob bent on terrorizing some poor shop owners just because they could. Just because it was fun to snatch and grab and run away.

What other secrets was her son keeping from her? Was he skipping school? Cheating? Using drugs? Drinking, the way Scott had once and probably still had been?

Maybe the bad gene had come from Scott, the ability to lie to her face without a flicker to betray him.

Mia was still meeting with Ophelia, Jonas, and Charlie when school got out at three, but she got the meeting to wrap up as soon afterward as she could. After they were gone, she closed the door to her office and dialed Gabe's cell number with a shaking finger, not bothering to go into her contacts list. She didn't have time to work her way through menus. She had to talk to him now.

"Hello?" Gabe's voice was nearly unrecognizable, slower and deeper. He must be drunk or high or both. Who knew if he had as many football practices as he said, or if he did, that he went to them? Maybe the reason the coach hadn't been putting him in was that Gabe never attended practice.

The words poured out of Mia as if someone had breached a dike. "You are grounded immediately. I'm sure you can guess why. And I don't want to hear one word of argument from you, young man. I trusted you, Gabe. I trusted you."

There was a long pause. Mia imagined him getting ready to spit out something defiant, and the muscles in her neck and shoulders knotted up.

Instead the voice on the other end of the phone said slowly, "Who do you think you're talking to? Because I think you might have the wrong number."

It took a second to reorient herself. "Um, isn't this 206 . . ." and she reeled off the rest of Gabe's cell number.

"My number's almost the same, but it starts with 204. I'm in Winnipeg."

"Winnipeg? Like in Canada?"

His voice—a voice that Mia now clearly recognized as belonging to a full-grown man—was amused. "Yes, Canada. Best of luck to you and your Gabe, though." And he hung up.

Part of Mia knew that someday she might find this funny. In about ten years. But the rest of her was still angry. Still, she decided it would be better to confront Gabe in person, where she could watch his expressions and his body language the way she would a suspect's.

She forced herself to work until five, preparing what she would say to the grand jury the next day. Then she drove home. How would Gabe react? Anger? Annoyance? Indifference?

When she walked into the kitchen, he was pouring applesauce into a bowl while Brooke waited. She turned and cried out, "Mommy!" in a happy voice.

Gabe's face went still and watchful when he saw her walk in so early. She felt herself grow hot with anger.

"What are you doing home so early, Mom?"

Instead of answering, she bent over Brooke. "Honey, can you go into the family room and watch TV for a minute? Your brother and I need to talk."

"Okay." Brooke was too young to be curious. Instead she took the bowl of applesauce from Gabe and walked off. It was too full and she would probably spill some. Mia didn't care. Let her ruin the whole carpet. Everything was already ruined.

She turned back to Gabe. "I think you can probably guess why I came home."

He kept silent, as if there was some faint chance that if he didn't cop to it he wouldn't get in trouble. Mia had seen this type of behavior more times than she cared to count. But always from criminals. She had never expected to see it from her own son.

"Today at work I saw a videotape from the Sunshine Mart that was taken on Saturday afternoon. And I saw what you and those other kids did." She forced herself to take a breath. "What were you thinking?"

"I didn't know what they were going to do until they were doing it." Gabe fisted his hands in his hair and tugged. "And by then it was too late. What was I supposed to do?"

"You were supposed to say no. You were supposed to say no and walk away."

"I didn't even take anything."

"I saw the tape, Gabe. You were holding a candy bar."

"Yeah, but someone tossed it to me and then I just put it down. I didn't take it!"

"If the police want to make a case, it doesn't matter if you didn't actually take possession of it. If you intended to steal, it could still be third-degree theft. Among other charges. And you know what else, Gabe? You could end up costing me my job."

"You? But you didn't do anything!" His voice was full of pain. "I'm the one who messed up. Not you!"

"Yes, but once it comes out that you're my kid, they could decide it's a conflict of interest for our office to prosecute it. Then it could be assigned to a multiagency task force to investigate. You could end up dragging my name through the mud. My boss would *not* like that." Which was an understatement. Frank would be furious.

"Tell me what I can do." Gabe's voice was high-pitched. Desperate. "Tell me what I can do to make it right!"

Mia had been mulling over this ever since she saw the video. "First of all, you're grounded."

"Okay."

He nodded eagerly, but she wasn't done. She wasn't anywhere near done.

"Second of all, I'm going to expect you to go into that store and give that shop owner fifty dollars and apologize. And then you are going to have to work to earn that fifty dollars to pay me back."

"Can't I just mail it to him?" Gabe scuffed the floor with the toe of his Vans.

"No. You went there in person to cause him trouble. You can say you're sorry in person too."

Gabe took a deep breath, and she saw him steel himself. "Okay. I'll do it."

"That isn't everything, Gabe. Right now we're going down to the police department, and you're going to tell them what you did. And not only that, you are going to give them the name of every kid you know who was at that store."

"What?" He began to shake his head. "No way! Those are my friends!"

"Friends? You don't need those kinds of friends."

"But you don't understand." His voice cracked. "I do need them! These guys like me even though I'm not very good at football and I have to watch my baby sister all the time."

"Do they really like you, Gabe? Like you for you? Or do they like you because they know you'll go along with them?" He started to open his mouth, but Mia held up her hand. "Don't answer me right now. I want you to think about it. And I also want you to think about this: if you don't stand up for small things, then by the time big ones come along, you won't be strong enough to stand up for them either."

"But you want me to tell on my friends." His look was anguished.

"I'm not saying it's not going to be hard. But it's the right thing to do. And look at this logically. The police already have the video. The visuals are clear. Including images of you. That shirt pulled over your nose and mouth isn't much of a disguise. It's only a matter of time before they figure out one or two of the people who were in there. And once they have one, that person will give up the rest. We have a bargaining position if you go there voluntarily." Mia hated to be thinking strategically. But this was her son. "We lose that once you're identified."

"But I didn't even take the stupid candy bar!" His voice rose. "I didn't take anything!"

"There could still be other charges. Conspiracy to commit theft. Disorderly conduct. Malicious mischief. They're talking about making an example of the kids who were there so it doesn't happen again. Even if you didn't take anything, it doesn't change that you were willingly there."

"Okay." Gabe's shoulders slumped. "Okay, I'll talk to the police."

At the police station Brooke tilted her head back to look at the high ceiling, slowing their progress, while Mia resisted the urge to tug her forward. Her heels echoed on the white marble floor. She asked the woman behind the bulletproof glass for Marc Stoker, the detective handling the case. Tracy had given Mia his name when Mia told her she might have recognized one of the kids on the tape. Mia hadn't said it was Gabe, and she had been relieved when she didn't recognize the detective's name. Bad enough to go through this with a stranger. Far worse to do it with someone she had worked with. Then she had called to ask if Marc could stay late to meet them.

Now they waited in silence. Her son stood two paces behind her with his head down. When the detective came out, Gabe's eyes widened. Marc Stoker's biceps strained the short sleeves of his black uniform shirt. He had a shaved head, a brown mustache, and a close-trimmed goatee.

"My son has a matter he wishes to speak to you about." Mia

didn't let on that she had paved the way for this. Let Gabe carry the burden.

Gabe's voice was low. "I went to that Sunshine Mart with those kids. The ones who stole things. But I didn't take anything."

"All right," Marc said. "Let's go on back and talk."

He took them to a room where a video player was set up. At first Brooke watched the tape with interest. She grew bored as Marc stopped and started it, walking Gabe through what had happened and writing down the names Gabe knew. Mia had tossed some crayons and a notebook into her purse before leaving home, and now she let Brooke draw while she half listened to what Gabe was saying.

Then she heard Gabe say Zach's name as he pointed at one of the boys wearing bandannas. Mia stiffened. The kid who had shaken her hand, looked her in the eye, asked about her job? The one who had made such a good impression? Maybe she was no better judge of character than Gabe.

Eventually Marc asked Gabe to look through yearbooks for kids whose names he didn't know but who had taken part.

"Where do you get the yearbooks from?" Gabe asked. He was starting to relax because he thought the worst was over. He didn't know Mia was planning one more stop before this day—which she hoped was the worst in his life—was over.

"Every year we ask the schools to send them to us," Marc said. "As you can see, they can come in handy." It was depressing to think that a percentage of the yearbook's smiling faces would someday be posing for mug shots.

While Gabe was looking through them, Mia stepped out into the hallway and made a phone call. Fifteen minutes later the detective said they were done and shook Gabe's hand. Gabe's shoulders straightened.

"There's one more stop we have to make," Mia said as they walked to the car.

He stopped. "What?"

"We're going to see your coach."

Tears welled up in his eyes. "Mom—no."

"I know there's a code of conduct for the team, and you violated it. I need you to tell Coach Harper that yourself."

Gabe was silent during the twenty-minute drive to the coach's house. Mia did not attempt to fill it. She hoped he was thinking. In the back Brooke had fallen asleep, her head at an awkward angle. When Mia pulled into the driveway, she hoisted Brooke onto her hip, ignoring her sleepy grumbles.

The coach answered the door. Standing this close to him, she realized with a shock that she was probably a few years older than he was. He had light red hair and eyes that slanted down at the corners. From the back of the house, Mia could hear the piping sound of a young child's voice and a woman's soft answer.

"Coach Harper," she said, shifting Brooke's weight so she could offer her hand. "I'm Mia Quinn. Gabe's mom."

"Hello." His expression was wary. Mia had given him the barest explanation of why they were coming.

"Gabe, can you tell the coach what happened on Sunday?"

In a few halting sentences, her son laid it out. He kept his eyes down until the very end.

The coach sucked in a breath. "And were there other players from the team involved?"

"Yes, sir."

He winced. "Under the code of conduct I had you all sign, you are held to the highest standards of moral behavior and character both on and off the field. What happened on Sunday clearly violated that code."

"Yes, sir."

The coach's jaw firmed. "Who were the other players, Gabe?"

Mia stepped forward. "The police are figuring that out now, and I expect there will be charges filed. Right now, the way I see it, this is between you and Gabe, between Gabe and his conscience, and between Gabe and me. The information about who else was involved is going to come out, but I don't think it has to come to you from Gabe."

Coach Harper looked up at the ceiling, thinking. Then he nodded.

"All right. I accept that." He turned to Gabe. "I'm glad you came to me. I'm guessing this was your mother's idea, but still, you're here and you're being honest. I respect that."

Gabe's shoulders relaxed the tiniest bit.

"But I also have to consider that you acted in a way that violated our ethics. I'm going to bench you for three games."

Gabe took a ragged breath and then nodded. "I actually haven't played once since the season started."

The coach nodded. "I'm aware of that."

"You are?" His eyes widened, and in her son's expression Mia could see how beaten down he had been feeling, sitting on the bench game after game.

"Yes."

"But why? What have I been doing wrong?"

Coach Harper's face was open. "What do you think, Gabe?"

Gabe hesitated and then said in a rush, "It could be because I'm not good enough. Or because I'm new and don't know the plays yet. Or because I missed that one practice."

"If you weren't good enough, you wouldn't have made the team." The coach put his hand on Gabe's shoulder. "It's the second thing you said—you don't know the plays well enough yet. But you keep studying the playbook and you keep showing up to practice, and you will." He squeezed his shoulder and then let go. "I have faith in you, Gabe."

"Even after today?" Gabe bit his lip. His eyes were shiny.

"Maybe especially after today."

CHAPTER 41

It happened again that night—Brooke screaming in terror, Mia unable to wake her, Gabe hovering, helpless and wide-eyed, at the end of his sister's bed. The only difference was that Mia knew she would be seeing their pediatrician the next day. She just prayed that Dr. Gibbs would know what was going on.

Mia had gotten the earliest doctor's appointment that she could—eight thirty. As she parked in front of the medical office, part of her worried that Frank would note her absence and be unhappy. But she was no Frank. Her kids came first.

When Dr. Gibbs came into the exam room, Mia immediately felt her shoulders loosen. As she looked into his calm gray eyes, caught in a net of wrinkles, she let her breath out in a whoosh. Dr. Gibbs was nearly seventy. He had once told Mia that he even had a few former patients whose grandchildren now came to him.

He patted the exam table. "Okay, Brooke, do you think you can get all the way up here for me?"

Excited by the challenge, Brooke scrambled up. Dr. Gibbs was a small man, nearly elfin, so he was only a few inches taller than Brooke as he listened to her lungs and heart and looked into her ears. Then he handed her a picture book from the rack on the wall. "Why don't you look at this while your mother and I talk."

He turned to Mia. "Has her father's death greatly affected her?" His soothing voice still held the hint of a Scottish burr.

"She was sad when it happened. But she's so young, I'm not sure how much she understands." Mia tried to swallow the sudden lump in her throat. It thickened when he patted her shoulder.

"Since this problem began, has she seemed different during the daytime? Is she unhappy? Lashing out?"

Mia thought back. "Not that I've noticed."

"And does she ever remember these episodes when she is truly awake?"

"No."

He nodded. "I think I know what we're dealing with."

Mia braced herself. Was it some kind of seizure? Mental illness? A brain tumor?

"What Brooke is experiencing is something known as night terrors." He patted her hand. "But they're more terrifying for the parents than the child. About one or two kids out of every hundred get them. They're not nightmares, and they're not the result of bad dreams. Some children's brains simply haven't learned how to transition from deep sleep to light sleep. The result is a night terror. It presents in a manner similar to sleepwalking. The brain waves, the sweating, the tachycardia—accelerated heart rate—and the increased respiration rate are similar."

Mia remembered what her dad had said. "My father told me I used to sleepwalk."

"There you go." Dr. Gibbs nodded. "There may be some genetic predisposition. But just as you did, Brooke will eventually grow out of it. You can help her by keeping a regular bedtime. Try putting her to bed at eight or eight thirty every single night. Don't let her fall asleep earlier than that, and don't keep her up later. And if she continues to have night terrors, you should pay attention to how long after she goes to bed they occur. Then try waking her up fifteen minutes before that time and keeping her awake for about five minutes. In a few months her brain should catch up with her sleep patterns and the night terrors should stop altogether."

Even though she barely made it back to the courtroom for her scheduled time in front of the grand jury, Mia felt oddly relaxed. Brooke was okay.

She began by bringing the grand jury up to speed on the events of the last few days. She put Charlie on the stand to testify about what Gina Miller had said about being near Colleen's house the night of the murder.

"And Gina Miller volunteered for a polygraph?" Mia asked.

"Yes." Charlie nodded. "I observed as it was administered. According to the examiner, she passed the test with no signs of deception." While the polygraph results weren't admissible in court, they could be helpful when considered in totality with other evidence. "We also took possession of a .22 caliber pistol that had been stored in a shoe box. She claimed the gun had not been fired in several years, but there is no way to test for that."

He also talked about the homeless girl who lived across the street from Colleen.

"And what efforts have you made to find her?" Mia asked. In a way, she was asking for herself as much as for the grand jury. She hadn't touched base with Charlie since they had spoken with Ophelia.

"I went to the local high school and determined that Ronni Slate has been attending this school year. However, Friday was the last day she was in school. I talked to several of her friends and encouraged them to have her contact me, but I haven't heard from her yet."

Finally Mia asked him to explain to the grand jury about Willy Mercer, who had been prosecuted by Stan for a little girl's murder and who himself had been murdered, targeted for a killing it later turned out he actually hadn't committed.

"And what have you learned since then, Detective Carlson?"

"Colleen Miller prosecuted the girl's real killer two years ago." He explained how the girl's stepfather had been the man who really murdered her. "The parents of Willy Mercer divorced after his death. I've spoken with his mother, and she denied any involvement in Mr. Slavich's or Ms. Miller's death. Willy's dad, Seth Mercer, has moved since his son was killed, and I'm trying to locate him for questioning."

Mia turned to the grand jury. "Do you have any questions for Detective Carlson?"

"How could everyone believe that poor boy was guilty?" a woman with red-framed eyeglasses asked.

Charlie sighed. "It's unintentional, but sometimes people see what they want to see. Given the previous charge that Willy Mercer had been a Peeping Tom, Stan Slavich focused on the things that linked him to this case. Unfortunately, Mr. Slavich was wrong."

Mia wondered if Stan had paid the ultimate price for his blindness. Public defenders like Eli Hall were often asked how they could defend a murderer or a rapist: what if a guilty man went free? But no one seemed to realize that the prosecutor faced a similar dilemma: what if an innocent man was imprisoned? Even if Stan had been right 99 percent of the time, that still meant that out of a hundred cases, one defendant he prosecuted might have been innocent, sent to prison for a crime he or she hadn't committed.

The same horrible statistic applied to Mia.

When there were no more questions, Mia said, "Okay, people, we'll take a ten-minute recess and then we'll turn to the case of Darin Dane."

Mia remained at her table, although she could hear the babble of the grand jurors' voices as they took their chance to grab a snack and discuss what they had just seen and heard.

Ten minutes later the court reporter swore in Reece Jones. Today he was dressed in a navy blue suit that set off his blue eyes and dark hair. The suit was perhaps a mistake on the part of his attorney, because it made him look several years older than fourteen.

"Now, Mr. Jones, could you please tell us where you go to school?" Mia asked.

Reece looked down at a yellow piece of paper that he clutched in his hand.

"On the advice of my attorney," he said, "I must respectfully decline to answer and assert my constitutional right to remain silent." His voice started out small and then got louder as he went along.

Reece might have an attorney, but the attorney was not allowed to accompany his client into the grand jury room. Instead he was forced to wait on one of the narrow benches in the hall and hope that his client didn't decide to disregard his script.

"You seem to be reading from a piece of yellow paper, and there is some writing on that paper," Mia said. "Is that writing what you have just read to us now?"

Reece hesitated, then finally said, "Yes."

"And did your attorney write that out for you this morning?"

After a moment's pause, he looked back down. "On the advice of my attorney, I must respectfully decline to answer and assert my constitutional right to remain silent."

The jurors looked at each other with raised eyebrows and shakes of the head.

"Did you know Darin Dane?"

Another glance at the paper, although by now Mia thought Reece should have had it memorized. "On the advice of my attorney, I must respectfully decline to answer and assert my constitutional right to remain silent." When Reece raised his face, he was smiling.

No, scratch that, Mia thought. He was smirking.

She fought to keep her own voice neutral. "Did you ever physically strike Darin Dane?"

A hint of singsong crept into Reece's voice. "On the advice of my attorney, I must respectfully decline to answer and assert my constitutional right to remain silent."

Murmurs now.

"Did you ever hack into his Facebook page and put up malicious postings?"

Reece's eyebrows drew down. He opened his mouth, closed it, and then finally read his prepared statement again. "On the advice of my attorney, I must respectfully decline to answer and assert my constitutional right to remain silent."

As he spoke, a few jurors began to mutter impatiently.

"Okay, Mr. Jones, I understand that your lawyer has instructed you to not answer today. We"—she indicated the grand jury—"would like to hear from you if you change your mind. Until then, thank you."

Reece left with a bounce in his step.

Next, Brandon Shiller was brought into the room and sworn in. His hair, so stiff with gel it angled straight out from his head, made Mia think of a character from one of the video games Gabe liked to play. She wondered how seriously he was taking all of this. But then she looked into his wide-spaced brown eyes and saw fear. Secretly Mia was glad. How frightened must Darin have been of Brandon?

"Mr. Shiller, where do you go to school?"

"Independence High."

"What year are you in?"

"I'm a freshman." He kept his eyes on his folded hands.

"And who are your close friends at school?"

"I don't know. Reece, I guess. And Conrad. Zane."

"Could you please give me their last names, Mr. Shiller?"

"Um, okay. It's Reece Jones, Conrad Silcox, and Zane Appall." His fingers were still folded, but now the knuckles were white.

"And are you involved in any sports at Independence High?"

"Right now I play football."

"And those other boys you mentioned, do they also play football?"

He nodded.

"Mr. Shiller, would you mind answering that question out loud for the court reporter?"

"Oh." He cleared his throat. "Okay. They all play football."

"Did you know a boy named Darin Dane?"

His shoulders tensed. "Yeah."

"For how long?"

"Since sixth grade, I guess."

"What did you think of him?" Mia asked. Brandon might look like a cartoon character, but he probably wasn't stupid. He knew he was suspected of bullying, so he would try to minimize the distaste he had felt for Darin.

"I don't know." A shrug. "I didn't know him that well."

"You just said you've known him since sixth grade."

"Yeah, but it's not like we hung out." He pressed his lips together. "We were never friends."

"You seem pretty adamant about that. Did you dislike Darin?"

"No." He shook his head a little too hard.

"No?"

"We were just different types of people, that's all."

"What do you mean?"

"I play sports, like you said. Darin isn't like that. Wasn't."

"Well, what was he like?"

"He was different. All his friends were girls."

"It seems like a boy your age might like to have a girlfriend."

His face reddened. "That's not what I mean. I mean, it was like he was a girl too."

"And did you ever verbally tease him about these differences?"

"No."

"Really?" Mia said. "Remember, you swore to tell the truth. It's an oath. Is there anything you want to change about what you said, anything at all?" She would have loved to have leaned into his face when she asked the question, but in a grand jury trial the prosecutor always remained seated for the questioning.

"Well, maybe I teased him a little bit. But it was just being funny and stuff. Anyway, if he had tried harder to act normal, maybe nothing would have happened."

A few jurors recoiled. Mia knew she had them now, that they were already making up their minds about this boy.

"These things that just happened—did they involve any physical contact?"

Brandon played dumb. "What do you mean?"

"In PE, for example, did you ever snap him with a towel?"

"Maybe a couple of times."

"Did you ever push him in the showers?"

Brandon was silent for a long moment. "Maybe. Maybe once or twice."

"Did you ever trip him?"

Silence.

Mia repeated, "Did you ever trip Darin Dane, Mr. Shiller?"

"A few times. Not that many."

"And did you ever strike Darin with a closed fist?"

"I don't . . . I don't remember."

"You don't remember." She said it flatly, not phrasing it as a question.

"I might have, once," Brandon said. "But other people did that too. It wasn't just me. I wasn't the only one."

"Can you tell me their names?"

"Those guys I said before. Reece. Zane. Conrad. A few more."

"Tell me, Mr. Shiller, is there a name for people that Mr. Jones beats up?"

"Yeah." His voice was nearly inaudible. "We call them Reece's Pieces."

One of the jurors gasped.

"I'd like you to look at three notes, Mr. Shiller." She leaned forward and handed them to him. "They are numbered exhibits 39, 40, and 41. Now, first, looking at number 39—and please don't take it out of the plastic—do you recognize the handwriting?"

"Maybe. It's hard to say."

"Whose handwriting does it resemble?"

"Reece's. Maybe."

They already had a handwriting expert who would testify the handwriting belonged to Reece, but there was no point spending the money twice on an expert witness. She would save it for the trial. Mia felt she had more than enough for the grand jury to indict. When it came to the grand jury, they weren't looking for guilt beyond a reasonable doubt. They were simply looking for a preponderance of evidence.

The exhibits were passed from hand to hand. A couple of the jurors shook their heads when they read the more violent threats.

"And do you know what happened after Darin received the note labeled number 41?"

"He went out to the track and someone beat him up."

"Do you know who did it?" she asked.

Brandon bit his lip. "You won't tell him what I said?"

The jurors were quiet now, listening intently.

"These grand jurors are all sworn to secrecy. They can't talk about what happens in this room. So you are safe telling them everything you know and everything you believe."

"Reece beat him up." He was talking to his lap now, shoulders slumped.

"And what about Darin's Facebook page. Did you ever post on it?"

"A couple of times."

"What specifically did you post?"

"Called him some names. You know, like queer."

"And did you hack into his Facebook page and post invitations as if you were Darin for boys and men to come to Darin's house?"

He looked her in the eye. "No, I didn't do that."

If it hadn't been Brandon, it had to have been Reece, although it really seemed more like something Brandon would have done. "Do you know who did?"

The rule of thumb was that you should never ask a witness a question to which you didn't already know the answer. But there wasn't really a way around it when you had a hostile witness in front of the grand jury.

"Yeah." He looked up at her. "It was Jeremy. Jeremy Donaldson did it."

CHAPTER 42

Charlie was just opening a big manila envelope holding an accident report he had ordered when his phone rang.

"Detective Carlson."

"It's Mia. I just finished questioning the two boys about Darin's death in front of the grand jury. Reece Jones took the Fifth, but Brandon Shiller answered all my questions. He admitted to harassing and physically abusing Darin, and he also implicated Reece."

"That all sounds good." So why did her voice sound so shaky?

"There's one problem, Charlie. He says neither he nor Brandon hacked Darin's Facebook. He said it was Jeremy Donaldson."

"Jeremy?" Even as he phrased it as a question, Charlie knew in his bones that it was really a statement.

"I want to reinterview him."

"In front of the grand jury?"

"If I send him a target letter, he might lawyer up—pull a Reece and never admit to anything," Mia said. "But I felt like you and I made a connection with Jeremy. He might still be willing to talk to us."

He wondered if she was right. "I'll call his mom and see if we can go over there as soon as school lets out. I also think I've managed to locate Seth Mercer, Willy Mercer's dad. The last report is that he's living in a trailer park between here and Tacoma."

Less than an hour later Charlie and Mia were in Jeremy's living room. On the coffee table was a tray of chocolate chip cookies. But today not even Mia was eating them.

"So did you get those guys?" Jeremy asked. "Brandon and Reece and the rest of them?" He ran his thumbs up and down the outside seams of his pants.

"Actually, Jeremy," Charlie said, "we're here because we're wondering if you've told us the whole truth." He didn't say anything more. Silence could be a more powerful weapon than any accusation. To someone who was feeling guilty, it could be nearly unbearable.

"I don't know what you mean." The kid's legs began to jig up and down. "I told you what I know. About how those guys beat Darin up and stuff."

Charlie and Mia didn't move, didn't speak. They hadn't planned this tactic in advance, but Charlie could feel Mia settling into the silence along with him.

The kid bit his thumbnail, scrubbed his hands across his face, raked his fingers through his hair. "Is this about Darin's Facebook page?"

Again they gave him no answer, just kept their eyes fixed on his face. And it was their calm expressions that broke him.

When he spoke next, his voice was high and hesitant. "Look, I just wanted to teach him a lesson. That's all. I didn't think it would go as far as it did. And I never, ever, ever thought he would kill himself." His voice broke.

"Tell us what happened," Mia said in a soft voice.

"See, Darin came over to my house this summer. I guess he thought we were still friends. But we really don't have anything in common anymore. I tried to tell him that he needed to change the way he acted. Maybe in middle school everybody accepted it if he wore blue sequined pants that he got at the thrift store, you know, 'cause people said, well, that's just Darin. But I knew high school was going to be different. Kids from four different middle schools go there, and not everyone was going to be so understanding. I told Darin he had to try to be more normal. Even if he was acting." His eyes swung from Mia's face to Charlie's. "You can do it, you know? You just watch how other people do things, and you do what they do. You don't stand out. You don't make a fool of yourself. And you don't get beat up."

Old memories bubbled up in Charlie, but he tried to ignore them. His high school years were long behind him now, but there were times the memories were as fresh as newly spilled blood.

Jeremy twisted his hands together. "But Darin wouldn't listen to me. I mean, he wore that rainbow-striped scarf the very first day of school. And a few days later, when he saw me in the hall, he threw his arms around me and gave me this big hug." At the memory, color rose in his cheeks. "Everybody stared. Guys don't hug. Darin should have known that! So I decided to teach him a lesson. See, when he was here that one day over the summer, my mom said I had to take the garbage and recycling out to the curb before the truck showed up. So I said Darin could use my computer to check his Facebook. Later I realized that it saved his password."

"So what did you do to his Facebook?" Mia asked.

"I posted some stuff. You know, like I was really Darin. I thought I could show him the way things were going. I thought he would notice and change how he was acting. But he didn't. So the next day I made it worse. I know I shouldn't have." His hands twisted on his lap. "But then some other kids found out about it and started talking about it at school. Everyone was looking at his page and commenting on it and sharing it on other people's pages. But you have to believe me, I didn't know Darin would kill himself." Jeremy's voice cracked. "He always seemed so happy and clueless."

"But wasn't there a reason that Darin didn't know?" Mia's blue eyes were flinty. "Why wasn't he notified when people posted on his wall?"

In a small voice Jeremy said, "Because I turned off notifications."

"And you unfriended his close friends, like Shiloh and Rainy."

He nodded and hung his head.

How was Darin supposed to learn his lesson if Jeremy had systematically eliminated any way that he might?

"Of course I wouldn't have done it if I'd known what was going to happen. And I feel terrible." He raised his head. "But it's not all my fault. Darin just wouldn't play along. He wouldn't even try to fit in. And all those other things that happened to him—I didn't do them. I never hit him. I never pushed him down. I never threatened him. I never called him names. All I tried to do was to give him some advice about how he needed to change. But he just wouldn't—"

"You mean he wouldn't be the same as everyone else," Mia said flatly.

"Isn't that the definition of normal?"

She sighed. "Look, Jeremy, there's one more thing I'm going to need you to do for me. I need you to go before the grand jury and talk about what you know. That would be about the assaults the other boys made on Darin. It would also be about what happened with his Facebook page."

Charlie noticed that she had switched to using the passive voice, as if the Facebook account had somehow managed to hack itself.

"Will they understand that I didn't know he would kill himself?"

"You can tell them that yourself, Jeremy. You can explain it to them just like you did to us."

On their way out, Mia told Jeremy's mother that her son would need to go before the grand jury. Charlie waited for her to object or say she wanted to get a lawyer, but she kept on chopping vegetables for some kind of stew and nodded.

How much did she know about what her son had done? Charlie wondered as he drove them to the trailer park that was Seth Mercer's last known address. How much did she want to know? His eyes focused on the road in front of him, but his mind was still back in the cheerful blue-and-green living room with the cowering kid at its center. Jeremy had done what he thought he had to do. When you were afraid of being bullied, sometimes the best thing to do was to become a bully yourself.

Mia's voice interrupted his thoughts. "Charlie, every time we talk to these kids about what happened to Darin, I can see it on your face."

His shoulders tensed and his hands tightened on the steering wheel. "What?" There was no way she could see anything, guess anything, tell anything. That part of Charlie had been buried long ago.

"Did something happen to you when you were in school?" Her voice was soft, coaxing, nearly maternal. "Were you picked on?"

Charlie knew Mia wouldn't stop asking questions until he told her the truth. And he found himself wanting to give it to her. To prove to her that she hadn't been wrong about him. His lips twisted into a bitter smile. "Not exactly."

"What do you mean?"

"You're right that Darin's case brings back bad memories. But you're wrong about what they're of." He took a deep breath. "The truth is, Mia, that in high school I was the bully. I was my high school's Reece Jones."

Her eyes went wide. "What—what do you mean?"

"When I was in high school, things happened." Charlie heard himself minimizing, using the passive voice himself, and forced out the truth. "I made them happen. I didn't get my growth spurt until I was a senior. So what do you do when you're six inches shorter than everyone and you dress in clothes from the thrift store? I had already been jumped a couple of times. I decided that the best way to protect myself was by hurting other people first. I figured if I hurt them, they would be too scared to hurt me." His voice roughened. "And you know what? It worked."

The rest of the drive to the trailer park was completely in silence. Charlie told himself it didn't matter if Mia had lost every shred of respect she had ever had for him. He was sure it hadn't been a lot to begin with.

Twenty minutes later he checked the address again to make sure that this trailer was the one where Seth Mercer lived. If these homes in the Lonely Pines Park had ever been mobile, that had been years in the past. The one Mercer lived in was baby blue, about twenty feet long, with four tiny windows. Topping the flat white roof was a rusting TV antenna. Living in the trailer would be like living in a tin box.

They got out of the car, still not speaking. Charlie knocked on the front door. It sounded hollow and flimsy, barely protection from the elements, let alone from anyone who really wanted to get inside. Mia stood behind him on the cement slab porch, which was set off by a six-foot-long wrought-iron railing painted white.

"Who is it?" a man's voice growled.

"Seattle Police. We're looking for Seth Mercer."

After a pause the man said, "Okay. Just give me a minute."

Time stretched out. Surely longer than a minute. Charlie was just turning toward Mia when the door began to creak open.

"Took you guys long enough." The man had three days' growth of silvery beard and was dressed in jeans and a red-plaid flannel shirt. But it wasn't his words or his appearance that drew Charlie's attention.

It was the rifle in his hands. The rifle leveled right at Charlie's chest.

Charlie shouted, "Gun!" He pushed Mia sideways with one hand as he drew his Glock with the other. "Take cover!"

CHAPTER 43

"Take cover!" Charlie yelled as he shoved Mia out of the way.

She scrabbled sideways, her eyes fastened on the gun. Her toe caught on a crack in the cement. She fell to one knee, her hands scraping across the cement. Not feeling the pain, she pushed herself back to her feet, stumbled off the porch, and scrambled for the car and whatever cover it could provide.

She couldn't die. Not now. Not when her kids were so young. Not when they had already lost their father.

Crouching behind the front wheel, she risked peeping over the hood. Seth Mercer still stood in the doorway, holding the long gun with the barrel only a few inches from Charlie's chest. Homicide detectives normally wore plain clothes—which meant Charlie wasn't wearing a bulletproof vest under his shirt. Over the years Mia had seen enough autopsy photos to know that at this range, Charlie would be dead the second Mercer pulled the trigger.

Only a few minutes earlier she had been sickened by Charlie's admission that he had once been a bully. But now, as he stood nose to nose with a man bent on killing him, she knew she would do whatever she could to save him.

"You don't want to do this," Charlie said calmly. He had raised both hands. The one holding his gun was turned so that it pointed off to the side.

Yanking her phone from her purse, Mia dialed 911 by touch, then held it to her ear.

"911. Police, fire, or medical?"

"Police," Mia half said, half whispered. "There's a man holding a police officer at gunpoint."

"What do you know about what I want?" Mercer said. His lips twisted into a sneer. "You don't know anything."

"What's your location?" the dispatcher said in Mia's ear.

"A trailer park between Seattle and Tacoma. It's called the Something Pines." *Think, Mia, think!* "Whispering Pines—no, *Lonely* Pines. Unit Seven."

Charlie's voice was unhurried. "I know that your son Willy was wrongly convicted of murder."

Mia risked another peek over the hood. Charlie had lowered his gun, but not holstered it.

"I know that he was murdered in prison. That's what I want to talk to you about."

"The guy's name is Seth Mercer," Mia told the dispatcher. "And he's got a rifle pointed right at Charlie Carlson from Seattle's Homicide Division."

"Too little and far too late." Mercer shook his head. "I've been waiting for you guys to show up for nearly five years."

"Why don't you put the gun down and we can talk about it." Charlie's tone was conversational. "I want to hear what you have to say."

"We've got units on the way," the dispatcher told Mia.

"Even the Bible talks about an eye for an eye," Mercer said. He kept the rifle where it was, so close that if he moved it forward four inches it would touch Charlie's chest. Touch the skin right over his beating heart.

"So because your son was wrongly convicted and then murdered in prison," Charlie began, "you . . ."

"I shot Stan Slavich." There was no emotion in Mercer's voice. He was simply stating a fact.

"Why did you shoot him?" Charlie's voice was as steady as if he were in an interview room and not a second away from being shot himself.

"Didn't I just tell you?" Mercer said angrily, and everything inside Mia tensed as the distance between the end of his rifle and Charlie's chest narrowed to nothing. She ducked back down behind the wheel well, praying without words that Mercer wouldn't pull the trigger.

"Slavich decided my son was guilty, when he was innocent. Not only that, he charged him with *first*-degree murder. Because he said Willy had planned it. When Willy couldn't plan what to have for dinner. But Slavich had the power to do that. One person—one—decided to put my son on trial and what the charges would be. And the moment he did that, he ruined my son's life forever. Even if Willy had been found not guilty, that's not the same as being found innocent."

"You're right," Charlie said simply. "It's not."

In the distance sirens began to wail.

"Right!" Mercer agreed. "Everyone would have looked at him sideways, even if he was acquitted. But of course even being acquitted didn't happen. And then he was murdered by a piece of scum. Murdered for something he didn't do. And all the guards did was watch."

"So you decided to do something about it."

Mia risked another look. The rifle was no longer pressed against Charlie's chest. Mercer had moved it so that it pointed off at an angle. The barrel drooped. Now if he fired, the bullet would punch a hole through Charlie's liver and intestines. But maybe he would live. Could Charlie rush Mercer and push the rifle even farther down so that it fired only at the ground?

"When Willy was murdered, I thought about how Slavich would continue to walk through this world untouched. He showed Willy no mercy, so I showed him no mercy."

"And so you shot him?" Charlie prompted.

"Yeah. A clean kill. Not like my boy, left to bleed out in the yard until the guards decided it was safe enough to drag his body away."

Mercer made a grating sound, a nightmare version of a laugh. "And then I waited for you guys to come looking for me. But it was like you'd already forgotten about what you had done. When the truth came out about who really killed that poor little girl, no one even apologized to my family. My son paid the price for Slavich's mistakes. My family did. We went bankrupt trying to defend our boy. And after he was dead, my wife and I divorced."

The sirens were getting louder, converging from all directions.

"And then what happened?" Charlie prompted, his voice still conveying no urgency.

"Nothing. I just waited for you guys to show up. Waited and waited."

"What about Colleen Miller? When she convicted Laura Lynn Childer's stepfather, did you feel that she should have known from the beginning that he was the real killer? Did you decide that justice called for something to be done about her too?"

Silence. Mia peeked again over the car's hood.

Mercer tilted his head, squinting. "What?"

And then three police cars screamed into the trailer park, light bars flashing. Cops spilled out with guns drawn, crouching behind their open doors. Charlie took one step back, two, and then his hips were against the white wrought-iron railing. The cops shouted commands for Mercer to put down his gun, to put his hands up.

Charlie shouted, "No! No! Don't do it!"

But Mercer kept raising the rifle, pointing it past Charlie to the cops who had just arrived.

Charlie rolled back off the railing and onto his belly.

And nearly half a dozen shots drilled into Seth Mercer.

As they waited to be debriefed in a sad cinder block building that was rather grandly known as the trailer park's community center, Charlie sat with his arm around Mia. He smelled of blood and gunpowder, and his clothes were freckled with red. Outside the investigators and crime-scene technicians buzzed around Mercer's trailer, measuring, photographing, videotaping. The man at the center of their activity lay covered with a white sheet.

Every time Mia thought she was finished crying, it would start up again. The horror of thinking she would die, the horror of truly watching Mercer die. The fear she had felt for herself and for Charlie. The sadness for all the lives lost: Laura Lynn, Willy, Stan, Colleen, and Seth Mercer. One of the cops had come up with a box of tissues before leaving them in this room with a Ping-Pong table, a pile of old magazines, and a half dozen folding chairs. Mia had already gone through half of the box.

She scooted a little bit away from Charlie, who took back his arm. She blew her nose. At each loud watery honk, he flinched—and then smiled, just the slightest bit.

The crumpled tissue went into the nearly full wastebasket. "You heard him, Charlie. Seth Mercer didn't know anything about Colleen's murder."

"He didn't say that." Charlie rubbed his temple.

"He clearly didn't know what you were talking about. That's the same thing."

"Maybe he was stalling for time. Maybe he was embarrassed that he shot a woman."

"Or maybe he didn't kill her," Mia insisted. "We've got nothing to tie him to Colleen's killing."

"So? We've got nothing to tie him to Stan's murder either, except for his confession." Charlie repeated the aphorism. "The absence of evidence is not evidence of absence." He shook his head. "Just because we don't have any physical evidence linking Seth Mercer to Colleen's murder doesn't mean he didn't do it."

CHAPTER 44

"I'm sorry, but you can't smoke in here," Eli told Ben McFadden, one of Tami Gordon's former clients. Judging by the stink of cigarette smoke that wafted from Eli's chair cushion every time he sat down, this rule had not been enforced by Tami when it had been her chair and her office.

From what Eli had heard about Tami, she had not been much for following rules. The only thing she believed in was her clients' absolute innocence. In Eli's view, it was the judge or the jury's job to determine guilt or innocence based on the evidence and the arguments presented; it was his job to make as effective a case as possible. Most defendants were neither completely innocent nor completely guilty. The truth was a slippery thing.

The skinny man sitting across from Eli plucked the unlit cigarette from between his lips and began to tap it on the edge of the scarred desk, flipping it over and over. The tips of his fingers were stained yellow with nicotine.

"I still don't understand." McFadden's hazel eyes flashed up to Eli's and then back to his cigarette. "Who are you? Why did you call me to come down here? Where's Tami?"

"Tami's no longer employed by this office. I've been asked to take over her cases. She left in something of a hurry." This was a euphemism for what happened when you were caught having sex with one of your clients—a suspect in a double homicide—in an attorney-client visiting room on the eleventh floor of the King County Jail.

Eli had heard that Tami claimed it was all a misunderstanding. That while she took full responsibility for not stopping her client from hugging her, all that had happened was a simple embrace. That the deputy hadn't understood what he was seeing.

"But I want to talk to Tami," McFadden said, chewing on his lower lip. "I need to."

Eli's gut clenched. Was McFadden another "special" client of Tami's?

"I'm afraid that's impossible."

"Am I still going to be able to plead out? She promised I wouldn't go back to prison."

"I'll be talking later today to the prosecutor, Katrina Nowell. I'm going to make sure she's still on board with the offer she made you."

McFadden's hands stilled. "Why wouldn't she be? It was her idea."

According to Tami's notes, the plea deal called for McFadden to give up the names of the people in the identity theft ring, plead guilty, and accept eighteen months of probation. It was a very good deal. Maybe better than McFadden, who had never managed to keep his nose clean for more than three months in his adult life, deserved.

"I just need to make sure we're all on the same page," Eli said patiently.

"I can't go back to prison. I won't." McFadden had been in and out of prison since he was nineteen. Now he was thirty-four and could pass for fifty-four. With trembling fingers, he pushed up the sleeves of his gray long-sleeved T-shirt. His right bicep was tattooed with SS lightning bolts. The underside of his left forearm bore a spiderweb tattoo, common among racists who had spent time in prison. Sometimes you earned it by killing a minority inmate, although when he looked in McFadden's haunted eyes, Eli hoped fervently that this was not the case here.

"So you're in the Aryan Brotherhood?" The white power group

preyed upon the confused, the angry, the troubled, and the weak. It made men who had never felt special for a single day in their lives believe that they were part of something important, something bigger than themselves.

"I was. But I'm not anymore. Not since I got me a half-black girlfriend. But the Brotherhood says the only way you really leave them is in a body bag. If I go back to prison, both sides will be after me. I'll be lucky to come out alive. You need to remind Katrina that I kept up my end of the deal."

"You've already given up the names of your accomplices?" There had been nothing about it in Tami's notes. If you could call them notes.

His nervous eyes skittered over Eli's face. "Right. That's what I did."

From what Eli had been able to figure out from Tami's fragmented files, Tami had made a number of plea deals with Katrina Nowell, more than with any other prosecutor in Violent Crimes. Maybe Tami had found the sweet spot in the King County District Attorney's Office—a prosecutor with a kind streak.

While a defense attorney couldn't steer a case to a certain prosecutor, you could request that a case be assigned to one who had been involved in any area of your case—even just a bail hearing. Tami might have taken advantage of that perfectly legal tactic to ask for Katrina whenever possible.

Some prosecutors were mirror images of Tami, viewing all defendants as guilty, guilty, guilty. They saw it as their job to demand a maximum sentence with no leniency or allowances. As a defense attorney, you wanted a prosecutor who understood that while clients were often no angels, many had also suffered from chaotic upbringings, lack of schooling, and crippling addictions that sometimes led them to make poor choices.

But it was the prosecutor alone who ultimately decided whom to charge, what to charge, and what sentence to recommend—or whether to accept or offer a plea bargain. Frank D'Amato and the heads of the various departments didn't have time to monitor everyone's cases. It was called prosecutorial discretion. And Katrina had exercised hers on McFadden's behalf.

"I'll talk to Ms. Nowell today and let you know what she says," Eli said.

But McFadden didn't seem reassured at all.

The secretary gave Eli directions to Katrina's office. When he turned the corner, he saw a woman with a long, slender back and blond hair pulled back into a low bun walking ahead of him. Eli's heart took a stutter step.

"Mia?"

She turned. "Eli." Her smile didn't reach her shadowed eyes. This morning word had gotten around his office that the man responsible for murdering Mia's friend and another prosecutor had killed himself just as he was about to be arrested.

"I'm here for that meeting with your co-worker." He hesitated and then said, "I heard about what happened. You must be relieved that it's over."

Instead of answering him right away, Mia closed her eyes and pressed her lips together. Finally she said, "You might not have heard everything. He committed suicide by cop, right in front of us. It was awful. This was one of those cases where there are no winners."

"I'm sorry." Eli wished he had more than just two overused words to offer her.

Charlie Carlson came up behind Mia, standing a little closer than Eli thought was strictly professional. As if he and Mia were a team, and Eli the interloper. He thought about that moment Friday night under the hood of her car, that second when they had nearly kissed. How much of an accident had that really been?

"Charlie," Eli said, nodding. The bottom of Charlie's tie bore a yellow stain that looked like mustard.

"Eli."

A woman with a head full of frizzy blond curls popped her head out of an office a few doors down. "Did I hear someone say Eli?"

"That's right. You must be Katrina." Nodding at Charlie and Mia, Eli walked past them to shake Katrina's hand.

As they settled in her office, she said, "So you're the new Tami?"

"I guess you could say that. Without some of her"—he hesitated—"quirks."

"I actually like Tami. I also realize I might be the only one in this office who would say that. She's caring. Committed. And very smart." One corner of Katrina's mouth turned up. "Except maybe when it comes to matters of the heart."

Eli chose to neither confirm nor deny. "Well, as you probably heard, she left rather abruptly, and as a result her files are a little disorganized. I just wanted to make sure you were still on board with the plea bargain for Ben McFadden."

"Yes, he was very helpful. He's provided some information that's going to help us roll up the whole thing."

"He'll be glad to hear that. He was in my office today, and he was quite anxious."

"Anxious?" Katrina's brows pulled together. "Why?"

"It's not really what he said. It's more what he showed me."

She cocked her head. "Oh?"

"His tattoos."

Her face cleared. "Oh yes. I was thinking about them when Tami and I were discussing the plea bargain. I knew that once he got into prison he'd probably end up dead or in solitary confinement for his own safety. What can I say?" She smiled and shrugged. "If someone seems like they just made a mistake, I'm willing to think about going outside the box a bit, especially if he could help us catch some bigger fish. Plus, the courts are clogged enough as it is. Why go to all the expense of a trial when I can guarantee he'll be supervised for the next eighteen months?"

"It's a good deal," Eli said. "A very good deal."

"I was feeling generous that day." Katrina's eyes went oddly flat, like a doll's. "I can stop feeling generous, if that's what you want."

Eli hurriedly backtracked. "No, no, I didn't say that." If there was one thing he didn't want to do, it was to get off on the wrong foot with the one prosecutor who might be more inclined to be on his side.

CHAPTER 45

"Come in, come in," Frank called to Mia when she peeked in his half-open door. Judy had said he wanted to see her. "Come in and sit down."

Mia took a seat in the visitor's chair, wondering if the Frank she had first worked with years ago would even recognize this man who had other people do his summoning.

He reached across the desk to give her a two-handed shake. "I'm sorry I wasn't here earlier to congratulate you on tracking down the man who killed Stan and Colleen."

Mia's morning had been filled with her co-workers' attaboys and applause and a few tears. Frank had been out of the office in meetings—including a quickie press briefing where he announced that the killer had chosen death over arrest, and promised to reveal more details later.

"Charlie Carlson's the one who figured out where Seth Mercer was. And he's the one who almost got killed." Mia pictured Seth slumping to the ground, his chest a red mess, but in her mind's eye he wore Charlie's face.

"From what I hear, you were smart enough to get out of the line of fire and then alerted more cops before Mercer could kill anyone else." Frank made Mia's panicky dash sound smart and nearly heroic.

"Charlie pushed me out of the line of fire, and then he got Mercer to confess. And Jonah's the one who figured out what Colleen and Stan had in common." Mia decided to simplify things by not mentioning Ophelia's contribution.

"You're the one who thought to ask for Jonah's help," Frank said. "You're the one who wouldn't stop digging."

Mia was beginning to realize there was no point in arguing. "This is Colleen we're talking about, Frank. Of course I didn't."

"That's why I asked for you." He blinked rapidly and then sniffed. "Because this is Colleen we're talking about."

For a minute Mia saw a flash of the old Frank, the one who gathered with them around takeout pizza in the break room on crazy nights. Back when Frank was passionate instead of carefully calibrated. Back when he was one of the team instead of the man who had his secretary summon you to his office.

Then Frank's expression shifted, became unreadable. The switch made Mia tense.

"And I'm hearing you even have some kids on the hook for Darin Dane's death."

She nodded. And waited.

"And you got permission from Jeremy Donaldson's mom to question him? Alone?"

Uh-oh, Mia thought. "Of course we did, Frank."

"Well, Jeremy's father called me and said his wife didn't know what she was agreeing to. That she felt threatened and intimidated because you two went to her home. According to Mr. Donaldson, she didn't know she had a choice to say no. Supposedly she's claiming it felt almost like an invasion."

"An invasion! That's ridiculous. She gave us snacks! And then when we told her what would happen next, she just kept chopping vegetables. She didn't seem fazed at all."

"Her husband's threatening a suit based on prosecutorial misconduct, even a civil rights violation. He says his kid's rights were violated under color of law. Do you understand how this looks, Mia? He's saying he's going to go to the media."

"Let him," Mia said flatly, thinking of how Mr. Donaldson's son had tormented the boy who had once been his friend. "Jeremy freely confessed to us. And nobody likes a bully."

"Exactly." Frank leaned forward and put his hands flat on his desk. "And that's what you and Charlie look like. Picking on some poor kid until he broke down in tears and didn't know truth from falsehood, until he told you anything just to get you to leave him alone. Mia, you have to figure a way out of this before it goes viral. This guy is well connected, and he can make some noise. I do not need my campaign derailed just weeks before the election. I do not need to give my opponent a boost. He'll be saying we railroad minors, that we interfered in the relationship between parent and child. You need to take care of this."

Without speaking, Mia stood up and walked to his door. She was trembling. Before she could think of whether it was the right thing to do, she turned and said, "This isn't about your reelection, Frank. This is about a dead child." She left while he was still opening his mouth to rebut.

What was the right thing to do? she wondered as she walked back to her office. Did these boys deserve to spend years in a detention center? Would it teach them a lesson? Would it prevent future Darin Danes? She sat for a long moment and then called Nate Dane.

She was just hanging up the phone when Katrina poked her head into Mia's office. "Hey, are you still planning on having that garage sale?" Katrina the ever-practical.

The garage sale. Mia flashed back to Colleen's Fleetwood Mac albums, to the last conversation she had had with her friend.

"Yeah, I am. In a week or two." Even a few hundred could be put to one of those Visa bills.

"I have some ski equipment I'd like to sell. Can I drop it off at your house after work?"

"Oh, sure. If I'm not there, you can leave it on the porch." Mia gave her head a little shake. She didn't have time to think about garage sales, bills, or even Colleen. Not right now. Not when she needed to be thinking about what she might say to Nate Dane. Not when she needed to be worrying about the potential fallout from her retort to Frank.

Katrina tilted her head. "Are you all right, Mia?"

"Just tired."

"You should be proud that you found the guy who killed Colleen and Stan. You figured it out."

Yesterday Mia had found so many answers, but instead of filling her up, they had left her feeling hollow. Colleen was dead, but so was her killer—and Mia had been a witness to both deaths. The boy who had tormented Darin the worst had turned out to be the same boy who had once been his friend. Even the reason for Charlie's behavior had proved to have a dark side.

"Seth Mercer suffered a lot too," Mia said. "His son was innocent, and not only did we convict him, we let him get killed. We made mistakes we could never undo."

"What's done is done." Katrina shrugged one shoulder. "Sometimes you just have to move on." And with that she took her own advice and exited with a little wave of the fingers.

Mia sat for the next twenty minutes without doing a single thing. Without even thinking. Then Judy called to say that Nate Dane had arrived. Mia met him in the lobby and walked him back to her office, trying not to wrinkle her nose. A fug of stale cigarettes hovered around Nate like the cloud of dirt that followed Pig-Pen in the Charlie Brown comics.

"I know what you want to talk to me about." Nate stared down at his big hands, twisting in his lap.

"You do?" That was a relief. Mia hadn't been looking forward to explaining the decision she had reached.

"Let me just say right up front, I'm sorry."

She had been bracing herself, but not for this. "What are you talking about?"

"For scaring you. I'm sorry. I shouldn't have done it. But when it's your child, you just get obsessed. I needed to know you were making my son's death a priority."

Mia looked at him more closely. Nate Dane was wearing a dark hoodie. Mentally she added a baseball cap and pulled the hood up to hide his face.

"You. You're the one who followed me."

"It seems like you've been spending a lot of time not even thinking about Darin. Like teaching at that school."

"I'm teaching future lawyers who will go out and fight for people like your son."

"And then you showed up at the football game on Friday. Charlie was there too, but he was the only one really paying attention to what was going on. And then I realized you weren't there to investigate. You were just there to cheer on your son. When my son is dead."

Mia ticked off the possible charges in her head. Stalking, menacing . . . But Nate was right. His son was dead. And Nate was lost to grief.

"Despite what you think you've seen, Mr. Dane, I have been working hard for your son. We've had several hearings in front of the grand jury. I can't tell you what's been said, because everyone in that room is sworn to secrecy. About all I can say is there have been no surprises. However, yesterday, outside of the jury room, Charlie and I learned the identity of the person who hacked your son's Facebook."

He straightened up. "Who was it? That Reece? Brandon Shiller?"

"It was Jeremy Donaldson."

His face crumpled. "But they were friends."

She thought of Gabe, of Charlie. "Sometimes it's friends who hurt us the worst." Was that what she was planning to do now? What if Frank hadn't talked to her? Would she still say what she planned to next?

"Here's the thing, Nate. I feel sure we can get an indictment against Jeremy and Reece and Brandon."

He started nodding before she even finished saying their names. "They deserve that. They deserve to suffer. They killed my son."

"But these are minors, teenagers who are fourteen or fifteen.

Kids who don't have criminal records. You may want them to rot in prison, but the reality is even if they are sentenced, it will be as minors, not adults. And there are no guarantees we will win. Juries and even judges can be unpredictable. To make sure they are punished, I'd like to offer them a plea bargain."

Nate was already shaking his head. "No."

She had known this wasn't going to be easy. "The outcome of this trial is unpredictable. With a plea bargain we can guarantee that they receive some punishment."

"But it would be to a lesser charge, right? That's not acceptable. I want them to get the maximum."

"The thing is, Nate, the juvenile justice system in Washington State is geared to rehabilitation." Gabe's face flashed into her mind. "Not punishment. Not even deterrence. No one, not even Jeremy, is likely to be sentenced to a juvenile facility for this. It's even possible that they could be acquitted. However, if we offer a plea bargain, then we know for sure that they will be punished." He hadn't interrupted her yet, so Mia continued, "We could propose that if they plead guilty to criminal harassment, they will be on probation until they're nineteen. And that during that time they must be in school or employed. And that they'll have to complete, say, forty hours of community service."

"A hundred. Forty hours isn't enough."

Mia nodded. "Okay."

"And part of that time they have to speak to schools about bullying. Get up in front of everyone and admit the part they played."

Mia thought about it. Would Reece, in particular, go for it? She thought the answer might be yes, given that the alternative could be harsher. "Okay."

"And on every anniversary of his death they have to write me a letter saying how they are doing and telling me what they imagine Darin would be doing right now."

"Okay," she said again.

After Nate left, Mia picked up the phone and started calling lawyers.

She had just finished talking to Brandon Shiller's lawyer when her phone rang. It was her direct line, not a call that had come through Judy.

"Hello?"

A girl's voice said, "You said I should call you if I wanted my stuff back."

It took her a minute to reorient herself. "Ronni?"

"Yeah. And I can't sleep without my bear." Her ragged voice bore testimony to the truth of her words. "I don't know why. I just can't. Do you have him?"

CHAPTER 46

A woman clutching a Seattle's Best coffee cup walked by and gave Mia an odd look, as if trying to figure out what category she belonged to. Occidental Park, in the heart of Seattle's Pioneer Square district, attracted all kinds of people, from tourists to the homeless to office workers taking a quick break. But Mia bet this might be the first time that a professionally dressed woman had sat on one of the park benches with a worn brown teddy bear perched on her lap.

Mia's heart ached for Ronni, so alone that a worn stuffed animal was her only comfort. "I have everything of yours that was in the house," she'd told her. "Your bear, your textbook, your clothes, your sleeping bag. Just tell me where you are and I'll meet you."

"How do I know you won't turn me in to the authorities?"

"Your birthday was three days ago, Ronni." Charlie had gotten the girl's birth date from her school. What had it been like, marking her birthday all alone and in hiding? "You're eighteen now. In the eyes of law, you can stay on your own. Even if that means you're living on the street. And since you didn't do any damage to your old house when you were staying there, the bank isn't interested in pressing charges."

"I can't go back there, can I?" Ronni asked. "I tried my key, but it didn't work."

"No, I'm sorry, you can't. They changed the locks, and the real estate agent will be going inside more often."

They had agreed to meet at three. Now Mia and the bear sat looking out over the park, facing one of the four carved totem poles that reminded visitors that long before Seattle was a city, this area had been home to native tribes. Pigeons bobbed and cooed at her feet. Even a few gulls patrolled the brick pavement, looking for crumbs from workers' lunches or from treats purchased from one of the coffee shops that ringed the park.

Mia checked her watch again. Ten after. Charlie was at the other end of the park, pretending to read a copy of *The Stranger,* Seattle's alternative weekly. She had noted his presence and then not looked at him again, except out of the corner of her eye.

Charlie a bully. The idea still shocked her. Mia imagined him with bloody fists, standing over some crying, cowering boy. She tried to put an expression on his teenage face, but couldn't.

What kind of bully had he been? Smirking like Reece? Pitiful like Jeremy? Given Charlie's age, he had to have been a hands-on bully like Brandon and Reece. There'd been no Internet to hide behind.

And why had he been a bully? Although, did it matter where it came from? Weren't all bullies insecure, maybe even in pain? He had claimed he had acted out of fear, but maybe he had enjoyed the power.

Knowing that Charlie had been a bully changed everything. Didn't it?

Mia remembered his compassion with Shiloh and Rainy when they talked about Darin. Even with Jeremy he had been gentle.

Especially with Jeremy.

If you had done something wrong, were you unforgivable?

Could you change your past? No.

Could who you were now offset who you were in your past?

Mia considered her dad. Which was the real man? The father who had kept his distance, barked orders, didn't pay his child support? Or the kind dad who only wanted to help her?

A little boy laughed behind her, and she turned. A father held the hand of a three- or four-year-old boy as he walked up a tilted slab of granite that was part of a memorial to four fallen firefighters. The granite slabs were meant to evoke a collapsed building. Bronze statues of the firefighters—two kneeling and two standing—memorialized the men who had been killed in the collapse of a deliberately torched warehouse twenty years earlier.

For a moment Mia envied the dad and his young son. Life had been easier when Gabe was three, when he willingly held her hand. She had had to let go, let him make his own mistakes. She only hoped he was learning from them.

And what about Charlie? Yes, he sometimes flouted the rules. But Mia had also spent the last week in his company. He hadn't hesitated to leave a crime scene to help her family. He had let out a relieved sigh at the news that Brooke would outgrow her night terrors. Even when Seth held a rifle on him, he had treated him with something approaching kindness. And then he had held Mia while she cried.

And it wasn't as if Charlie had changed only because being a cop had forced him to. Just because you were a cop didn't mean you couldn't be a bully too. Mia had even prosecuted one, a cop who broke a woman's arm and claimed she had been resisting arrest—until a neighbor's cell phone video showed he was lying. But despite Charlie's reputation for being gung ho, Mia had never heard anyone even whisper that he was too quick to use force. And yesterday it had been clear that he had wanted to bring Seth in unharmed.

When a girl began walking slowly toward Mia, her mind was brought back to the matter at hand. The school had given them a photo of Ronni. Her hair had been worn down around her shoulders. Now it was tucked back behind her ears, exposing black plugs that stretched her lobes. Her hair was dyed black except for a three-inch stripe of brown at her crown. She was bone thin, and even her skinny jeans looked too loose.

"Ronni? I'm Mia."

The girl didn't say anything, just snatched up the bear. She stepped back and hugged it close, burying her face in it and sniffing it.

"Why don't you sit down?" Mia patted the bench beside her.

The girl did, keeping a good three feet between them. She sniffed again, then wiped her blotchy cheeks on the bear's face. Mia had thought she had been inhaling the bear's comforting scent. Now she realized Ronni was really using it to hide her tears.

"Where's the rest of my stuff?" the girl demanded.

"In my car. We can get it in a few minutes." Mia picked up the brown paper bag that sat between them. "I got you a bagel and a coffee in case you're hungry."

The words were barely out of her mouth before Ronni was biting into the toasted bagel with a little moan. Mia could smell the warm rich scent of melted butter.

"How did you end up living in your old house?"

Ronni spoke with a full mouth. "We got foreclosed on in July. My mom took me and my brother and we went out to Spokane to live with my uncle. But it was pretty clear he didn't want us, and there wasn't any room anyway. And I love my school. I'm a good student, you know? But if I had stayed with my mom, I would have had to go to a new school and try to study in a tiny house with two bedrooms for ten people. And I thought—our old house is empty, and I still have a key. Why can't I just live there and keep going to school? So I came back about a week before school started. The water still works, so it's not that bad."

"Does your mom know where you are?"

A shrug. "Yeah. She's not happy, but she didn't try to stop me either."

Mia tried to imagine being that hands-off, but couldn't. "So you started back at your old school?

"I just showed up on the first day like always, and no one asked any questions. When I filled out the forms, I just did it like I was my mom. We already qualified for free lunch, and the school serves breakfast too." Her bagel had disappeared, and now she licked her shiny fingers.

"What about weekends?" Mia asked, thinking of the peanut butter and crackers. "How have you been eating then?"

"Sometimes I panhandle. But I don't like it because then people stare or make rude comments. If I get really hungry, I go to that one fountain, the one in front of the bank, and fish out the coins. But you have to be pretty desperate to do that, since they're mostly pennies."

It would take a lot of pennies to add up to something to eat. "Where have you been staying since Saturday?"

"There's this Laundromat? I've been sleeping under the folding tables. Or if people are still there, I put an out-of-order sign on the bathroom and lock the door. But like I said, I can't sleep without my bear." She hugged it again.

"Why not go to a shelter?"

"I'm not like those people," Ronni said. "People with no teeth and track marks on their arms. I'm normal. There's lots of homeless kids in Seattle, kids who won't go to a shelter because they're runaways or they don't like the rules or they're scared of the other people. But I don't want to be like them either, sleeping behind hedges, hoping some old homeless guy or meth addict doesn't find you."

At a nearby bench was a reminder of the world Ronni was trying to avoid. A scrawny man with a snake tattoo coiled around his neck sat with his eyes half closed. Next to him was an older woman with rotted teeth. She held a rope leash, and on the other end was a pit bull named Diablo that she petted and praised.

Ronni's gaze skittered over them. "I've heard of kids who hide in a library or a school after closing time, just to have someplace safe to sleep. But I was worried if I got caught they would turn me over to the police for trespassing."

"So were you in your old house ten days ago? On a Sunday night?"

"Yeah." She squeezed the bear.

"Around eight?"

Ronni nodded, her hair falling in her eyes.

"Did you see Colleen get shot?" Mia held her breath as she waited for the girl to confirm that Mercer had been the shooter.

"No. I didn't see it."

Mia exhaled, and then Ronni added, "I heard it. And then I looked out the window."

"What did you see?"

"Nothing that will help you, to be honest. Someone dressed all in black was looking in the window. Part of it was broken, but the rest was still in the frame. He put his hand up next to his eyes like this"—she cupped her left hand around the outside of her left eye—"so he could see inside. He was wearing gloves. Another man was standing on the curb holding something in his right hand. When I saw that it was a gun, I dropped to the floor. I was so afraid he would turn and shoot me."

"Did you see their faces?"

"Only the guy with the gun. And it was more just like an impression. About all I could tell you was that he was white. Once I saw the gun, that was all I could see."

"Was he fat, thin? Tall, short?"

Pressing her lips together, Ronni shook her head. "Average height, average weight. I guess."

"Old? Young?"

A shrug.

"What did you do then?"

"I didn't know what to do. I don't have a phone anymore. They're too expensive. And the nearest pay phone is at least a half mile away. While I was still trying to decide, I heard the sirens. When I peeked out, the men were gone, so I pulled the blinds back down and watched through the crack." She sighed. "But the police were too late. Colleen was already dead. And I didn't even see how the guy who killed her left or what he looked like or anything. I didn't see anything that could help you find whoever killed Colleen."

Mia didn't tell her not to worry, that the killer was already dead. Because something Ronni had said didn't fit.

CHAPTER 47

Charlie glanced sideways at Mia as she drove through Seattle's stop-and-go traffic. The last twenty-four hours had been a roller coaster. Jeremy, who was supposed to be on their side, was actually the one who had hacked Darin's Facebook. Charlie had admitted his shameful secret to Mia. And then both of them had watched Seth Mercer die right after hearing him confess to murder.

Charlie had spent enough time with Mia in the past week that he could see on her face the toll it had taken: her shadowed, slightly puffy eyes, her downturned mouth. And now Ronni had given them something new to think about. After talking to her, Mia had waved Charlie over, introduced him to the skittish girl, and then had her repeat what she had seen.

Ronni had not understood their interest. She was sure what she had seen had been too little to help them. And maybe she was right. But Charlie couldn't wait to get back to the office to check Colleen's murder book. Something the girl had told them didn't jibe with what they remembered.

But first they had to figure out what to do with her.

There was no easy answer. Ronni was an adult, so they couldn't force her to go back to live with her family in an overcrowded house. Besides, what kind of mother would let her daughter squat in a foreclosed home? Charlie might not be a parent, but even he knew that was wrong.

The problem with Ronni was that she didn't fit neatly into any charity's mission. Still, Charlie had his contacts and so did Mia. They would spread the word, in the hopes that a church or even a family might take her in and allow her to finish her senior year at the same high school.

Mia nosed her car into a parking space in front of the Crown Royal Motel. As a stopgap measure, Charlie and Mia had decided to pitch in and pay out of their own pockets for three nights. Charlie knew the motel well because he had made a number of arrests here. The staff were cooperative with police and the rates were low. And it was safe enough if you didn't leave your room at night.

"For you, we give discount," the clerk said. Her name was Ksinia, and she had brown, deep-set eyes. Charlie had dealt with her a time or two.

"Oh, that's not necessary," he said. But after she insisted a second time, he took it. Thirty bucks was thirty bucks, and it wasn't as if he had flashed his badge and asked for it.

He came back to the car, and then he and Mia carried Ronni's stuff inside. The carpet was sticky, the walls were smudged, and there were cigarette burns on the bedspread, but at least the room had a dead bolt. Ronni put her teddy bear down on the thin pillow and pronounced it perfect. They gave her a few more dollars for food. Before they left, the girl hugged both of them. When her thin arms went around his neck, for some reason Charlie found himself having to clear his throat.

Mia drove them back to his office. Without Ronni in the car he was free to talk.

"It doesn't make any sense, Mia. I remember what that spot was like in front of Colleen's window. Soft. Even muddy. But the crime-scene techs didn't pick up any strange prints from her yard. How could someone have pressed up against the window and not left any marks on the ground?"

Inside the station, she followed him into his cubicle, where he flipped through the murder book until he came to the photos of the crime scene. Mia pointed. "I thought you said there weren't any prints."

One photo, taken just outside the shattered window, showed a clear boot print plus a smudged partial. The center of the full print had an indented narrow oval. Each side of the oval was marked by a distinctive zigzag pattern. Underneath the arch of the foot you could clearly read the word *Danner.*

But just because there was a boot print didn't mean it was a clue. In fact, this was the exact opposite.

Charlie explained it to her. "I wasn't saying there weren't any prints at all. All the crime-scene techs wear that style of Danner boots." Wearing the same boots meant they could easily distinguish their own prints from those of the bad guy as well as the victim and witnesses. For exclusionary purposes, the crime-scene techs had taken photos of the bottom of Charlie's shoes as well as those belonging to the uniforms and the paramedics.

"So some crime-scene guy stepped on the real print and obliterated it?" Mia asked, her brow furrowing. "That's pretty clumsy of them, tromping on the evidence."

Charlie took a magnifying glass from his drawer and held it over the boot print. The full print was clear, the mud on either side of it untouched. It didn't make any sense. Even if the crime-scene tech had deliberately lined up his boot with the existing print, it still shouldn't be that clear.

Mia took the magnifying glass from his hand. "Look at it." She jabbed it with her finger. "Do you see what's wrong with it?"

Now Charlie focused on the boot print itself, not the soft ground around it, but he couldn't see what was causing her excitement. "Actually, I don't. I don't see anything wrong with it."

"That's the thing, Charlie. That looks like a brand-new boot. The tread is perfect. There're no marks, no defects, no signs of wear."

He looked closer. "You're right."

"So what are the chances that one of the crime-scene techs has brand-new boots *and* is clumsy enough to step on the evidence?"

They both knew the answer. Zero. The chances were zero. Charlie reached for his phone. "I'm gonna call all the team members to see if anyone has new boots."

"And if they don't, then the person wearing those boots wasn't a tech. It was one of the killers—and they wore them because they knew that was the brand the crime-scene techs wear."

Charlie said, "And the only people who know that . . ." His voice trailed off.

Mia looked around the room to see if anyone was listening. In a voice barely above a whisper, she finished the thought for him: "Are people who work in law enforcement."

If what they were thinking was right, then whom could they trust? On the short drive back to Mia's parking lot and then as they made their way to her office, they talked about what they had just discovered. But they stopped whenever anyone else was within earshot. Had Colleen tangled with a judge, a criminal defense attorney, even a cop? For now it seemed safer to keep their suspicions to themselves.

Judy let Charlie into Colleen's office. For the hundredth time he began to page through her files. But this time he was looking for clues that someone inside the system had been the killer. Looking for evidence that Colleen had stumbled across something she shouldn't have known, that she had rubbed someone the wrong way, that she had had a secret relationship with a judge or a cop or even a defense attorney that had turned sour.

Mia knocked softly and then opened the door and stuck her head in. "I'm going home."

"Okay. See you tomorrow." He paused. "And watch your back."

Mia's eyes met his for a long moment, and then she nodded.

Charlie continued to search, continued to ponder, but finally he had to give up. He used Colleen's keys to relock the file drawers. He fingered the keys on the ring. He had already established that there were no mystery keys. Instead, there was the key to her Volvo and the black fob to unlock it. Keys to the front and back doors of her house and the mailbox on the curb. A small brass key fit the fire safe he had found in Colleen's home office. It had held Social Security cards, passports, birth certificates, and even the license for her long-defunct marriage to Martin.

The three small silver keys he had just used were for her filing cabinets. They had been unlocked when Charlie originally searched Colleen's office. But then again, she wouldn't have needed to take the extra step of locking the filing cabinets if her office was locked at the end of the day, which seemed to be the norm here.

All the keys were accounted for.

Suddenly Charlie straightened up.

It wasn't what was on the ring that was a clue.

It was what *wasn't* on the ring.

Where was the key to Colleen's office? Judy had let him in today, just as she had the day he first searched it.

No wonder he hadn't found anything in Colleen's office.

Someone had been here before him.

He grabbed his phone and punched in Mia's number, but it went straight to voice mail.

CHAPTER 48

For the last two days Gabe's school had been buzzing. On Tuesday Zach had been spotted being escorted down the hall by the school's "resource officer"—a.k.a. cop—with his hands cuffed behind his back. In five minutes the news had spread all over school via whispers and texts. That same day four other football players had been pulled out of class and not come back—including Eldon and Rufus. Gabe had spent the remainder of the school day feeling sick, wondering when someone was going to point and call him a snitch, but no one did. Coach Harper had canceled Tuesday's practice and announced that on Wednesday they would have a meeting to discuss the team's code of ethics.

Because Gabe had come forward, and because he hadn't taken anything, Tracy Lowe, the lady from the Juvenile Unit where his mom worked, the one with long red-painted nails that looked like daggers, had decided not to charge him. He didn't know whether to feel relieved or guilty. Tracy had told his mom that most of the others would likely be sentenced to community service. All of them would probably also have to pay a fine.

Except for Zach, the rest of the football team was back in school on Wednesday. After school, the team gathered in the locker room and waited without speaking. Most of the guys—most of the school—knew by now what had happened at the Sunshine Mart on

Saturday. Gabe and Eldon and Rufus and the other two guys who had been there looked at each other, but didn't speak. When Coach Harper came in, everyone straightened up.

"You have probably heard," he began, "about the incident that happened Saturday. A flash mob that included some members of our team robbed a convenience store. When I heard about it"—he paused while they all waited, not even breathing—"I won't lie to you, I felt low. Very low. You all signed a code of conduct. But our ethics are more than words on paper. Our ethics are about much more than being a football team. They're about what makes us men." He looked from face to face, lingering on those who had been involved. "And real men acknowledge when they have made mistakes and ask for forgiveness. I think those who participated owe the team that."

Gabe was the first on his feet. He felt all those eyes fasten on him, but he just focused on Coach's face. "Coach Harper, I'd like to apologize to you, the other players, and to my friends and family for what I did."

"Thank you, Gabe. I appreciate that."

One by one the others followed. A few minutes later Coach Harper dismissed them, shaking hands with each of the boys as they filed out. When it was Gabe's turn, he gave him a nod and tightened his grip. Gabe looked him straight in the eye and didn't flinch. He left feeling oddly light. The worst was over.

Forty-five minutes after leaving the meeting, Gabe was in his kitchen, sliding a grilled cheese sandwich out of the frying pan and onto the cutting board. His mouth watering at the aroma of toasted bread and melted cheddar, he took one of the knives from the wooden block. A chef's knife, he thought his mom called it. She didn't like Gabe to use her "good knives," but he had planned to wipe it on the kitchen towel and slip it back into the block with no one the wiser.

He was cutting the sandwich in half to share with Brooke, who was upstairs playing in her room, when he heard someone walk onto the porch.

Who could it be? The mail had already come. He waited but

didn't hear a knock. Gabe's heart started to pound. He tried to remember what his mom had said to do about strangers who might come to the door. Was he supposed to ignore them? But what if they knew someone was home? Was he supposed to talk to them through the door without opening it? Open it but keep his hand firmly on the knob? He thought of Colleen, shot through a window. It was all on his shoulders to decide what to do. He was the one in charge. Had he turned the dead bolt as his mom was always nagging him to?

The knife in his hand was big, maybe ten inches long. Gabe carried it with him as he tiptoed down the hall. Finally he risked a peek through the small paned windows at the top of the door.

His breath let out in a whoosh. It wasn't a stranger. It was that lady from his mom's office. The one with the frizzy blond hair. The one they had sat by at the funeral for Colleen. Katrina. That was her name. She was holding some ski equipment. When she saw him, she gave him a wide smile, and his racing pulse began to slow.

He set the knife down on the entryway table, turned the dead bolt—he *had* thrown it—and then the doorknob.

"It's Gabe, right?"

He nodded.

"Sorry if I scared you. Your mom said I could bring my stuff for her garage sale."

"Sure. Let me help you."

He took the skis from her, but then, not knowing what to do, he laid them flat in the hall, against the wall. Katrina put the ski poles next to them. She stopped short when she saw the knife on the table.

"Oh, Gabe, did I scare you? Did you bring that knife out to defend yourself?" She threw a smile over her shoulder, a smile that said the knife was sort of pathetic.

From inside her purse, her phone began to play music that sounded like the beginning of a symphony. Horns, the clash of cymbals, some kind of stringed instrument.

A ring tone. Gabe had heard that snatch of sound once before. But when?

And then it clicked into place. He knew exactly when he had

heard it. That ring tone had been the last sound he had heard on the phone right after Colleen's bubbling breath stopped. He had heard the same series of sounds repeated twice. Right before he dropped the phone and ran in to see why Brooke was screaming.

He had thought Colleen had been listening to music, music he could finally hear because she had stopped struggling to pull air into her lungs.

But no. He had actually heard the ring tone of someone who had been there when she died.

The snatch of music played again.

The ring tone that belonged to Colleen's killer.

Katrina. The woman standing in front of him.

The murderer his mother had been hunting? It was someone who worked beside her.

Gabe kept his face blank.

Katrina reached into her purse and pressed a button to silence the phone. And when she did, he saw something else in there, glinting darkly. Gabe couldn't be sure, but he thought it was a gun.

What was she really here to do? And how could he stop her? The knife was on the hall table, which was right next to Katrina. One phone was in the kitchen, another in the family room, a third upstairs.

All too far away to help him.

Katrina was looking at him curiously now. And then her gaze sharpened. Her eyes narrowed and her lips thinned. And looking at her bony face, her flat blue eyes, Gabe knew that whatever she was thinking was bad. Very bad.

"Is something wrong, Gabe?" Katrina's voice was precise and ice cold.

For an answer, he leaned down and grabbed his skateboard from underneath the entryway table. Then in one motion he stepped back while hoisting it over his shoulder.

And with every ounce of strength he had, Gabe swung the skateboard at her head.

CHAPTER 49

When Mia turned onto her street, a strange car was in the driveway. Although it wasn't completely unfamiliar. She had seen the car someplace before, but it didn't belong to any of her friends. And it wasn't the car that Zach from the football team had been driving. Still, seeing it made her uneasy. Her cell phone started ringing, but she ignored it.

Through the windows at the top of the front door, Mia glimpsed something that turned her blood to icy slush. A blur of moving heads, swinging arms—it looked like there was some kind of a *fight* going on inside her house.

Throwing the car into park and turning it off, she scrambled out so fast that she left the keys still in the ignition and the car door wide open. All Mia's energy was concentrated on getting to her kids.

At that moment she wasn't a prosecutor. She wasn't anything but a mother.

She ran up onto the porch and threw open the front door. Too late, she realized that Gabe was just on the other side. He let out a grunt as the edge thumped into his left shoulder.

At first she couldn't understand what she was seeing. Gabe was gripping the tail of his skateboard. He held it cocked by his right ear as if it were a bat. His teeth were bared in a grimace. He looked like an animal.

The other person standing in the entryway was Katrina. Bright rivulets of blood were running down her face from a nasty-looking gash on her left temple. She raised her hand to it and pulled back fingers that looked like they had just been dipped in red paint. Her eyes widened.

"What's going on?" Mia demanded. Had Gabe gone berserk?

"Mom—she's the one who killed Colleen!"

Shaking her head, Katrina looked at her with pleading eyes. "Your son's gone crazy, Mia—you've got to help me!"

If the past few days had taught Mia anything, it was that teenagers couldn't be trusted. That even her son was capable of lying.

She hesitated.

Katrina's expression hardened. She wiped her fingers down the front of her trench coat, then slid her hand into her purse. When it reappeared, it held a small black pistol. A pistol that she pointed at Mia's chest. "Put down the skateboard, Gabe. Or I'll shoot your mom."

Mia's mouth fell open. Nothing made sense. Gabe set the skateboard on the floor.

"Now roll it down the hall and out of the way," Katrina ordered.

He complied, at the same time turning his head to give Mia a look that mingled fear and determination. The skateboard came to a stop near the kitchen.

"What's happening?" Mia said. "I don't understand." Her thoughts were sludgy. They kept getting stuck on Katrina's icy eyes. On the blood that was now dripping from her cheek onto the floor. On the round eye of the gun pointed right at Mia's heart.

It was Gabe who answered her. "When you had me listen to Colleen, I heard something right after she died. Like classical music. I thought she must have been listening to the radio, and that I could hear it because she stopped breathing. But it was Katrina's ring tone. She's the one who really killed her."

Katrina puffed air out of her pursed lips. "I came over with my ski equipment like I told you about, and then all of a sudden your son picked up his skateboard and hit me in the face. He's gone crazy,

Mia. I had to threaten you to protect myself. To stop your son from hitting me again."

What was the truth? Whom should she believe? But Mia's brain was picking up speed. And Katrina hadn't put down her gun.

She looked from Katrina's eyes to Gabe's. And then she made her choice.

"So why did you do it, Katrina? Why did you kill Colleen?"

Mia watched her decide whether to continue to lie. But then she shrugged and said, "Colleen didn't understand."

"What didn't she understand?"

"She didn't understand that you could still do a good job even if you were getting a little something extra."

"Something extra?" The light dawned. She remembered what Eli had said about a plea bargain that seemed too good to be true. "You mean like bribes?"

"I'm just keeping the court system from getting clogged," Katrina said. "But then Colleen started poking that big red nose of hers where it didn't belong."

Mia remembered Colleen's words. *"If there's one thing this job has taught me, it's to turn over rocks—but sometimes you don't like what you find underneath. Lately I've been thinking how flat-out ugly it can get."*

"Colleen asked me about it over lunch. She was all lovey-dovey, pretending she understood. Like she was my mom and I was her little girl. I finally told her that I had helped out a couple of poor souls. And of course I said there was no money involved, just me trying to give a few people a second chance. That's the kind of sappy stuff she liked. I gave it my best, but I could tell Colleen wasn't buying it. And that it was only a matter of time before she took it to Frank."

Mia nodded. She was listening, sickened, but her mind was also working double time. Where was Brooke? She wasn't even going to mention her. Mia just hoped that she was safe upstairs. That her daughter had escaped Katrina's notice.

"When Colleen went to the bathroom, I took her office key. And over the weekend I went through her files. I found a notebook she'd been keeping. I took that home and burned it. And then I cut another special deal with one of my defendants to help me take care of the problem."

Gabe was looking, not at the gun, not at Katrina, but at Mia. He cut his eyes away to something behind Katrina. He did it again. Her son wanted her to notice something. But what?

"But we didn't find any evidence at the scene." Mia hoped that Katrina didn't notice her eyes searching for what Gabe wanted her to see. "How did you manage that?" She managed a note of admiration.

"I got us both the same Danner boots the crime-scene techs wear." There was a weird glint in Katrina's flat eyes. Something oddly like pride. "I knew we could tramp all over her yard and no one would ever see it."

Katrina must think there was no chance they would repeat her boasts. Which meant that she was going to kill both of them. Everything was lost, Mia realized. Everything. It wasn't enough that Scott was dead. Now her family was going to die. And for what? For what?

She sent up an incoherent plea, a plea that wasn't even really words. *God, help us. Help my children.*

Then she saw what Gabe had wanted her to notice. On the entry table behind Katrina was something flat and silver.

A knife. It was a knife. And it looked like a big one. Now was not the time to wonder why her chef's knife had ended up on the entryway table.

Mia looked at Gabe and then the door. With both hands, she made a steering motion. Katrina's face screwed up in puzzlement. Then Mia drove in hard, pushing Katrina's gun arm up, while groping desperately for the knife with her other hand.

The gun fired into the ceiling, filling her nostrils with acrid smoke. Her ears rang as if they had been boxed.

"The keys are in the car," Mia yelled. "Go get help!" Gabe didn't even have his learner's permit, but if he tried to run to the neighbors, Katrina might shoot him dead on someone's doorstep. He fumbled open the front door and ran outside. Mia grappled for Katrina's gun with her left hand while straining for the knife with her right.

Katrina elbowed Mia in the face, knocking her sideways. The gun fired again. It felt like someone had punched Mia in the shoulder. She staggered back, one step, two, as her left arm turned hot and tingly. Only the adrenaline coursing through her allowed her to ignore it.

Katrina stepped over the threshold and began to aim.

Mia lurched forward and grabbed the knife. She saw Brooke at the top of the stairs, her thumb in her mouth. "Go back to your room!" she screamed and then followed Katrina out the door.

Outside, Gabe was hunched over the steering wheel. Mia heard the engine turn over, but it didn't catch.

The battery. The stupid battery that had been on Mia's stupid to-do list. Too late now. Far too late.

Gabe jerked his head up and around. He saw Katrina and threw himself sideways. Just as she fired.

Mia ran toward Katrina, the chef's knife clenched in her hand. Screaming, "No!" she raised it high overhead and brought it down, aiming for Katrina's shoulder.

Katrina spun sideways, and the knife caught her in the bicep. Her gun went skittering across the driveway.

Mia yanked the knife free, yelling, "Get the gun, Gabe! Get the gun!"

Gabe scrambled out of the car. He had just picked up the gun when Charlie screeched into the driveway.

If it had been any other cop but Charlie, she and Gabe could easily have been shot. A cowering woman with obvious wounds facing a woman armed with a knife and a boy with a gun—who was the victim?

Instead, Charlie aimed his gun at Katrina and said, "Katrina Nowell, you are under arrest for the murder of Colleen Miller."

CHAPTER 50

Mia watched Eli walking toward her, toting the table saw. It was heavy, but he handled it easily. He set it on the card table Gabe had put up in the yard this morning, then handed Mia three crisp twenty-dollar bills. Brooke was under the table, leaning against Mia's leg and whispering to herself. She seemed to be pretending she was in some kind of hideout.

"That's a good deal." Eli tapped the side of the saw blade. "It doesn't look like it's ever been used."

"My husband was going to add on to the deck, but I think buying that saw is as close as he got to doing it." Scott had been great at starting things.

"You sure you don't want to hold on to it?" Eli pushed it toward her a half inch, and the card table rocked a little bit.

"Positive. You're saving Gabe from sawing off his fingers. Or at least me from worrying that he will."

Mia thought about her own fingers. Had Eli noticed the pale band of skin on her left hand, the one poking out of the blue cloth sling? The bullet had cut a clean path through her shoulder, missing any vital structures. At the hospital they had removed her wedding band, worried that her hand might swell. The ring had been returned to her in a plastic envelope, and she hadn't put it back on. Last night she had held it in her palm for a long time and then locked it in the fire safe.

"If you're sure." He hefted it under his arm.

"I am."

"I still owe you that cup of coffee," Eli said. "Maybe I can buy it for you over lunch sometime."

She didn't know what to say, so she was surprised to hear herself answering, "I'd like that."

Eli stepped back to let a woman deposit all of Mia's mismatched plastic storage containers and a stack of paperbacks on the card table. She gave him a wave with her good hand, which he returned before turning and carrying the saw to his car.

In quick succession she sold a step stool, more books, and a game of Monopoly with London place names. The garage sale was doing brisk business. A lot of purchases were being made by curious neighbors who wanted to know more about what had happened. Gabe was talking to one of them now, a girl who lived down the street and who seemed to have shot up three inches in the last three months. By the way he was swinging his arms, Mia guessed he was retelling the story of how he had fought off Katrina with the help of his skateboard.

Katrina was sitting in jail, as was the man she had offered a plea bargain to in exchange for providing the gun and pulling the trigger. Ben McFadden had thought he was trading Colleen's life for his freedom, but now both were gone. Mia's co-workers had been combing through Tami's and Katrina's files, looking for more plea bargains that might have been the result of bribery. Katrina wasn't talking, and Tami claimed she had had no knowledge of any, but Mia suspected that this was as spurious as the idea that Tami had only been hugging that inmate. She had always been willing to claim anything in the courtroom in the hopes that her clients might go free. Now it looked as if she had been willing to let anything happen outside the courtroom as well.

Ronni put down two of Mia's old sweaters and then reached into her pocket.

"Your money's no good here, I'm afraid." Mia started to put the sweaters into an old brown paper grocery bag, but it was hard to do. It was amazing how much you needed two hands to do things well—or at all. Cutting up food, using a computer, getting dressed, driving. Even sliding a sweater into a grocery bag was nearly impossible. Mia promised herself that when she got this sling off she would be forever grateful for the use of both of her hands.

"I owe you too much already," Ronni said. Thanks to Mia's suggestion that Ronni house-sit for Violet while she was at college, the girl now had a place to live.

"You don't owe me anything." Mia had to raise her voice over the sound of the shop vac, which an old man in high-waisted jeans had turned on to see if the homemade sign that read Works Fine was really true. "Except to keep your grades up."

"Then all I can say is thank you." Ronni took the grocery bag from her, folded the sweaters neatly, and placed them inside. She smiled at Mia before stepping aside for an older woman who was toting Brooke's old high chair.

"That will be seven dollars," Mia said.

"That's my chair." Brooke stood up with her lower lip pushed out.

"But you're a big girl who sits in a big chair now," Mia said. "Can you press the buttons on the cash register for me? It's a seven and then zero, zero."

Distracted by her new adult role, Brooke did as she was asked. She hadn't had a single night terror since Mia had adjusted her bedtime. With a ding, the red plastic drawer popped open. Mia told Brooke where to put each of the bills. Scott had bought the cash register a year ago, when paying thirty dollars for an "educational" toy had seemed like a good deal.

While Mia was recuperating, she had gotten started on refinancing the house. Yes, she would be sixty-seven when she finally owned it free and clear, but a re-fi would allow her to pay off the debts and give her some breathing room.

A familiar figure walked into the yard. Charlie. While Mia was being treated at the hospital for her gunshot, he had gruffly admitted that he had thought the worst when he pulled into the driveway and saw the blood.

He shot her a crooked smile, waved at Gabe, and then began to browse. Finally he came up to her card table with a cast-iron frying pan.

"I really didn't figure you for the cooking type, Charlie."

He shrugged. "Things aren't always what they seem."

She thought of Katrina. "I guess we both learned that, didn't we?"

He looked away. If she didn't know it was impossible, she would have said Charlie was acting shy.

"I also wanted to see how you were doing."

"Pretty well, all things considered. The doctor says I can go back to work on Monday. And the sling can come off in another week."

"Actually . . ." Charlie glanced down at Brooke and back up at Mia. "I've been looking into an old case and I'd like to talk to you about it."

"Sure." He probably wanted her opinion about whether it could be prosecuted. There was no sense in reopening a case if the prosecutor felt there was little or no chance of winning a conviction.

"Maybe over lunch?"

Two requests for lunch in one afternoon? Then again, it was only lunch. With people she worked with.

She realized Charlie was still waiting.

"I'd like that." She held out her good hand. "Aren't you forgetting something?"

Gingerly, he took it. His fingers were cool. "What?"

"You owe me two dollars."

READING GROUP GUIDE

1. On her eHeartMatch profile, Colleen lies about her weight and age. Vincent lies about his appearance and occupation. Do you feel that you have a different level of trust for what you read on the Internet as opposed to what someone tells you or what you see in the newspaper or on TV? Do you think that the truth has become more malleable in your lifetime? Or is it perhaps easier to discover?
2. Her husband's death made it necessary for Mia to go back to work. Many women juggle duties both at home and at a job. Is it really possible to have it all? How can we find balance? Have you ever felt torn between competing needs?
3. Nate says about his son Darin, "A long time ago, I realized I could spend all my time wishing for the son I never had or I could love the son who was standing right in front of me." Have you ever struggled with loving someone just the way they are? Do you think in some cases it's not possible?
4. Teens these days interact with so many different kinds of social media: Facebook, Twitter, Tumblr, Pinterest. They can access social media on their phones, computers, tablet computers, or netbooks. If you have kids, how have you tried to manage or oversee this? Have you put the computer in a common area? Do you look at their texts, their Facebook posts, their e-mails—or is that any different than eavesdropping or reading their diaries?

Is it even possible to successfully monitor their interactions? Would you ever consider putting spyware on your child's phone or computer?

5. Darin was bullied. Were you ever bullied as a kid—or perhaps even on the other side? Do you think that bullying is more prevalent today or is it something we are simply more aware of? What do you think are the best ways to help prevent bullying?
6. Gina's and Martin's adopted child might be autistic. Doctors say he needs thousands of dollars worth of therapy. Have you known anyone who has struggled with autism?
7. Gabe's coach keeps him on the bench instead of putting him in to play. Do you think high school sports should focus on winning or on letting more kids on the team play? Does that change if you're talking about a JV team?
8. Mia discovers that Scott has left their family in debt. Do you think she should have pursued bankruptcy? Do you know someone who has been affected by foreclosure or overwhelming debts?
9. Brooke has night terrors. Have you ever known a child with night terrors? Have you dealt with a child who had a mysterious illness?
10. One of the main themes of *A Matter of Trust* is that appearances can be deceiving. Ronni is homeless yet determined to finish school. One of the boys who tormented Darin turns out to have also been his friend. Do you think as you have gained more experience in life that you have gotten better at seeing below the surface? Or are we all so busy that we are often forced to rely on the surface and to make snap judgments?

ACKNOWLEDGMENTS

Dear "Mia," even though you are a figment of my imagination, thank you for letting your story be told. In some ways, you are more truth than fiction, and so near and dear to my heart. Telling your story brings me closer to you and will, I hope, inform women who see themselves in your proverbial shoes. Tread wisely, my friend.

Speaking of friends: Thank you, O'Reilly, from Wiehl. And Roger Ailes, an intrepid leader. And Dianne Brandi, daughter of Dolores.

Research is the key to any good story, so thank you, Joe Collins (paramedic and firefighter), Robin Burcell (author and former cop and forensic artist), and all our friends in law enforcement who consulted and advised without attribution.

Thank you to the amazing team at Thomas Nelson! Their spirit for the story never ceases to amaze. It is with much gratitude that we thank Daisy Hutton, Vice President and Publisher (spirit, charm, and smarts all wrapped up in one amazing person); Ami McConnell, Senior Acquisitions Editor (she was the first to really "see" Mia . . . I will always love her for that); Amanda Bostic, Acquisitions Editor (I love how she thinks); LB Norton, line editor (with her keen eye, quick pen, and great sense of humor); Becky Monds, Associate Editor (I don't ever think she doesn't have a smile on her face, love that); Jodi Hughes, Editorial Assistant (and destined for great things, I feel it in my bones); Kristen Vasgaard, Manager of Packaging (she makes book covers sing); Ruthie Dean, Marketing and Publicity Specialist (she gets it all done . . . not quite sure how, but she does); Laura

Dickerson, Marketing and Publicity Specialist (so glad to be part of her team); Kerri Potts, Marketing and Publicity Coordinator (the inspiration behind my Facebook); and, finally, with special thanks to Katie Bond, Director of Marketing and Publicity (I'm so proud of you, friend. We have shared so many stories, and have many more ahead). We love this team!

Special thanks to our book agents, Todd Shuster and Lane Zachary of the Zachary, Shuster, and Harmsworth Literary Agency, and Wendy Schmalz of the Wendy Schmalz Agency—you made the Mia novels happen.

To my mom and dad. I still aim to follow the moral compass you set years ago.

All of the mistakes are ours. All the credit is theirs. Thank you!

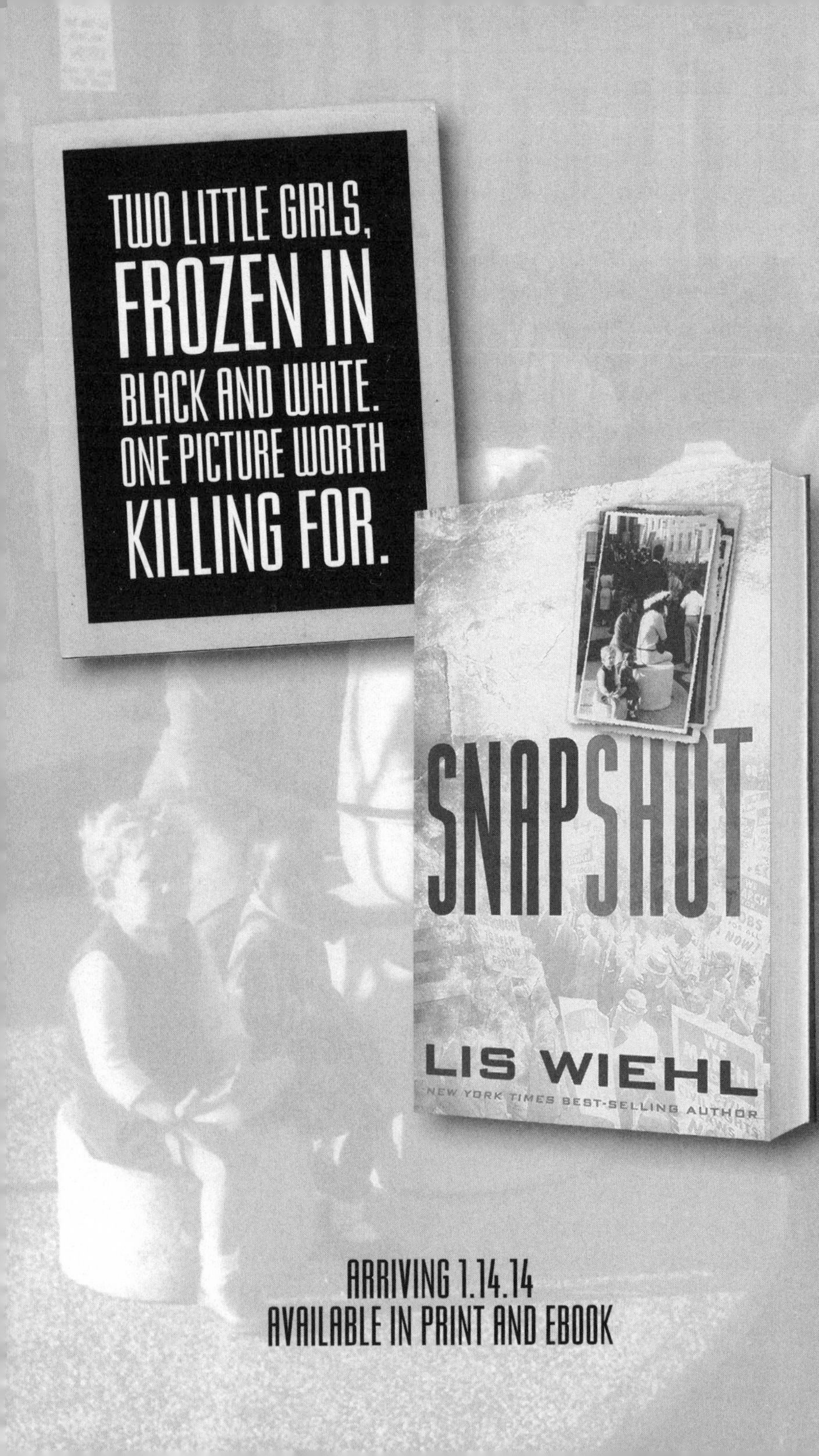

9781595549068-A

AN EXCERPT FROM *SNAPSHOT*

PROLOGUE

APRIL 10, 1965

Fort Worth, Texas

Special Agent James Waldren reached around his jacket and felt the Smith & Wesson .38 Special concealed at the small of his back. He scanned the pedestrians up and down the street before responding to the tugs at his sleeve.

"Daddy, look. Daddy, I'm skipping." Lisa took off in an awkward hop and skip up the sidewalk.

"Wait for me," James said, picking up his pace. The camera hanging around his neck slapped his chest as he reached out for her arm. "Hold my hand now."

"And look both ways," Lisa said as they reached an intersection. The light turned green, and they crossed the street with a growing crowd hurrying forward.

James was keenly aware of the glances, and of how people moved ever so slightly away—some even crossed to the other sidewalk—when they saw him. This wasn't a neighborhood where a white man and his blond-haired daughter would normally be seen. Lisa skipped along, oblivious.

The sounds of cheering and shouts echoing through a bull-horn increased as they closed in on the throng of people. As a tall man raced by, the placard he carried clattered to the sidewalk. Lisa released James's hand to run a few steps ahead, reaching the sign as the man bent to pick it up.

"Here you go, sir," Lisa chirped. She picked up the edge of the sign that had FREEDOM NOW painted in bold red against the white.

The man glanced from Lisa to James, then back to the child. She pushed the end of the wooden pole as high as she could with two hands.

"Thank you, li'l miss," the man said.

"You're welcome, sir," Lisa said, smiling back as he picked up the placard.

He gave James a tentative nod before racing up the street, sign in hand.

As the sidewalk congestion grew, James scooped Lisa into his arms, eliciting a joyful squeal. She rested in the crook of his elbow, and her soft hand reached around his neck, curling her fingers into his hair.

At the corner, the streets lined with tall brick buildings opened to a small park and public square. The air was electric with the energy of the growing crowd.

James surveyed the plaza where at least a hundred people lined the adjacent street, waiting for the approaching marchers: women in Sunday dresses, many with hats and white gloves, pantyhose, and dress shoes; men in crisp button-down shirts and slacks, some with ties and jackets even on this warm spring morning.

"Where is the important man, Daddy?" Lisa craned her neck.

"We'll see him very soon," James said, moving closer toward the parade route. His eight years with the Bureau had altered training into instinct, but in the eighteen months since President Kennedy's assassination in Dallas, every important event held the threat of danger, no matter how peaceful it was planned to be.

James had spent countless hours and overtime investigating the

JFK assassination. He was assigned to the killer, the deceased Lee Harvey Oswald—his activities, friends, coworkers, family, and especially his Russian wife, Marina Oswald. Good ole cowboy country hid numerous underground connections and secret groups throughout Dallas, Fort Worth, and outward from the South and across the nation. There were Russian expats with connections in the USSR, hidden KKK members in political positions, and a growing group of black freedom fighters.

But today James tried to blend in. Just another bystander, a normal guy who'd brought his daughter to witness a historical event. Just any white dad who happened to have a revolver and FBI credentials in his wallet. The truth was, James couldn't be just a bystander. A special agent with the Federal Bureau of Investigation was never off duty, and an event like this had layers of possible intrigue. His wife would be furious if she knew he'd brought Lisa with him. She thought they were going to the park.

"Here he comes." James lifted Lisa onto his shoulders. She patted the top of his head, bouncing up and down with the cheers erupting around them. "See that man, the one in the middle?"

"The man with the big hat?" Lisa leaned down toward his ear. The girl was hat obsessed. She'd wanted to break out her Easter bonnet today, but his wife wanted it saved for Easter Sunday.

"Not that one. The shorter man with the red necktie." He lifted his camera with one hand and snapped a picture, then advanced the film and snapped another.

"I see him," she said, bouncing again.

"He's an important man, a very good writer and speaker."

James took pictures as they watched the progression down the street. Benjamin Gray was surrounded by marchers holding signs, the cry for freedom and equality on their lips. The crowd took up singing "We Shall Overcome." Benjamin Gray carried a Bible under his arm and slapped his hands together as he joined in the singing.

Lisa wiggled on James's shoulders, trying to slide down just as he spotted his partner, Agent Peter Hughes, up a block and across the street.

"Want down, Daddy," Lisa said.

The marchers made a sharp turn and moved into the square where Gray and other leaders would speak to the crowd.

James set Lisa on the ground, holding on to her arm, but she tugged away from him.

"Wait!" he called, weaving through the crowd after the blond head.

James watched as Lisa stopped a few feet from a little black girl close to her age who sat on a cylindrical concrete seat. The girl stared back at Lisa, then smiled when his daughter waved. Lisa clambered up the seat, pushing higher with her toes. It seemed that thoughts of parades and important men were pushed aside by the more interesting distraction of a potential playmate.

"I'm four," Lisa said as she held up three fingers, then the fourth.

James didn't hear the other girl but saw her show Lisa four fingers back. A nearby woman in a large white hat kept a watchful eye from an adjacent, slightly taller bench.

"Can I take a picture?" he asked her.

She leaned back, studying him and then the two girls before winking and breaking into a smile.

"Go right ahead," she said, and returned to watching the progression of marchers as they looped from behind them to curve around James toward the central square at his back.

He clicked several photos, struck by the poignancy of the images. These two little girls, one white and one black, sitting side by side, were the symbol of today's event.

James snapped another picture as the two girls leaned close, smiling and talking as if already friends.

A gunshot pierced the air. Then another.

James jumped to shield Lisa as he grabbed his gun. He moved the two girls directly behind him. His eyes jumped around the crowded plaza behind him, where the shots had come from.

The rally turned into instant chaos, with people running in all directions.

The black girl's mother screamed at James, hitting him with her purse as she reached for her child.

"It's okay, I'm FBI." He flipped out his wallet with the large letters clearly visible, but the woman continued to cry out, gloved hands at her mouth. James passed the child to her, and they were immediately enveloped into the crowd and out of sight.

"They shot him! Help, please help!" someone screamed.

Through the commotion James glimpsed a man on the ground. Beside the body, a Bible lay covered in blood.

James pushed forward with Lisa held against his chest. "Close your eyes," he demanded.

The faces around him reflected terror and confusion.

As he turned toward the man on the ground, James was certain that Benjamin Gray was already dead.

NOVEMBER 1971

Queens, New York

Former Special Agent Peter Hughes sat with the gun on the desk beside him as he looked out the second-story window at bare trees reaching like hands toward a gray sky.

Outside, Peter knew, people were preparing for the holidays. Thanksgiving was a week away, and Christmas carols already played in the stores. Peter wondered if Lisa was performing at her elementary school. He wished he could be there and see her wave to "Uncle Peter" as she'd done last year from the stage. He hoped she knew that he didn't want to go away.

Peter reached beneath the desk to the very far corner. He pulled back the wood and removed the object he'd hidden there.

He held up an old brass key and set it beside his revolver. He recalled watching as Robert Kennedy used the key to unlock a drawer. Together they'd admired the craftsmanship of the massive cabinet.

"Every drawer has a unique key. Isn't that remarkable?" Bobby had said.

"Sounds like a lot of work to me. And a lot to keep track of," was Peter's response.

"Brilliant, really." Bobby told Peter how the queen of England had given the cabinet to his brother John when he was elected to the presidency. Originally it had been given to the royal family three hundred years earlier.

Peter and Bobby believed they were doing the right thing that day, locking away the proof of a crime. It was for the greater good, and for only a short time. Bobby would be president, probably within the next few years. He'd pick up his brother's mantle and bring some right back to all that was going wrong. They'd wait just a little while longer, till Bobby was in office, then set everything right.

Bobby had turned the key, locking the secrets away.

And then he was shot dead, just when change seemed within grasp.

Peter wanted to fix things, but every attempt seemed to dig him in deeper. First he couldn't find the key. Then the cabinet was moved, along with the secrets it held.

Now he had the key. Right here in his hands. But he was hated and reviled by those he loved most. Peter knew his old friend James Waldren could right the wrongs.

A car turned around in front of the house and parked on the street.

He peered down and saw a young man rise from behind the driver's seat. The kid took a worn briefcase from the backseat, adjusted his tie, and moved up the walkway.

Peter recognized the look on the young man's face. He'd once had such dreams, and a belief in a world that could be better than it turned out to be.

The doorbell rang, and Peter heard his sister's footsteps moving toward the door.

He thought of little Lisa Waldren again. How many times he'd wished he had a child like her of his own. But that, too, could never be.

Peter placed the key and letter into a large envelope and sealed the top as he heard his sister talking to the visitor at the door. He set the envelope in the top compartment of the desk.

"There's someone here to see you, Peter!" his sister shouted from downstairs.

Peter looked again at the empty trees. Then he picked up the gun, placed it beneath his chin, and pulled the trigger.

CHAPTER ONE

PRESENT TIME

Boston, Massachusetts

Moakley Federal Courthouse

She needed air.

Lisa Waldren's quick footsteps were lost in the noise filling the marble corridor as she slung her satchel over her shoulder and wove through huddled groups of jurors, family members, and legal teams. She didn't turn toward the elevators that led to her office, but instead focused her steps toward the fresh ocean air waiting outside the building.

"Lisa, wait," someone called behind her as the glass rotunda entrance came into view.

She didn't slow until she'd pushed out the glass doors into the curved courtyard of Moakley Federal Courthouse. The scent of the sea filled her lungs and cooled her face, a welcome relief from the recycled air of the courtroom. But in her hurry to escape, Lisa had forgotten that the press would be waiting. They recognized her as the lead federal prosecutor and hurried toward her.

"Ms. Waldren, are you pleased with the sentencing?"

"What did Radcliffe say to you? Did he show any remorse?"

The faces, cameras, and microphones pressed around her.

"We have an official press conference at two o'clock." Lisa pushed through the net that circled and squeezed in. Someone grabbed her arm, but as she protested, Lisa recognized a familiar face pushing around and leading her through the mob.

"That's all for now. Sorry, folks, more in a few hours," Drew Harman said with a commanding tone that brought a smile to the edge of Lisa's lips.

"Hey, Drew, you got an exclusive with her or what?" The reporter gave him a sly expression as a few others broke into laughter.

"You'd like to know," Drew said. As they moved beyond the gathering, he shook his head as if disgusted. "Sharks."

Lisa couldn't help but laugh, given that Drew was a former newsman himself.

"I'd say thank you, but that wasn't necessary. I have plenty of experience shoving past the press."

"Don't I know," Drew said with a wicked grin.

Lisa ignored the remark. "Do you have time for lunch? I'm starving."

"Sentencing bad guys to thirty years in prison works up an appetite, I'm sure."

The breeze wafting through the landscaped courtyard carried the scent from a Sicilian restaurant, teasing her grumbling stomach with visions of homemade linguini and fresh seafood.

"Today was good news," Drew said, and Lisa realized he'd been studying her expression.

He was right. A bad guy was going to prison, and that should make her feel good. But for the past three years, Lisa had spent countless hours with the victims of the multistate extortion case. A hundred and forty-three victims had been taken by a swindler—that's what it came down to. They were humiliated and disillusioned, but even worse, most had lost nearly everything they had. Lisa could see the faces and hear their stories:

the Huffs had to move in with their married children after losing the home they'd had for forty years; elderly Maryann Brown was scouring the job market after losing her entire life savings; Blaze Hampton survived being a POW in Vietnam but had lost his finances to a man claiming to be another veteran . . . the stories went on and on.

Sending Gerald Radcliffe to prison for thirty years didn't help the victims.

"Yes, good news. At least it's over." Lisa tried to muster up some acceptable enthusiasm.

They walked toward the blue waters of Boston Harbor that gleamed beneath the noonday sun. A large catamaran cut through the choppy waves, reminding Lisa of days when her husband was alive and he'd coax her and their young son out for a day at sea. The memory no longer stung but served to soften her mood and remind her of how time passed and healed. And tonight was one of her two regular weekly video chats with her now college-aged son from his dorm in London.

"It is actually over. That is a relief." Lisa glanced at Drew as the weight finally began to lift.

"You need to take that vacation now. Celebrate this and don't just hop on the next case. It's a huge victory. I know one thing—Radcliffe thought he was getting away with this, but he didn't expect Federal Prosecutor Lisa Waldren. You did good, so be proud of yourself." Drew's white smile beamed against the darkness of his skin.

Lisa nearly brushed away his words by saying that she'd been part of a great team and all the usual things people were supposed to say. But Drew knew the hours she'd put in and how determined she was to get the last nail hammered into Radcliffe's coffin. She'd followed a paper trail after it virtually disappeared, found family members that Radcliffe had thought he'd left behind and a partner in exile he wanted dead. Without her determination fueled by the victims' stories, Radcliffe would have never gone to trial, let alone been found guilty.

"I guess I did do all right," she said, breaking into a smile of her own.

As they stepped onto the harbor walkway, Lisa's phone rang. The name on the screen stopped her.

"My father?" She held up the phone as if to confirm that her eyes weren't tricking her.

"You should answer it."

Lisa hesitated a moment longer.

"Dad?"

"There you are. I didn't know if you'd be in court." The voice struck her as so familiar that the time since she had last seen her father disappeared in a moment. They spoke in short greetings on holidays and birthdays, though Dad had forgotten most of Lisa's. They were family, yet neither of them knew the details of the other's life.

"I just left a sentencing and am going to lunch. How are you? Is everything okay?"

"I want to talk to you about something. Time is critical with this."

"What's it about?" Lisa braced herself for the news she was about to receive.

"There's too much to go over right now. But do you remember when you were little, really little, I took you to a civil rights rally?"

Lisa frowned, trying to gauge where this was going.

"It was in Fort Worth. There was a shooting?"

"Do you mean the rally where that civil rights leader was killed?" Years ago, after her mother had brought up how upset she'd been that a man was killed so close to her daughter, Lisa had researched the event.

"Yes, exactly. His name was Benjamin Gray."

Lisa caught the rise of excitement in Dad's tone. She shifted from one leg to the next as Drew took the heavy satchel from her shoulder and motioned toward a bench near the water's edge. Lisa followed him and leaned on the thick chain railing.

"Didn't the shooter get the death penalty?" she asked.

"Yes, but he didn't do the crime. The wrong man has spent more than four decades in prison for the Gray killing."

"And?" A headache was growing in her temples, and she wanted to ask what this had to do with her, with them, with his abrupt phone call out of the blue.

"I want to right that wrong."

"That's admirable of you."

This was not like her father at all. Special Agent James Waldren had retired with accolades from the FBI over a decade earlier. He fit the G-man role naturally. He didn't share his feelings with anyone, he'd never go to therapy, and he wouldn't see the point of losing sleep questioning life decisions. Yet now Lisa detected the tone of someone impassioned by a cause.

Had he become obsessed with this case? Was he losing his mind? Words like *dementia* and *Alzheimer's* made her pulse race.

"It's not admirable; it's what should have been done long ago. And I need your help."

"Me? What can I do?"

"I don't know what you remember from that day, but the real killer couldn't have been in the spot where they arrested Leonard Dubois—the man convicted of the shooting.

"There were many inconsistencies and reports that never sat well with me. I have several files for you to look through, and much more here in Dallas. I know I'm dumping a lot on you at once, but we're running out of time. In seven weeks, the wrong man is going to be executed. We have to work quickly."

We? Lisa didn't know what to say. Her father obviously believed she should care. After all this time he popped into her life, not to know her better, but because of some old case from the sixties.

She hadn't spoken to him since she'd called him at Christmas. There were no inquiries about her son, his grandson. No sharing of pictures or telling stories of John going off to England, or how she'd slept in his room the first week or how empty the house felt without him. Nothing about her, nothing about them, nothing a father and daughter might usually share. No opportunity to mention that she'd just won one of the biggest cases in recent Boston history.

She closed her eyes against the throbbing headache, then she remembered the time.

"Dad, I have to hold a press conference in an hour. Can I call you when I'm home?" She couldn't give a flat-out no to her father, even if he'd turned his back on her more times than she could count.

"Oh yes, I heard something about your big case. Congratulations."

"Thank you." Lisa was surprised that he knew anything about it at all.

"Will you have some time off now? I wondered if you might come down here."

"Go to Texas? You're still in Dallas, right?" It was a question for a casual acquaintance, not a father.

"Of course. If you could see all this evidence and these pictures, and the letter Leonard Dubois wrote me from prison."

"I have a vacation sort of in the process."

Drew raised his eyebrows at her semi-lie.

"Well, I'm sure you deserve it. I can try mailing you copies of the snapshots I took at the parade. Maybe you'll remember something. But it'd be best if you came here."

"Why don't you e-mail or text them to me."

"I can't do all that stuff. Just call me back as soon as you can. There's a lot at stake here."

"Okay, Dad." Lisa would hear him out; she'd give him that at least.

She hung up the phone and stared across the water. The catamaran had sailed beyond view.

"He wants me to go to Dallas."

"You should consider it." Drew motioned for them to walk. He kept her satchel on his shoulder as he led the way toward the quaint cafés and shops across the bridge. A historic fishing vessel knocked against the dock and strained its mooring lines.

Lisa couldn't enjoy the walk as she normally would. She might have known Drew would side with any chance of her reconnecting with her father. In their eight years as friends, Drew had never met him. He'd met her mother and stepfather on numerous occasions, and Lisa knew Drew's family well. But Dad had never visited her in Boston, not once, while Lisa's career and single parenting had kept her from returning to Texas. When her son was young, she'd tried developing a relationship between her father and her fatherless son. But Dad had never particularly enjoyed children, and she eventually gave up.

Now Dad called, acting as if he regularly phoned for a friendly father-daughter chat and that it wasn't outside of normal to request her help on an old case.

Why was this case so important to him?

"There is absolutely no way I'm going to Dallas."

Drew didn't look toward her as they walked.

"I think that you will."

ABOUT THE AUTHORS

Lis Wiehl is a *New York Times* best-selling author, Harvard Law School graduate, and former federal prosecutor. A popular legal analyst and commentator for the Fox News Channel, Wiehl appears weekly on *The O'Reilly Factor* and hosts her own weekly radio program, *Legal Lis*.

April Henry is the *New York Times* best-selling author of mysteries and thrillers. Her books have been short-listed for the Agatha Award, the Anthony Award, and the Oregon Book Award. April lives in Portland, Oregon, with her husband and daughter.